Brain-Based Parenting

Brain-Based Parenting

*The Neuroscience of Caregiving
for Healthy Attachment*

Daniel A. Hughes
Jonathan Baylin

Foreword by Daniel J. Siegel

W. W. Norton & Company
New York • London

For information about permission to reproduce selections from this book, write to Permissions, W. W. Norton & Company, Inc., 500 Fifth Avenue, New York, NY 10110

For information about special discounts for bulk purchases, please contact W. W. Norton Special Sales at specialsales@wwnorton.com or 800-233-4830

Manufacturing by Quad Graphics, Fairfield
Book design by Martha Meyer, Paradigm Graphic Design
Production manager: Leeann Graham

Library of Congress Cataloging-in-Publication Data

Hughes, Daniel A.
 Brain-based parenting : the neuroscience of caregiving for healthy attachment / Daniel A. Hughes and Jonathan Baylin.
    p. cm. -- (The Norton series on interpersonal neurobiology)
(Norton professional book)
Includes bibliographical references and index.
ISBN 978-0-393-70728-1 (hardcover)
1. Parent and child. 2. Attachment behavior in children. 3. Parenting. I. Baylin, Jonathan F. II. Title.
BF723.P25H84 2012
649'.1019--dc23
                    2011046056

ISBN: 978-0-393-70728-1

W. W. Norton & Company, Inc., 500 Fifth Avenue, New York, N.Y. 10110
                    www.wwnorton.com
W. W. Norton & Company Ltd., Castle House, 75/76 Wells Street, London W1T 3QT

1 2 3 4 5 6 7 8 9 0

I would like to dedicate this book to my parents and to my children. They have helped me to understand the magic of the parent–child relationship from both sides. —DH

I would like to dedicate this book to my wife, Sarah, and to my sons, Benjamin and Zachary. —JB

Contents

Acknowledgments

Over the years, Allan Schore and Dan Siegel have given me much time and encouragement to develop my thinking around interventions that are congruent with the emerging insights that we are getting from the new research into the structure and functioning of the brain. Their theory of Interpersonal Neurobiology has provided much of the impetus for this work for me.

This book would never have been written without the enthusiasm, knowledge, curiosity, and creative ideas regarding the brain and nervous system that my coauthor has brought to these pages. He understands the research involving the brain much more than I do and he is always quick to move us both into discussions about the implications of this research for clinical applications. Jon is truly a renaissance man—those who know his musical interests and abilities as well as his continuing prowess on the baseball field will attest to that. I am fortunate that he is my colleague in this and other endeavors. I am even more fortunate that he is my good friend.

—DH

Because this book has been nearly 67 years in the making, many people in my life have contributed to its creation. My parents, George and Sarah, gone now, would be thrilled just to see that I finally wrote a book. My marvelous brothers, Eric and Steve, continue to inspire me every day; Eric, with his endless creativity in the realms of art, teaching, and poetry; and Steve, with his world-class work in cancer research and his full-bore engagement with life, including being the world's oldest catcher, slapping on "the tools of ignorance" in the blistering Phoenix sun. Beth, thanks for the close reading of early drafts and helpful feedback. To the staff of Delaware Guidance Services where I spent thirty-some years growing up professionally, many thanks. A very special shout-out to Carl Chenkin, friend and fellow traveler. Thanks, Carl, for your humor, wisdom, and encouragement. And to Dawn and Christine, thanks for being such early and constant supporters and creative consumers of brain knowledge. To the folks in IOP and Day Treatment who really work in the trenches with the most stressed-out families, I hope our many discussions about blocked care made your work a bit easier. To the staff at High Road School, you guys have really made me work to put brain science into action. Brain group, you know who you are, just a really brainy group of wonderful people who've met regularly over years now to talk about all things "brain." To members of the South Jersey Indians, the great senior baseball "kids," thanks for all of the Sundays where I've had to put aside book-writing duties to concentrate on bad hops and getting the bat on the ball. To all at Broudy and Associates, thanks for many years of being great colleagues. And to you, Dan, my coauthor, thanks for being my long-lost third brother from Pittsburgh. I have learned so much from watching you in action, connecting with kids that I haven't connected enough with over many years of trying. You've made me a believer in PACE.

Most importantly, to my wife Sarah, my life's companion now for over fifty years, you are the constant source of all things good. Your patience with cluttered surfaces has been almost limitless; your love and encouragement have been limitless. And your greatest gift of so many, giving birth to Ben and Zach. Thanks guys, for being who you are and for teaching me all the best I know about being a father.

—JB

Foreword

This important book offers parents and other caregivers, as well as professionals who work with families, a useful, neuroscience-inspired framework for understanding and improving the experience of raising children. By carefully revealing the science of the caregiving brain, the authors provide an inside view of the experience of being a parent, and offer practical suggestions for how to use this fascinating knowledge to improve the day-to-day ways we care for our children.

Modern research reveals at least five "systems" or clusters of neuronal circuits that enable fundamental aspects of the care of children to occur. The authors have creatively described these systems and demonstrate the powerful benefits when a parent understands them in daily family life. These basic parenting circuits include (1) the *approach system* that allows us to connect rather than withdraw from our children; (2) the *reward system* that makes parenting pleasurable; (3) the *child reading system* that enables us to see the mind of the child, or have "mindsight," as we reflect on the inner experience of a child, and not just respond to their behavior; (4) the *meaning-making system* that enables us to have a coherent understanding of ourselves; and, (5) the *executive system* that coordinates and balances the other four systems and enables us to become attuned to ourselves and to our child and also to repair ruptures in such attunements when they inevitably occur.

When parents and others provide care for a child, these five systems should work well together. When things get tough, when moments of conflict arise between a parent and a child or within the inner life of the parent's own mind, the care systems can become "blocked." Hughes and Baylin brilliantly describe the ways in which a given child can induce a momentary blockage in care, or how extended "blocked care" can occur, compromising the child's healthy development. Having insights into how and why blocked care happens can open a window of opportunity for a parent to reflect on what is going on interpersonally as well as internally so that such toxic blockages can be identified, internal shifts can be initiated, and interpersonal repair can occur. This is an important way we can parent from the inside out. Each of the five parental systems can contribute to blockages, and knowing how our own brain functions as caregivers can be an empowering knowledge that sets the stage for conscious, intentional parenting.

Our authors serve as empathic and wise guides through the intricacies of both detailed brain circuits and helpful parenting strategies. We, the fortunate readers, are taken on a powerful journey that illuminates ways of improving our efficacy as parents and enhancing our pleasure in the experience itself. Because these examples include interactions between the clinician and family/parent clients, professionals reading this book will also find direct assistance offered by experienced clinicians working with families from an attachment-based model.

In the Norton Series on Interpersonal Neurobiology we aim to include books that demonstrate in helpful ways how relationships and the brain interact to shape our development across the lifespan. *Brain-Based Parenting* offers a practical, science-informed, in-depth exploration of just these sorts of issues in our social brains. If you are a parent or other care provider, this book will be a welcome resource for understanding your own inner subjective and neurological experience. Why is this important? We know from careful research in the field of attachment that the most robust predictor of a child's attachment to you, as a parent, is your own self-understanding. This book will serve as a useful guide in building aspects of that insight. If you are a professional who helps parents and families to thrive, then this book will reveal the powerful and creative framework of the parenting brain by two highly skilled colleagues. Though this book is written directly in a way that addresses parents themselves, I am convinced that clinicians will find this book a very useful resource in their professional work.

In interpersonal neurobiology we build our interdisciplinary field on scientific research and then we seek to apply that knowledge in practical ways in therapy, education, organizational and community functioning, and everyday life. Naturally, the examples of moment-by-moment, parent–child interactions described in this book were not carried out in mobile brain scanners. The authors have taken the important step of incorporating what is known from empirical studies of the brain to create a science-based framework for how to under-stand the neural systems underlying the experience of parenting. They have then taken the necessary next steps and applied this framework to everyday parenting to demonstrate in practical ways how knowing about the neural science of parenting can deepen our understanding of what is likely to be occurring—and then illustrating how this understanding, when applied, can actually lead to new and effective approaches to improving parent–child relationships.

Interpersonal neurobiology is more than just summarizing and synthesizing science; it is a field that translates science to try to improve lives. Clinicians and parents alike can see for themselves how this framework offers practical ways to deepen our understanding of—and even pleasure in—the parenting experience. As any parent of an older teen or an adult child will tell you, while the days of parenting may seem so long, the years are so short. This book will help you to find the gratitude and balanced perspective we need to greatly enhance this important, challenging, and life-changing relationship. I wish you all the best in the days and years ahead. Enjoy the journey!

 —Daniel J. Siegel, MD
  Founding Editor, The Norton Series on Interpersonal
  Neurobiology; Executive Director, Mindsight Institute;
  Clinical Professor, UCLA School of Medicine

Brain-Based Parenting

Introduction

Maternal love is essential for preservation of the human species.
—Noriuchi, KiKuchi, & Senoo (2008, p. 415)

This is not a parenting book in the traditional sense. We do not promise to deliver advice about all parenting challenges and worries. What we do promise is to help parents—and the therapists who may be working with them in a family therapy setting—think of parenting in a fundamentally different way. Our goal is to help parents to deepen their connections with their children, and therapists to deepen their work with stressed-out parents.

As two aging clinical psychologists who grew up in the pre-brain era of mental health, we became intrigued by the exciting new information coming from the rapidly expanding field of neuroscience. Most recently, we discovered two closely related specialty areas of this vast field of brain science, research dealing with:

1. how life experiences affect the brain development of children, and
2. the neurobiology of parenting, concerned specifically with the brain processes that support caregiving

We want to share core aspects of this new knowledge with you, hopefully allowing you to feel some of the excitement we feel about this new window into how the minds and hearts of parents affect the developing brains of our children and how our children change our brains and hearts.

We have tried our best to make our brain-based model of caregiving accessible and useful to both therapists *and* parents, because we feel both audiences can benefit from this new material. While discussions about the brain can be quite technical, a brain-based approach to understanding the caregiving process and working with stressed-out parents has so much to offer that it is important to make this rich information available to a wide audience. We have tried our best to keep the material "jargon free" and digestible while respecting the complexity of both the underlying neuroscience of parenting and the therapeutic processes required for helping stressed-out parents improve their parenting.

We want parents to understand that the knowledge emerging from studies of the parental brain can literally change your life, helping you to better understand and empathize with yourself. Since we assume that you are smart and curious, we don't take the "brain-for-dummies" approach. We want to give you enough real, in-depth information about the brain to enable you to appreciate the importance of a healthy brain to parenting. We want to take you on a journey inside the workings of this most amazing part of ourselves, the part of us that orchestrates everything we think, feel, and do, including all aspects of how we parent our kids. Perhaps our most important goal is to motivate you to care about your brain because the health and well-being of your loved ones, especially your children, depends so heavily on how well your brain is working. And for therapists, we want to give you an improved model for understanding and working with stressed parents who need your help to recover their capacity to care about, and connect with, their children.

Going forward, we explain and explore how parenting can sometimes be hijacked by stress and what parents—and therapists from whom they may be seeking help—can do to restore good brain functioning and avoid compromised caregiving—what we refer to as *blocked care*—and sustain a caring state of mind. Exciting new brain research has provided a new knowledge base for understanding how parents form loving bonds with their children and stay motivated to care for them despite inevitable personal and interpersonal conflicts. This research sheds light on the role of the brain in parenting—which brain systems are involved in all the characteristics we consider crucial to "good parenting," and what happens in those brain systems when parents get stressed out and their caregiving suffers.

What is good parenting from a brain-based perspective? It is . . .

- Being sensitive and emotionally responsive to children's needs for attention.
- Comforting children effectively and consistently when they are stressed out (what clinicians refer to as *co-regulation of affect*).
- Being a good first companion as children are initially learning how to enjoy and stay connected to other people.
- Knowing when to let kids struggle and work through challenges to build their own resilience.
- Protecting children from the dysregulating effects of our own negative emotions by using our powers of self-regulation and stress management—by being the "adult in the room."

Good parenting involves qualities that both protect the child's developing brain (referred to as *neuroprotective factors*) and stimulate brain growth (*growth-enhancing factors*).

The science that digs deeply into the neurobiology of parent–child connections goes by the fancy name of *developmental social neuroscience*. While this is a mouthful, the content of this research, as presented in books such as *Handbook of Developmental Social Neuroscience* (deHaan & Gunnar, 2009), is intriguing. This research deals with the impact of a child's experiences with other people, especially parental figures early in life, on his or her development, revealing in ways we have never been able to know before, how early experiences literally "build" a child's brain. Amazingly, this research now involves studying the way that early life experiences affect the activity of a child's genes—his or her DNA. This line of research, which is referred to as "experience-dependent" or "epigenetic" effects on brain development, may currently be the hottest area in the field of neuroscience. Although we do not try to explain a lot about this highly detailed and complicated research, stay tuned, because this area of developmental brain science has huge implications for our whole understanding of how human beings develop in response to the interaction of our DNA with our environment (Champagne, 2008; Canli et al., 2006).

Brain-based research has begun to influence both psychotherapy and the development of intervention programs for parents and young children, with the explicit goal of improving early brain development. Whereas in the 1990s, some researchers were just beginning to make the case that early caregiving affects the development of the infant's brain (Schore, 1994), now many brain scientists concerned with child development consider it to be a fact, not just a theory, that parenting affects children's brain development in lasting ways. Research from developmental social neuroscience is now considered to be the best information we have for understanding child development and for designing intervention programs through which parents can enhance children's development (National Scientific Council on the Developing Child, 2010; Shonkoff & Levitt, 2010). We see a brain-based approach to understanding parenting as consistent with, and essential to, this new paradigm for improving services for parents and children.

The large body of social neuroscience research also provides the knowledge base for a new model of brain-based therapy, called *interpersonal neurobiology* (Siegel, 2010). This model is currently the most influential one in terms of integrating brain science and mental health interventions, and the concepts we present in this book are consistent with this rich model.

The study of the inner workings of the parenting brain is a fairly recent branch of brain science. Early pioneering work with animals

(Numan & Insel, 2003) laid the foundations for this line of research, which has blossomed in recent years. The flowering of this research can be seen in a volume called *Neurobiology of the Parental Brain* (Bridges, 2008). This wonderful, if highly technical, tome is the outgrowth of a conference that took place in Boston in June, 2007, called "Parental Brain Conference: Parenting and the Brain."

In essence, research on the parental brain shows that human parenting rests squarely on a core foundation of mammalian care-giving, to which we add our uniquely human powers of self-under-standing, "people reading," reflection, emotion regulation, and capacity for growth and change in response to new experiences in life. Our brains link the core system of caregiving inherent in all mammals to our fancy *prefrontal cortex* (a "higher" set of brain regions that are more developed in humans) to form a dual-level parenting system. This dual-level functioning allows us, at our best, to experi-ence the deepest, most heartfelt emotions about our children while also being able to think clearly and creatively about all aspects of parenting, constructing rich meaning and a sense of purpose about our precious roles as parents. In coming chapters, we describe how these interlocking brain mechanisms—the age-old parenting system we share with creatures great and small and our uniquely human thinking, reflecting brain—combine to give us the brain power we need to raise our children well.

We also explore how this dual-level brain system of "bottom-up and top-down" circuits is affected by the inherently stressful process of parent–child interaction. We use the term *bottom up* to describe the more automatic, emotion-driven aspects of parenting that we inherited from mammalian evolution. Certain brain regions (e.g., the amygdala)—those formed early in primate evolution—mediate these functions. The term *top down* refers to those higher, more uniquely human "executive functions" such as problem solving, emotion regu-lation, and reflection, which are mediated by higher regions of the brain, particularly the prefrontal cortex. By combining knowledge from research on this dual-level parenting process and research on stress, we developed the concept of *parental blocked care*, or simply, *blocked care*, to describe how stress can suppress a well-meaning parent's capacity to sustain loving feelings and empathy toward his or her child.

Research on the neurobiology of parent–child interaction, the parenting brain, and the development of the stress response system provides a rich blend of knowledge for understanding the importance of parents' brain health for their child's development. This combined research builds on animal studies (Champagne, 2009; Sapolsky, Meaney, & McEwen, 1985; Suomi, 2003) with primates and rodents showing conclusively that early care affects the development of the stress response system in the young in ways that can last a lifetime. This research is now being extended to humans in a variety of ways, including a study exploring the impact of sensitive foster care on children's stress response systems (Dozier, 2001), and research exploring the neurobiology of sensitive parenting using brain-imaging studies along with observations of parent–child interactions (Lorberbaum et al., 2002; Swain, Lorberbaum, Kose, & Strathearn, 2007).

In short, a wealth of neuroscientific research now makes it abundantly clear that *parenting matters*, and it especially matters early in a child's life when the brain is in a sensitive period for social, emotional learning and is vulnerable to stress. It is not an exaggeration to say, based on research across mammalian species, that good parenting sculpts the child's brain for emotional resilience and social competence while developing the child's capacity to trust other people and to sustain positive, caring relationships. Sensitive parenting builds resilient, caring brains, and children who receive good care are better equipped to be nurturing and effective parents when the time comes to raise the next generation. In sum, this exciting research shows that sensitive, attuned parenting provides children with a "secure base" from which to explore their world; a first companion to share their discoveries with; and the brain systems needed to embrace and cope effectively with life's inevitable challenges, including the challenges of parenting the next generation.

All children deserve the kind of caregiving that fosters the development of secure attachment and puts them on a trajectory toward social and emotional resilience. Too many children only know the kind of safety that comes intermittently and disappears with a parent's inattentiveness, defensiveness, disinterest, or loss of control. This kind of fleeting, sporadic safety forces children to play defense much too early in life, making them hypervigilant in the one setting where they should be able to relax deeply and feel "safe to the bone." The intergenerational repercussions of impaired connections that result from this defensive style of relating to other people are all too common.

But providing the kind of sensitive, attuned care that research now strongly confirms is so helpful to children's development isn't easy. Parenting is an inherently stressful process, and even the most sensitive, empathic parent sometimes loses the capacity to care about a child in moments of anger, fear, or fatigue. At times, we all are challenged to keep our lids on. In brain terms, when we are under intense stress, we are all prone to briefly dismantling the vital brain connections that make it possible to keep our cool under fire, to "feel and deal" (Fosha, 2000). This disconnection is much more likely to occur in a stressed-out parent's brain, and it is harder to recover from it because the consequences are quickly visible in the child.

In brain science terms, when we're stressed out, we "go limbic." The limbic system is essentially our primal, "emotional brain," our "affective/visceral" core (Panksepp, 1998). When we're in a state of parental frustration or stress, the deep parts of our brain that are tightly connected to our bodies are strongly activated, briefly suppressing our higher cognitive capacities for self-regulation, self-awareness, and empathy. While we're in this state of mind and body, we are essentially "mind*less*," not "mind*ful*" (Siegel, 2010). This temporary disconnection or "uncoupling" of our lower and higher brain systems puts us and our children at the mercy of our more primitive, poorly regulated emotions and actions. Fortunately, many parents are able to recover quickly from these "unparental" moments and repair their connections with their children, preventing more enduring breaks in the relationship. But when parents get stuck in defensive states of mind and do not engage in timely repair efforts, they are at risk for developing *blocked care*, which entails the suppression of their nurturing for their children.

To our minds, the body of research on the parental brain highlights five different key domains of caregiving (we take a closer look at these domains in Chapter 2, and then, in Chapter 3, we look at how they can be impaired by stress, leading to blocked care).

The 5 Domains of Caregiving

1. The *Parental Approach System* enables parents to be close to children without becoming defensive;
2. the *Parental Reward System* makes it possible for the parent to experience pleasure from parenting;
3. the *Parental Child Reading System* supports the ability of a parent to understand and empathize with a child's inner subjective experiences;
4. the *Parental Meaning Making System* allows the parent to construct a working narrative or story about being a parent, and;
5. the *Parental Executive System*, the brain system that relies upon higher brain regions, helps the parent to regulate the lower, more automatic brain processes. The executive system helps parents to monitor their own feelings and actions, as well as the state of attunement or misattunement with their child. This system also is crucial for resolving conflicts between parental and unparental feelings, and reflecting on our experiences of being a parent. The Parental Executive System, heavily dependent on the functioning of the frontal lobes, helps to keep the other four systems "on" and working.

By explaining these basic domains of caregiving and how the inner workings of the brain are involved, we hope to help parents and therapists shift from a behavioral view of kids and parenting (focusing on how they act out and what they do to misbehave) to a relational one (focusing on trying to understand what their behavior signifies) in which close connection and mutual understanding (or *intersubjectivity*) are key. After all, parenting—even when it is impaired or blocked—is fundamentally a two-way relationship.

When parents are experiencing blocked care, they often focus narrowly on the behavioral difficulties that they are having with their children. Under stress and with the impairment of any or all domains of care, mentioned above, parents often hope to just "fix the problem" without first making sense of the relational difficulties they are experiencing with their children. In this book we hope to show parents the bigger, relational, brain-based picture that will help them to provide care without experiencing blame or shame.

CHAPTER 1

Parenting Is a Brain Thing

Sarah, mother of 12-month-old Vincent, is watching videos of her son while having her brain imaged. She is watching two different scenes. In one video, Vincent is laughing gleefully as Sarah blows big wet bubbles at him. In the other, Vincent is crying because Sarah has just left the room. As Sarah watches the happy Vincent scene, parts of her left hemisphere light up on the imaging screen—parts of the brain known to be connected to what brain scientists call the *reward system*. Although we cannot see it on the screen, chemicals, including oxytocin and dopamine, are flooding these regions of Sarah's brain. In contrast, as Sarah watches the scene of Vincent in distress, parts of her brain on the right side become very active—brain regions associated with responding empathically to a loved one's pain. Now, different chemicals, including one much like adrenaline, are spurting into regions of Sarah's brain that ramp up her vigilance and make her intensely and somewhat painfully aware of Vincent's distress. We are watching the healthy parenting brain in action.

Sarah's Brain:
Seeing the Healthy Parenting Brain in Action

Creating stable structures lasting over many years for the protection and rearing of children is essential, as our offspring, compared to those of other mammals, are the weakest and require the longest care.
— Donatella Marrazziti (2009, p. 265)

Like Vincent, our precious children depend completely on us, as parents, and perhaps more specifically, on the healthy functioning of our brains to parent well. Children's brains thrive when interacting with adults who have the brain capacity to love them unconditionally, experience joy from being with them, pay close attention to them, and understand them deeply. In short, nothing is more important to parent–child relationships and to children's development than the health of parents' brains.

We have to be moved by our interactions with our children if we are going to be responsive to their needs and stay connected to them. It's not enough just to notice that your child is upset; you have to *feel* something in response to seeing and hearing your child's distress. We take this process of being moved as parents for granted, but in this book, we are going to take a close look at what neuroscientists have learned about how we are able to feel these essential parental feelings, how our brains and bodies talk to each other in ways that enable us to be parental, to be caring and sensitive with our kids.

Although the process of becoming a parent may seem a "no brainer," the process of parenting taps all of the brain power we can muster. Parental love and sensitive, responsive parenting are made possible by a core brain system that emerged in the transition from reptiles to mammals, a process that involved essential changes in the structure and chemistry of the brain. Mammals acquired new brain structures, such as the cingulate, the insula, and the orbital cortex, and brain chemicals such as oxytocin, vasopressin, and prolactin, that made it possible to develop a lovely obsession with taking care of babies—a parental preoccupation with offspring that can be seen in mammals great and small, from mice to whales and elephants. Sea turtles, meanwhile, lacking these structures and chemicals, invest all of their parental energy in laying and protecting eggs. They then return to the sea, leaving their offspring to their fate.

At its core, parenting is an emotional process emanating from deep within our brains, from a set of tightly connected regions, called the *limbic system*, which is in constant communication with our bodies, especially with our hearts, lungs, and gut. Literally, parenting rests on connections between the brain and the body that enable us to generate loving feelings and to be intensely motivated to care for our children. While we use higher, more uniquely human parts of our brains in our parenting, we rely heavily on the same core system of parental care that evolved millions of years ago to make parental love possible (Fleming & Li, 2002).

Being Parental: Love versus Self-Defense

The parent–child relationship can foster feelings of deep love and empathy, but it can also trigger self-defensive feelings and give rise to impulses that are "unparental." Loving feelings and trust are rooted in safety, in the kind of "felt safety" that is more primal and instinctive than the knowledge that you *should* feel safe. In order to sustain an empathic style of parenting, you have to have a visceral sense of safety as you interact closely with your child, both in times of quiet joy and in times of conflict. Love is a state of openness to another person, and it competes in our brains and bodies with closed states of self-defense. Parenting well requires the ability to stay open and engaged with our children most of the time, not closed off to them as we defend ourselves against feeling unsafe or insecure.

In neuroscience terms, parenting rests upon a process of regulating our internal "states of mind," a so-called *state regulation system* that is under development in early childhood (Porges, 2011). Parenting relies upon our social engagement system, a brain–body state that enables us to get very close to other people without getting defensive. Our state regulation system orchestrates internal shifts in our approach behavior (typically open and non-defensive) and our avoidance (defensive) behavior. Our brains mediate these shifts by using automatic, unconscious, bottom-up processes and by using more conscious, "top-down," and effortful processes. Becoming aware of this bottom-up and top-down state regulation process helps us to understand ourselves as parents and how we manage to stay parental in spite of the stresses and strains we inevitably experience along the way.

Being Open to Your Child:
Parental States and State Regulation

In particular, parenting rests upon the development of strong connections between our brains and our hearts. This brain–heart connection is based on a branch of a complicated, wandering nerve called the *vagus* nerve. The whole vagal system travels from our digestive tract all the way up to the brainstem, connecting all regions along the way to our brains. This system is the basis for that part of our nervous system called the *parasympathetic system*. In contrast to the *sympathetic nervous system* that ramps us up, increasing our heart rate when we need to be mobilized for action, such as in the defensive modes of fight and flight, the parasympathetic system is active when we are in relatively immobile states, relaxing, digesting, watching a movie, and so on. The bottom parts of the vagal system connect the gut to the brain and orchestrate basic relaxation, digestive processes, and the freeze/immobilization mechanism that we can use as a defense if we encounter an inescapable, life-threatening threat. The upper vagal system connecting the heart and lungs to the brain is a more recently evolved system that only exists in mammals. This is the system that supports social interaction and makes it possible, neurologically, to connect deeply with other people rather than become defensive and attack or run from them. It is this upper vagal system that is essential to good parenting.

Stephen Porges (2011), a neuroscientist who has devoted his career to understanding how humans are able to be such social creatures, calls this upper vagal system the "smart vagus" because it allows us to regulate our heart rate and our breathing very flexibly across a wide range of feelings without shifting fully into a defensive reaction. This is the system that enables a parent to stay grounded and emotionally "present" when the parent–child relationship becomes stressful or strained. The smart vagal system supports social engagement, connection, and mutual understanding by helping parents to stay in tune with a child's experience and to keep their lids on even while their usually loving son is blowing his top.

The smart vagus not only effectively connects the lower regions of the prefrontal cortex to the heart and lungs; it also controls the muscles of the upper parts of the face that we use to express positive emotions. This smart vagal system (which Porges also calls the ventral vagal system) also orchestrates voice quality or "prosody," the musical quality of the voice, as exemplified in "motherese," the way parents typically vocalize to their babies in higher-pitched, sing-song tones. Furthermore, Porges explains, this vagal circuit has a connection to a muscle in the inner ear that is vital to the process of tuning our hearing to the frequencies used in human speech. This connection allows us to be good listeners and to attune to both the content of speech and to the prosody, the subtle musical qualities of each other's voices.

When this smart vagal system is "on," in parents and children, both are able to feel safe enough to communicate openly. In this shared state of sociability, parents and children can sustain a deep level of engagement without shifting into defensive states incompatible with the uniquely human form of communication that Trevarthen calls "intersubjectivity" (Trevarthen, 2001; Trevarthen and Aitken, 2001) . Intersubjective communication is the sharing of inner experiences- thoughts, feelings, dreams, misgivings- between parent and child, as opposed to more superficial kinds of behavioral interactions that are often necessary, but do not promote deeper understanding of each other and a deepening of emotional connections. Open-minded parenting, resting heavily on the smart vagal system, promotes intersubjective communication, the kind of parent-child communication that helps children feel deeply understood and valued by their parents. The smart vagal system helps parents to stay in this open-minded internal state much of the time, regulating competition between this openness and defensive reactions that are usually false alarms and don't really require self-defense. When parents have a well-developed social engagement system, they can stay open and receptive to a child's full range of emotions and to their own internal feelings without defaulting to a self-protective, self-centered state of mind. In a sense, good vagal tone—that is, a well-developed smart vagal system—provides the brain support for a parent's tolerance of the stresses and strains of parent–child interactions. Parents with good vagal tone have larger windows of stress tolerance and a greater capacity to regulate strong emotions than parents with poor vagal tone. Figure 1.1 illustrates the smart vagal system.

Figure 1.1 The Smart Vagus Connecting the Brain and the Heart
This is the circuit that supports social engagement and parental openness.

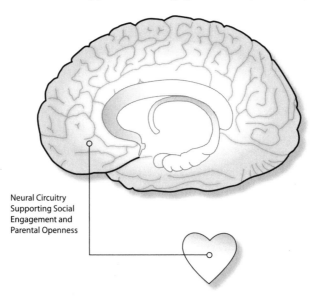

Neural Circuitry
Supporting Social
Engagement and
Parental Openness

The goal, then, is to stay in the open state of social engagement as much as possible, as illustrated in Figure 1.2. This is quite challenging for all parents because the process of interacting with children is inherently stressful and, inevitably, at times, triggers defensive feelings that are not consistent with the caring feelings we want to have. The social engagement system is only activated when we feel safe enough being near another person.

Next, we consider how our brains determine whether we are safe enough to stay focused on parenting rather than shifting our focus to our own physical or psychological well-being.

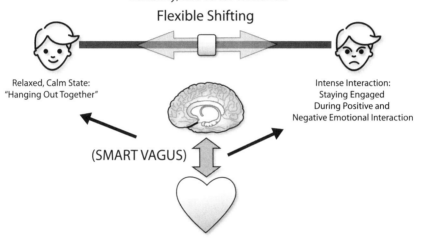

Figure 1.2 Using the Smart Vagal System to Support Flexible, Open Parenting.
Vagal tone in parenting terms translates into engagement, flexibility, and stress tolerance.

Flexible Shifting

Relaxed, Calm State:
"Hanging Out Together"

Intense Interaction:
Staying Engaged
During Positive and
Negative Emotional Interaction

(SMART VAGUS)

Taming Your Amygdala: Neuroception and Your Limbic System

To effectively switch from defensive to social engagement strategies, the mammalian nervous system needs to perform two important adaptive tasks: (1) assess risk, and (2) if the environment is perceived as safe, inhibit the more primitive limbic structures that control fight, flight, or freeze behaviors.
—Porges (2011, p. 57)

Our brains rapidly assess our social environment for safety or danger using an automatic screening process that works under the radar of our conscious awareness. Porges calls this the *neuroception system* to distinguish it from the more conscious process of *perception*. This neuroception system is orchestrated by a brain region called the amygdala (shown in Figure 1.3), the brain filter for all incoming sensory information as well as for all information coming into the brain from the body. The amygdala is part of what neuroscientists call the "limbic system," a group of structures in the mammalian brain that generate emotions and orchestrate the basic processes of approaching and avoiding things in life. As a key part of the limbic system, the amygdala receives input from all of the external senses and from the body and is able to detect a potential threat in less than $1/10$ of a second, much faster than the time it takes for our brains to create a conscious thought or feeling (Davis & Whalen, 2001). If the amygdala detects a threat, it can instantly switch our brain circuits from approach to defensive avoidance. If the threat level is moderate, not life-threatening, we are likely to activate our sympathetic nervous system, taking us into our fight or flight system, at least enough to raise our heart rate and increase our level of vigilance. If the threat is sensed as life-threatening or overwhelming and inescapable, the amygdala triggers our parasympathetic system, the lower vagal system that promotes immobilization, a shutdown response that, in effect, prepares us for a relatively pain-free death. This is the same system that animals use to "play dead" when they are about to be eaten by a predator and that we use to dissociate and to stop caring about what is happening.

If the neuroception system does not detect any real threat, it activates our social approach system, engendering a sense of safety and promoting trust between people. When this system is "on"—when, in effect, the amygdala has been tamed—other brain systems that mediate self-defensive reactions are "off." When we are able to activate this basic "approach" system as a parent, the rest of the parenting process, including the ability to experience intense pleasure from being with our children, turns on and fosters the development of enduring emotional bonds with our kids. Most of the time, these connections are robust enough to trump competing emotions inevitably triggered by interacting day after day with our children for the many years it takes for humans to reach maturity.

Figure 1.3 Location of the Amygdala

The amygdala has both input and output regions so that it can receive all kinds of sensory inputs, including the five basic senses, and from the visceral regions, including the heart and the gut. It then can use this input to either suppress or activate output pathways to the rest of the brain and to the body.

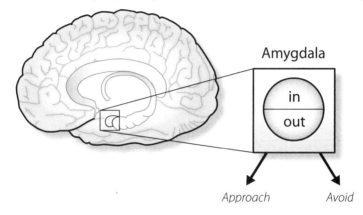

Although the amygdala reacts to both positive and negative stimuli, it appears to specialize in threat detection, fear conditioning, and harm avoidance, especially on the right side of the brain. It appears that the amygdala on the left side is more involved in generating conscious feelings and emotions related to approaching rather than avoiding things in life (Whalen & Phelps, 2009).

Since everything that we sense, both externally and internally, runs through the amygdala for a quick appraisal of its survival value, the amygdala plays a key role in the parental brain in quickly and roughly assessing whether it is safe to be close to and fully engaged with a child or whether there is something threatening about this intimate contact. This gives the amygdala a very important role in helping parents to orchestrate the process of staying parental and in connection with their child rather than shifting into a defensive state that disconnects parents and children from each other emotionally and psychologically. All mammals have the basic circuitry for performing this neuroceptive process.

According to Porges, "the neuroception of familiar individuals and individuals with appropriately prosodic voices and warm, expressive faces translates into a social interaction promoting a sense of safety" (2011, p. 58). In humans, the amygdala is very responsive to facial expressions, especially to eye contact and eye movements. This quick reaction to eye contact, which can be positive or negative, is thought to be one of the difficulties that people with social phobia and those on the autism spectrum have with sustaining face-to-face interaction with others. The amygdala is especially sensitive to changes in the region of the face around the eyes, including the lowering or arching of the brow, changes in pupil size and brightness, and shifts in gaze. Human eyes have the greatest contrast between light and dark, apparently a feature that helps us read other people's eyes to determine their trustworthiness. Even newborns pay more attention to a direct gaze than to averted eyes, whether it's a real face or a drawing. Although being eye-to-eye may engender intimacy and loving feelings, it may also set off a defensive reaction in the amygdala if someone stares at us in an unfriendly way. Living in a threatening environment can sensitize the amygdala to angry and fearful facial expressions, lowering the threshold for triggering defensive reactions to other people (Pollak, 2003).

A key area of the amygdala involved in parenting is called the medial region. The medial amygdala has much to do with our approach and avoidance reactions to other people (Mayes et al., 2009). This region is involved in rapid, automatic switching between these two responses of approaching versus avoiding (van Reekum et al., 2007). One of the ways that this switching is orchestrated without the involvement of a higher control process is through the release of oxytocin into the medial amygdala by pleasant experiences with other people, including "good touch" and warm, friendly voices. The amygdala has receptors for oxytocin and when these receptors are "occupied," this has a quieting effect on the amygdala (Veenama & Neuman, 2008, Domes, et al., 2007). In this way, oxytocin helps to inhibit the defensive, avoidant reaction system, enabling the social engagement approach system to stay on. In short, the release of oxytocin is an important automatic, bottom-up, process for helping a parent stay connected to a child rather than shifting into a self-defensive state that creates an emotional barrier between parent and child.

The amygdala is online and basically ready to work in the newborn infant's brain. Although there may be a brief period of time after birth that the amygdala is not yet very sensitive, it appears that exposure to highly stressful stimulation can override this early buffering system and activate the amygdala prematurely. At any rate, this threat detection system is available very early in the first year of life and orchestrates much of the infant's initial social and emotional learning, in conjunction with lower regions of the prefrontal cortex that have ties to the amygdala, especially the orbital region at the bottom of the prefrontal cortex.

BOTTOM LINE: In parenting terms, the amygdala mediates rapid assessment of safety or threat, thereby playing a key role in moving us instinctively toward, or away from, our children.

Keeping Perspective: The Role of the Hippocampus

In a healthy brain, the amygdala works in conjunction with a structure adjacent to it in the temporal lobe called the *hippocampus* (see Figure 1.4). The hippocampus is a crucial and intriguing part of the your brain because of its multiple roles. It . . .

- Constructs conscious, autobiographical memories.
- Helps to put emotional reactions in context of time and place.
- Gives birth to new brain cells (*neurogenesis*).
- Helps to regulate the stress response system (Andersen, Morris, Amaral, Bliss, & O'Keefe, 2007).

You can appreciate the many roles of the hippocampus if you have ever known someone with dementia; the hippocampus is eventually destroyed in patients with Alzheimer's disease.

Figure 1.4. The Hippocampus
This structure is essential for making parental memories, learning from parenting, dealing with stress, keeping the parental brain healthy, and making new brain cells.

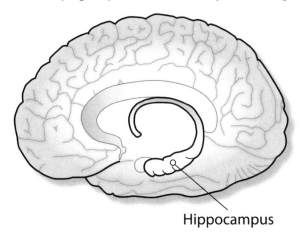

Hippocampus

In a healthy brain, the amygdala and the hippocampus work well together to help put emotional experiences into context. However, the hippocampus is slower to mature and come online in development than is the amygdala, and it is also quite sensitive to stress hormones. The slower development of the hippocampus has much to do with why early childhood is such a purely emotional stage of social learning and development, a period of life when many experiences are immediate, intense, and only remembered *implicitly*—that is, indirectly, in terms of unconscious clues such as smells, sounds, sights, and proprioception—rather than *explicitly*—that is, in terms of conscious and specific contexts often involving time and place and events (what is termed *autobiographical memory, one of several kinds of explicit memories*). The hippocampus is needed to make explicit autobiographical memories, the kind we usually are referring to when we speak of memory (Siegel, 1999; Wall & Messier, 2001). To summarize:

- *Implicit emotional memories* are nonverbal memories orchestrated by the amygdala and not involving conscious awareness. (There are other kinds of implicit memories that do not involve the amygdala, such as "procedural" memories of how to do various things in life, like riding a bike). Example of an emotional implicit memory: as an infant, Gail hears her father yelling at her mother and forms an implicit memory that associates males with feelings of fear. Then, later in life, being around men triggers extreme discomfort in Gail without her knowing what is really causing this reaction. These kinds of memories resulting from exposure to highly stressful or very pleasurable experiences very early in life are the basis of preverbal emotional conditioning that can cause strong reactions later in life to stimuli or events similar to those encountered in early childhood. These kinds of "triggered" memories seem to come from nowhere, causing feelings and bodily reactions that we don't understand.

- *Explicit memories* are verbal, conscious memories requiring hippocampal processing, only possible when the hippocampus is sufficiently mature and healthy. Example: When Jimmy was 5 years old, he was stung by a bee. Many years later, he could recall this experience and describe what it felt like. He tended to be quite afraid of bees and he knew why.
- *Autobiographical memories* are memories of events in our lives, including who, what, where, and when, and they require both the amygdala and hippocampus to capture both the feelings and context of the experience. Example: When Rob was 8, his Dad took him to his first major league baseball game, an experience that Rob recalled vividly at age 20, remembering being in the stands, having a hotdog, and hearing his dad rooting for the home team and then being sad when they lost.

As the brain develops, the amygdala and hippocampus work together to create emotion-driven memories that are embedded in time and place, memories that neuroscientists call *contextualized*. These are the kind of autobiographical memories that allow us to recall where we were, when we were there, and whom we were with when emotionally significant experiences occurred. These memories eventually get stored in our long term memory, but can be retrieved and compared to the present moment to tell if there is a difference or if there is a match between the present experience and past experiences. Before the hippocampal system really starts to work effectively, probably somewhere late in the second year of life, the brain is only capable of making *amygdaloid* emotion-based memories or procedural memories of how to do things.

Since the hippocampus is quite sensitive to stress hormones such as cortisol and to excitatory brain chemicals such as glutamate, it is a part of your brain that can be harmed by too much stress reactivity (McEwen, 2004). Poor hippocampal functioning and even structural changes to this region are common features of many psychiatric disorders, from depression and anxiety to posttraumatic stress disorder (PTSD) and schizophrenia. Protecting the hippocampus in early development is a very important goal from the perspective of promoting healthy brain growth and resilient functioning. Since the amygdala is closely connected to, and interacts with, the hippocampus, overactivation of the amygdala can be a source of toxic effects on the functioning, growth, and structure of the hippocampus.

BOTTOM LINE: In parenting terms, the hippocampus helps us put parenting experiences in perspective, manage stress, learn from our experiences, make new brain cells, and create rich memories of being with our children.

Building a Healthy Parenting Brain: Bottom Up and Top Down

The terms *bottom up* and *top down* refer to lower and higher brain circuits, or what brain scientists call the *ventral* (lower) and *dorsal* (higher) "streams" for processing information. (It helps to remember the difference between dorsal and ventral if you picture the dorsal fin of a shark sitting on the top of that big body.) The bottom-up stream in our brains is the one that is tightly connected to our visceral organs— our hearts, lungs, adrenal glands, and digestive tract—making this brain circuit the one that generates *affect*, meaning all kinds of feelings and sensations. *Affects* include all of our emotions, sensations, and visceral reactions to things we like and want to approach and things we dislike or fear and want to avoid. When this lower stream is activated, we feel something is happening *to* us. We have gut reactions and heart-felt responses that make us take things personally. This bottom-up stream, then, is the one that is really "on" when we are experiencing something from an egocentric or "me- centered" perspective. In fact, in people who have clinical paranoia (*clinical* means that the condition is severe enough to warrant a psychiatric diagnosis), brain imaging shows that only the bottom-up stream is on (Drevets, 2000); the upper stream is essentially out of commission, and this is why people with paranoia believe that everything they are experiencing is about them; they literally lack the brain power, at least in these moments, to distinguish between what is really "about me" and what is "not about me."

The upper stream of the brain is not directly connected to our visceral selves. We use this "cooler" brain circuit to understand or look at something more objectively, as if from above, less passionately and less personally. So, in an important sense, we need both of these brain streams, the lower and the higher, to be able both to feel our emotions and sensations—to "resonate" in response to our experiences—and to put our experiences in perspective by distinguishing between what is really personal and what is not (Beuregard, Levesque, & Bourgouin, 2001; Ochsner, Ray, et al., 2004). Since the bottom-up stream is the one that is tied to our limbic system, it is the circuit that is vital to our immediate survival, the system that performs the neuroceptive, unconscious "first-take" screening of the information coming from our external and internal senses. This is the system that we use to appraise everything in life first for its immediate survival value and for rapidly assessing whether we are safe or in danger.

The amygdala is part of the lower stream, whereas the hippocampus functions, in part, as a bridge between the two streams. The amygdala *receives from* and *feeds back to* every sensory region of the brain, whereas the hippocampus receives information that has already been highly processed in a multi-sensory fashion by other regions of the brain and then shares this well-processed information with higher brain regions (LeDoux, 2002). Both the lower and upper streams feed their "output" into the prefrontal cortex, making that region your headquarters for integrating the two streams, for putting your emotion-based, more subjective experience together with your more objective, cooler-headed, and "cognitive" way of making sense of what is going on. Damage to the prefrontal cortex makes this integration difficult or even impossible in more severe cases. (The most famous case in neuroscience is that of Phineas Gage, who suffered damage to his prefrontal cortex that destroyed the vital connections between his ventral and dorsal systems. Search "Phineas Gage" on the Internet to read about his 19th-century experience.)

The upper stream develops more slowly and works more slowly, creating a scenario in which the lower brain circuit can dominate the upper much more easily than the upper or top-down system can modulate the lower. Even as adults, then, we can still, at times, be at the mercy of our bottom-up brain–body system, temporarily losing the moderating functioning of our top-down system. Figure 1.5 shows the two streams connecting in the prefrontal cortex. As you can see, the lower stream is the one that is directly connected to your heart and to your smart vagal system. The prefrontal cortex is the integration zone for the lower and upper streams, making it possible for you to be aware of your feelings *and*, at the same time, to think about what is happening in your relationship with your child, to "feel and deal." Figure 1.5 illustrates the interaction of bottom-up (affect regulation) and top-down (reflective) processes.

BOTTOM LINE: In parenting terms, bottom-up and top-down brain processes integrate parental feelings and thinking in an adaptive, flexible way.

Early Childhood and the Parenting Brain: An Intergenerational Cycle

Developing the capacity for being a consistently nurturing parent begins in the *parents'* early childhoods. Early parent–child interactions

Figure 1.5.

The Ventral (Lower) and Dorsal (Upper) Brain Systems Meeting in the
Prefrontal Cortex, Which Integrates the Input from the Two Systems.
ACC = anterior cingulate cortex; PFC = prefrontal cortex.

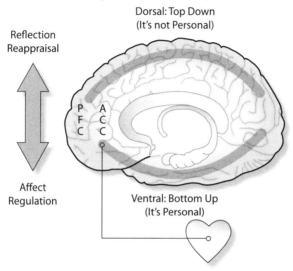

set the stage, not just metaphorically or psychologically, but neurobiologically, for the later capacity to be sensitive, caring parents. During
the first year of life, the child's brain starts to develop more connections between the lower and the upper streams of the brain. These
connections are essential for the regulation of emotion and for developing the ability to connect the processes of feeling and thinking, to
be able to deal with emotionally arousing events in life in a flexible,
resilient way. During the first 18 months of life, the child's amygdala grows two-way connections to higher brain regions located in
the lower parts of the prefrontal cortex (National Scientific Council
on the Developing Child, 2008; Schore, 1994). The two parts of the
prefrontal area that are most important in forming these *frontolimbic*
connections are the orbitofrontal cortex and the anterior cingulate
cortex (for short, just *anterior cingulate*), as shown in Figure 1.6.

The reason that the orbitofrontal cortex and anterior cingulate are
so important to child development and, ultimately, to parenting is that
these two regions can directly inhibit the activity of the amygdala and
help to modulate the threat-detection process (neuroception) and

state regulation process discussed above. In a healthy, mature brain, the orbital region and the anterior cingulate, working in connection with the amygdala, are more in charge of your emotions and your stress reactions than your amygdala by itself. This means that you have more power to regulate the way you react to emotionally arousing things in life, including things your child does that trigger unparental feelings in you. These connections between the orbitofrontal cortex and the nearby anterior cingulate with your amygdala are core elements of your "executive" brain, the system for regulating emotional reactions and orchestrating the process of staying in control of your actions even when experiencing strong negative feelings and impulses. This makes it extremely important that a child's brain grows good connections between the orbitofrontal cortex, the anterior cingulate, and the amygdala to form an effective executive brain system for self-regulation—a process that goes on very actively during the first 18 months of life and then continues as we mature.

Figure 1.6. The Frontolimbic System.
The orbitofrontal cortex (OFC) and the lower anterior cingulate cortex (ACC) connect to the amygdala to form a brain circuit for self-regulation.

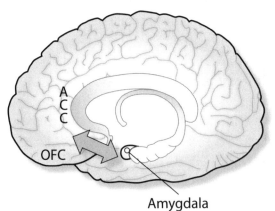

Neuroscience has revealed the process by which good parent–child and poor parent–child relationships are passed on, generation to generation. It is now quite well established by this body of research, which spans different species of mammals, that early care influences the development of offsprings' brains in enduring ways—ways that greatly impact the way adults are likely to parent the next generation (National Scientific Council, 2010). This intriguing body of research, called *maternal or parental effects*, is revealing, down to the level of specific gene activity, how the early environment impinges upon the brain (Francis, Champagne & Meaney, 2000). In essence, this research shows that early experiences "tune" and "sculpt" key brain circuits involved in stress responsiveness and in social–emotional processes. This programming of a child's developing brain adapts to this first social niche in ways that reflect the specific nature of the care the child encounters. In effect, this early "experience-dependent" process prepares the child's brain to live in a world that is similar to the first environment in terms of the level of safety and danger this environment presents.

Just as the child's exposure to a particular language in the first year of life tunes the language-learning circuitry to the specific sounds of that native tongue, and in doing so, makes it harder for the child's brain to hear all of the sounds of another language later in life, exposure to a particular social and emotional niche tunes the child's brain in ways that make the brain resistant later on to changing this basic social program for relating to other people. The developing brain is dedicated to learning a basic strategy for both staying connected to the vital lifeline that attachment figures represent and also for staying vigilant enough around these figures if they are not consistently safe to be near.

This preverbal strategy for relating to other people is called an *attachment style*, of which there are several, and these styles, whether secure or insecure, are rooted in early brain development reflecting the interplay of genes and environment (Siegel, 1999). Indeed, recent research using brain imaging of adults with different attachment styles shows specific brain "signatures" associated with these styles (Strathearn & Fonagy, 2009; Swain & Lorberbaum, 2008). At the most fundamental level, this is why these early attachment styles tend to be so enduring, often staying consistent from the first year of life into adulthood and affecting the style of parenting we adopt (Van IJzendorn, 1995).

The initial tuning of the social–emotional brain circuitry and stress response systems tends to endure and to keep running the same old programs even when presented with "new" information in response to the old behaviors. Nature has ensured that we will not give up original strategies for survival easily. Understanding the enduring nature of early programming of the social brain can go a long way toward helping both parents and therapists grasp why it can be so challenging to sustain the parenting process with a brain that has been tuned to living defensively rather than living in safe connections with others.

BOTTOM LINE: In parenting terms, early brain development lays the groundwork for self-regulation and personal security, helping to build a healthy parenting brain.

Priming the Parenting Brain: Hormonal Prepping of the Caregiving Process

While early development sets the stage for being a caring person, the actual process of becoming a parent promotes hormonal changes that help to shift the brain from a primary focus on one's own resources and competencies (i.e., the all-about-me phases of adolescence and young adulthood), which is developmentally appropriate, to an intensive focus on caregiving. While this hormonal "priming" of the brain for parenting is much more variable in fathers than in mothers of different species, becoming a dad also changes the brain in many species, at least enough to keep the fathers from harming their own infants (Veenama & Neuman, 2008). In some species, including humans, both mothers and fathers undergo powerful brain changes that shift the brains of both from other preoccupations to a keen interest in protecting and nurturing the young. In these co-parenting species, a similar process of brain changes typically promotes "pair bonding," or the development of lifelong adult connections after mating (Carter, 2005). In species such as prairie voles and titi monkeys that show these patterns of pair bonding and co-parental care, we see the origins of the kind of family systems that most humans value. And in some species, including humans, nonbiological parents can develop a nurturing brain; just being exposed to children can activate the caregiving system.

Neuroscientists such as Sue Carter opened a gold mine for understanding the brain mechanisms of emotional bonding by uncovering the role of *neuropeptides* (protein-like molecules used by neurons to communicate with each other), specifically of oxytocin and vasopressin, in promoting both adult bonding and parent–child bonding in animals (Carter, 2005; Insel & Shapiro, 1992). Oxytocin and vasopressin are active in the brains of both women and men, with oxytocin playing a bigger role in women, vasopressin in men. In both moms and dads, oxytocin plays a very important part in helping to promote the bonding process between parent and child. Parents whose brains release a lot of oxytocin into the limbic regions—that is, the amygdala, the hippocampus, and the orbitofrontal cortex —tend to be very nurturing parents who experience their interactions with their children as often highly pleasurable.

Oxytocin acts much like an antianxiety medicine in your brain, helping to keep your amygdala-driven alarm system calm while activating your brain's approach system, the smart vagal system that Porges describes as the neural basis for loving relationships. Vasopressin is more associated with persistent behavior and with aggressive "defense of the homeland," which may be why it is more of a "player" in the neurobiology of the father than the mother. Vasopressin in the father's brain probably helps to promote a fatherly preoccupation with the safety and well-being of his family at the same time that oxytocin helps the dad feel safe and comfortable when interacting closely with his kids (Bales & Carter, 2003). Maybe the different actions of oxytocin and vasopressin in fathers have something to do with why some dads are primarily motivated to be "bread winners," others really enjoy nurturing and playing with their kids, and some do both really well. More research is needed (and is underway as we write) to sort all of this out more clearly.

What neuroscientists found, when they set out to learn why parent–offspring and adult–adult bonds are much stronger in some species of mammals than in others, is that the big factor is loca-tion, location, *location*: where in the brain the receptors for oxytocin and vasopressin are most prevalent or "dense" (Carter & Keverne, 2002). All mammalian species appear to release oxytocin during lovemaking, a chemical reaction that can temporarily deactivate the defense systems that would otherwise make the process of mating impossible. But here's the key: In species that mate for life and form strong, enduring bonds between parents and offspring, there are lots of receptors for oxytocin in the reward center of the brain—in the nucleus accumbens region that is a critical part of our social engage-ment system and the parenting brain.

The nucleus accumbens is actually part of our motor system, key to what one neuroscientist calls our "seeking system" (Panksepp, 1998). When anything in life activates our nucleus accumbens by causing dopamine to flow into this region and activate receptors there, we get attached, even a bit addicted to, that thing, be it our spouse-to-be, our kids, our cars, our shoes, and, yes, drugs and alcohol. All things rewarding in life ultimately send a message to the nucleus accum-bens, using dopamine as the key transmitter. So, if in your parental brain, the activities of parenting light up your nucleus accumbens through a chain effect involving both oxytocin and dopamine, then you are going to experience being a parent differently from someone whose brain does not do this, or doesn't do it as strongly as your brain does. Furthermore, the density of receptors for both oxytocin and dopamine in a parent's brain depends, in part, on how that parent was parented, on the quality of care he or she received early in life. Good care promotes the "expression" of the genes for oxytocin and dopamine receptors, and this means that a child's well-cared-for brain makes more of these receptors.

This oxytocin–dopamine–nucleus accumbens scenario is also affected by your stress level. Under significant stress, even if you have a well-developed reward system, this system may be suppressed or knocked out, at least temporarily, by your stress reaction system—specifically, by stress hormones. So, when your stress system is on, your reward system is probably off; these two systems are basically in competition with each other, vying to "decide" whether you should be seeking something pleasurable or whether you need to be defending yourself. Your amygdala plays a big part in this "decision" process. People or animals with damaged amygdalas approach new things in life very readily, showing little concern about possible harm or danger. This is also true of kids with William's syndrome; these are super-friendly children who have underactive amygdalas and overactive people-processing regions of the brain. Becoming familiar with your amygdala and the kinds of things it reacts to in life is an important part of learning to regulate your own stress and manage your tendencies to approach and avoid things in your life, including your children.

Another area of the brain that is part of the parental priming process and is responsive to oxytocin is called the *medial preoptic area*. The medial preoptic area is a part of the hypothalamus, a collection of nuclei near the middle of the brain concerned with all of the basic drives in life: hunger, thirst, sex, sleep, and caregiving. In research across species of mammals, from rodents to people, the medial preoptic area has been shown to be a vital region of the brain for priming maternal behavior following the birth of offspring (Numan & Stolzenberg, 2008). Its role in fathers' brains is less clear because in males, the medial preoptic area is more strongly connected to mating behavior. In the generally more mysterious paternal brain, there appear to be interactions with other regions of the brain that help to suppress defensive reactions and enable a dad to be nurturing. At any rate, researchers have learned a lot about the parenting brain from studying how parenting is primed by certain hormones, shifting the brain into a state of readiness for a suite of caregiving processes, including building shelter, nursing, grooming, and retrieving the young when they get "lost." It is this priming process that helps make babies so endearing and irresistible to their parents.

What brain chemicals initiate this priming of the medial preoptic area? Estrogen appears to be the key here, and prolactin, best known for stimulating milk production in nursing mothers, also plays a very important role, surprisingly, in fathers as well as mothers. When estrogen is released into the medial preoptic area, it apparently sensitizes the receptors for prolactin and for oxytocin (which is produced and released from two other regions of the hypothalamus). When oxytocin is released into the medial preoptic area, after estrogen priming of this region, the medial preoptic area gets actively involved in promoting parental activity, signaling the body to rev up milk production, and signaling other regions of the brain, especially the reward system, to become highly responsive to infant stimuli, including odors, touch, facial expressions, and vocalizations.

In short, the priming of the medial preoptic area leads to the sensitization of the emotional brain and the people-reading regions of the brain to prepare the parenting brain to be especially interested in, and attentive to, the newborn child. Working together, these brain regions get the parenting process up and running, initiating a proactive suite of caregiving behaviors and making interactions with infants pleasurable. This bottom-up, hormonally driven scenario in the parenting brain constitutes the core mammalian systems of approach and reward that we call the Parental Approach System and the Parental Reward System. These two brain systems are shared across species for helping to ensure that parents are highly motivated to take care of their babies and to find the process memorable and essentially irresistible. These processes in the brain of the parent basically shift the brain's priorities from nonparental concerns to the tasks of parenting and help to maintain this parental state of mind for the duration of the period of time it takes to rear offspring to maturity. If this system for jump-starting and maintaining the parenting process does not work well or is suppressed for any reason, the whole parenting process suffers, creating a risk for blocked care. As we discuss more in Chapter 3, these systems can be suppressed by unmanageable levels of parental stress.

Experiments with rat moms show the power of this shift in priorities from before giving birth to after. "Virgin" female rats shun infant rats at first, either avoiding them or attacking them. "Primiparous" or first-time mothers, in sharp constrast, prefer contact with baby rats to a shot of cocaine. Their priorities then shift back over the time span in which baby rats mature up to weaning, so that by the time weaning is taking place, that cocaine is looking a lot better than it did when the kids were little (Fleming, Gonazalez, Afonso, & Lovic, 2008).

The parenting process is primed hormonally in human parents much as it is in simpler mammals. Although our parenting also involves the highest regions of our large prefrontal cortex, which give us greatly enhanced executive powers to regulate ourselves and to act in accordance with higher goals and intentions, we are still highly affected by the functioning of this mostly subcortical, bottom-up parenting system that we inherited from simpler species in the course of mammalian evolution. The role of the core parenting brain system in humans is demonstrated in many ways; for example, research shows that mothers and fathers release oxytocin during positive, pleasurable interactions with infants and that levels of prolactin rise in both mothers and fathers when both are involved in child care (Feldman, Gordon, & Zagoory-Sharon, 2010).

Parental Joy: The Dopamine Factor

One of the most intriguing findings in research on the parenting brain is that interacting with offspring powerfully activates the brain's reward system (Fleming et al., 2008). The reward system is heavily tied to the chemical dopamine, which is released into the nucleus accumbens when something pleasurable is encountered in life, including drugs of abuse. Once the dopamine system learns about a good thing, it stores a memory of it and then fires in anticipation of having that rewarding experience again. Research shows that our reward system is turned on by interacting with our children. This is an extremely important process that helps to ensure that we will stay engaged and highly motivated to care for our kids. In Chapter 3, we discuss how stress can suppress this system, making it very difficult to sustain the caregiving process. Suppression of the Parental Reward System is one of the core mechanisms of blocked care.

As we saw in the opening vignette about Sarah's brain, brain-imaging studies literally show the activation of the parental reward system in parents' brains when they are looking at pictures of their children or listening to recordings of their children's voices (Swain & Lorberbaum, 2008). Recent brain-imaging studies comparing the brain reactions of parents with secure and insecure adult attachments show intriguing differences, particularly in their brain activity when listening to recordings of their children crying. Whereas the securely attached parents appeared to activate their reward pathways in response to these sounds of distress, the insecurely attached parents showed a more complicated pattern of brain activity in which they appear to be activating conflicting systems of approach and avoidance (Strathearn & Fonagy, 2009).

BOTTOM LINE: In parenting terms, priming of the parental brain prepares the parent to become preoccupied with the well-being of the newborn child and to enjoy the process of caring for the child

---

Moved to Care: Parental Empathy and the Insula

In addition to this vital priming process, parents need to be moved emotionally and viscerally by interacting with their children in order to stay motivated to nurture them deeply, repeatedly, and for many years. In the literature on parenting, terms that appear frequently in describing rather intangible but important qualities of parental responsiveness to children are *empathy* and *warmth*. Actually, parental empathy and warmth are related to brain processes involving pathways that connect our bodily reactions to things in life to regions of our brains that allow us to be moved by these bodily reactions. So, empathy and warmth have to do with the ability to feel one's bodily reactions to things in life, to be aware of our gut reactions and the workings of our limbic systems. In order to experience empathy, these reactions have to register in brain regions that create the conscious experience of being moved by other people.

We focused earlier on the amygdgala as an important part of the emotional brain. A less well-known brain region, called the *insula*, is now receiving a lot of attention from brain scientists. The insula is now considered to be the "visceral" brain or the part of the cortex where information is received from the activity of our visceral organs, including the heart, lungs, and gut (Craig, 2009). People who are keenly aware of their bodily sensations, including the beating of their hearts, have very active insulas, especially on the right side of the brain. The activation of the insula is actually now thought to be a key part of the neurobiology of intuition, our "gut sense" about things that we cannot really explain but "just know." Like many brain regions, the insula creates a map of the information it processes—in this case, a map of the visceral systems of the body. Parts of the insula, when activated, trigger feelings of disgust and negative social emotions such as envy and jealousy. Other parts, in contrast, trigger positive, loving feelings that promote social engagement and intimacy (Cozolino, 2006).

Whereas people who experience intense feelings and tune in easily to other people's emotions show high levels of activity in the insula, people who report little awareness of feelings, including bodily sensations, have sluggish insulas and tend to lack intuitive knowledge about other people's internal states. In clinical terms, people who are *alexithymic*—that is, who are not aware of their feelings—have underactive insulas (Gundel et al., 2004). It is easy to see how the insula plays an important role in the parenting brain and how individual differences in insula reactivity could affect parental empathy—the ability to attune on a visceral, intuitive level, to a child's inner experiences.

Researchers make an important distinction between empathy and the more cognitive process of *mentalization* or what is often referred to, rather clumsily, as "theory of mind." Empathy is the more emotion-based, visceral attunement process that occurs quite automatically, whereas mentalization is a more intentional, cerebral process that involves the ability to understand a child's verbal and nonverbal communication. Mentalization involves higher regions of the parenting brain, including the middle region of the prefrontal cortex or the medial prefrontal cortex. Both empathy and mentalization abilities are important to parenting (Baron-Cohen, 2003).

As a key part of the parental empathy system, the insula, specifically the front or anterior region of this structure, is highly connected to another brain region that is very important to parenting, the anterior cingulate. This important insula–anterior cingulate connection is shown in Figure 1.7.

Figure 1.7. The Insula–Anterior Cingulate: Key to Parental Empathy

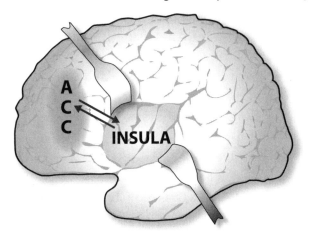

As mentioned earlier, the anterior cingulate is a structure that is basically nonexistent in the brains of reptiles. Its emergence in the transition from reptiles to mammals is thought to be strongly related to the emergence of sustained parental care in mammals, especially to the ability of a parent to respond to offsprings' distress vocalizations (i.e., crying). Destruction of the anterior cingulate in animals or people greatly reduces parental interest in offspring, leading to a lack of responsiveness eerily reminiscent of parental neglect (Cohen et al., 2006). It is clear from this research that the anterior cingulate is an essential part of the parenting brain. Later, we describe how the anterior cingulate also functions as a vital bridge between emotion regulation and reflective processes in a parenting brain, literally connecting the core parenting process to the highest human cognitive abilities (Allman, Hakeem, Erwin, Nimchinsky, & Hof, 2001).

A unique kind of brain cell, found only in mammals that exhibit heightened awareness of each others' emotions, especially states of distress, links the anterior insula to the anterior cingulate. These cells are called von Economo neurons after the man who discovered them. Von Economo neurons are most plentiful in humans, but are also found in a few other mammals that we know to be quite empathic: elephants, great apes, dolphins, and whales (Allman, Tetreault, Hakeem, & Park, 2011). (Although you might think, if you are a dog owner, that canines would certainly have these cells, they have not yet been found in this species.)

Intriguingly, people's brains show differences in the size of both the anterior insula and the anterior cingulate and differences in the density of von Economo neurons. And, even more intriguingly, these differences correlate with differences in empathy, both when measured in self-report tasks and observed in actual parent–child interactions (Cohen et al., 2006). So something very important is going on in these brain regions having to do with their connections and the actual number of VEN cells that connect them. Of great relevance to parents and therapists, there is evidence that the insula and the anterior cingulate respond to experiences in life by either contracting or expanding (Cozolino, 2006). Engaging in compassion meditation, for example, has recently been shown to foster expansion in both the anterior insula and certain parts of the anterior cingulate (Posner, Rothbart, Sheese, & Tang, 2007; Tang et al., 2010). This "experience-dependent neuroplasticity"—changes in brain processes or structure in response to lived experience—is very exciting to clinicians who are following this brain research (e.g., Siegel, 2010).

BOTTOM LINE: In parenting terms, the insula–anterior cingulate–von Economo neurons system promotes parental empathy and intuition, key components of the parental attunement process.

Attunement: The Work of Mirror Neurons

Another fascinating and groundbreaking finding in brain research was the discovery of mirror neurons: motor cells in primates that are activated by watching another primate or human engage in some type of intentional or purposeful action, such as reaching for something to eat. Since the accidental discovery of these mimicry cells by a group of Italian neuroscientists in the 1990s (Carr, Iacoboni, Dubeau, Maziotta, & Lenzi, 2003), brain researchers have found that humans have this same mirroring system. In fact, mirror cells are more abundant in the motor systems of humans than in the primates where they were first discovered. The mirroring process is an unconscious brain mechanism that is now thought to facilitate empathy and attunement between people, including between parent and child. Mirror cells are motor neurons that are activated either by our own intentional movements or by watching each other do things. This includes watching each other make facial expressions and gestures as we interact. Our voices can also activate mirror cells.

Mirroring leads to subtle activation of the same muscles that we use when we are engaging in the type of action that we are observing. On a simple level, the contagion of yawning is probably the work of the mirroring system. When we mirror each other, we also tend to feel, at least subtly, some of what the other person is experiencing. This is why many neuroscientists think that this mirroring process contributes greatly to empathy and to interpersonal attunement, including parent–child attunement. Young children have active mirror systems as well as parents, so mirroring is a reciprocal process (Norris & Cacioppo, 2007).

The mirroring mechanism occurs much more quickly in brain time than the time it takes to understand what another person says, so this system "trumps" verbal communication in its ability to affect the subjective experience of the "mirrorer." The mirroring process then primes our emotional responses to one another below conscious awareness and, often, in ways that are inconsistent with the content of our verbal messages. When the mirrored communication is inconsistent with the verbal messages, this inconsistency can be an important source of misattunement and misunderstanding between parents and children.

Mirroring in the parent–child relationship swings both ways: It has the potential to foster empathy *and* to engender mutual defensiveness, depending upon what is being mirrored. The potential for mirroring to be a disruptive influence between parent and child is heightened when a parent, without being aware of it, displays subtly negative facial expressions and tones of voice while thinking that he or she is communicating something quite different with his or her words. Or, a similar conflict can occur even in interactions with a preverbal child when the parent displays "micro" expressions, fleeting facial expressions, of fear, or anger, or disgust, which the child's mirror system detects even though these aren't known to the parent or consciously processed by the child (Tronick, 2007).

Parents with unresolved, stress-inducing memories from their past or parents who are experiencing current high levels of stress are likely to express the negative effects of these processes in their nonverbal communication while interacting with their children. Such a scenario can lead to the development of mutually defensive feelings between parent and child when the child mirrors the parent's stress and then exhibits signs of his or her own distress that the parent, in turn, mirrors back (Tronick, 2007). This process can create a negative cycle that is completely unintended by parent or child. These hidden interpersonal processes can foster blocked care as well as possibly transmitting trauma silently from one generation to the next in the absence of child abuse or neglect. This is why attachment-focused therapists and trauma specialists strongly recommend that parents find ways to come to terms with their own past experiences and to defuse the negative potential for unresolved painful memories to disrupt their parenting and their kids' development.

BOTTOM LINE: In parenting terms, mirroring strengthens the parent's ability to attune to a child's conscious or unconscious intentions as a part of the parent's child-reading system.

The Mature Brain: When Your Prefrontal Cortex Meets Your Limbic System

Although we rely heavily on the bottom-up, hormonally driven processes that foster and support the core caregiving process, we also need to use all of our great cognitive resources to parent well. Our brains have to have good connections between the deeper regions that generate emotion or "affect" and the higher regions that allow us to step back enough from our more primal reactions to reflect upon our experiences with our kids and to think about them and their needs.

Left to its own workings, our subcortical limbic system has a few basic interests: seeking, finding, and consuming the "good stuff" in life; detecting and defending ourselves against the "bad stuff"; and "connecting" with others, sexually and in other ways. The limbic system is essentially devoted to moving us rapidly toward or away from things in life that are relevant to our survival. If we want our children to develop their own powers of self-regulation, we need to regulate our limbic reactions in our dealings with them.

As we have seen, the top-down, bottom-up brain arrangement that supports parenting has to grow and develop. This process that begins very early in life extends at least into our early 20s when our prefrontal cortex "matures" enough to help us orchestrate our lives more "frontally" than we could even a few years earlier. This frontal power reaches a mature level when the prefrontal cortex is strongly connected both to the back of the brain, making a robust *horizontal* circuit, and to the limbic system, making a robust *vertical* or frontolimbic circuit (Giedd, 2010). The process of strengthening these connections has much to do with *myelination*, the insulation of brain wiring (axons) with a fatty substance—myelin—that greatly enhances the speed and efficiency of communication between different brain regions. Myelination produces the "white matter" of the brain. Recently, white matter is getting a lot more attention from brain scientists, in part because it has recently been discovered that experience affects the process of myelination, that is does not just occur entirely automatically (see *The Other Brain* by Douglas Fields for a fascinating discussion of the importance of white matter).

Figure 1.8 illustrates the horizontal and vertical brain circuits. When both of these circuits are well developed (myelinated), we have more brain power to delay gratification, control our impulses, plan ahead, and resolve inevitable internal conflicts between self-interest and our responsibilities to others, including our children. Trying to parent before our brains have reached this level of development—or when our frontal powers are being suppressed by stress reactions—is extremely difficult and prone to problems, including the development of blocked care.

Figure 1.8. The Mature Brain
When the prefrontal cortex is strongly connected to the back of the brain (horizontal) and to the limbic system (vertical).

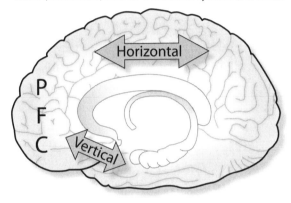

BOTTOM LINE: In parenting terms, you need a mature brain to parent well. It takes at least 20 years before your prefrontal cortex is developed enough to give you the powers of self-regulation that you need to parent well. Also, stress can impair your prefrontal cortex even after it has "matured."

Staying Parental:
The Role of the Anterior Cingulate Cortex

One of the most important brain structures for parenting is the anterior cingulate cortex (ACC for short). This is a structure that lies just beneath the neocortex, the outer layer of the brain, and runs in a narrow band along the midline of the brain from front to back. We focus on the front or anterior region of the cingulate, describing how this region serves as a "brain bridge" between the limbic system (the emotion-generating brain system) and the cognitive processes linked to the highest regions of the prefrontal cortex. By serving this bridging function, the anterior cingulate cortex helps parents connect their feelings to their thoughts in a flexible manner. This region is also an important part of the so-called executive attention system and of the self-monitoring system, making it a key structure in helping parents pay attention to their kids and to the feedback they receive from them.

Integrating Emotion Regulation and Parental Reflection: The Anterior Cingulate Cortex Bridge

Previously we described the role of the anterior cingulate in the transition from reptilian to mammalian parenting and its important contribution to parental empathy. In addition to its role in bringing feelings into awareness with the help of the insula and the amygdala, the anterior cingulate plays a vital part in helping to link the core processes of emotion regulation and self-reflection in the parenting brain. The anterior cingulate is the front part of the cingulate, a structure located in the middle of the brain just above the corpus callosum, that band of fibers that connects the left and right sides of the brain. Figure 1.9 shows the location of the anterior cingulate and the division of this region into three parts: the ventral, rostral, and dorsal. Also shown are the connections from the three anterior cingulate regions to the three key regions of the prefrontal cortex.

The reason the anterior cingulate is so important to parenting is that it connects both to the limbic system—the emotion-generating circuit—and to the three regions of the prefrontal cortex: the bottom region or orbital cortex; the middle region or middle prefrontal cortex, and the highest region, the dorsolateral prefrontal cortex (DLPFC). Because of its connections with all three regions of the prefrontal cortex, the anterior cingulate serves as a vital brain bridge that literally connects the emotion-regulating process at the bottom, in conjunction with the orbital region, to the reflective process of the middle prefrontal cortex, to the conflict resolution and planning processes of the dorsolateral prefrontal cortex at the top.

Figure 1.9. Connections between the ACC and OFC.
The ventral, rostral, and dorsal regions of the ACC connect to the OFC, MPFC, and
DLPFC divisions of the prefrontal cortex and to the smart vagal system.

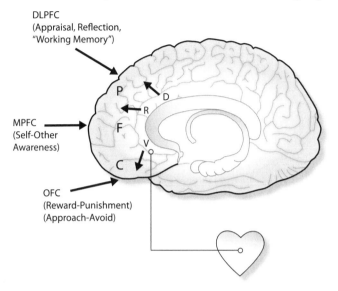

The bottom part of the anterior cingulate goes by several names in the brain science literature, including *ventromedial, subgenual,* and *ventral* anterior cingulate. (These terms all refer to the location of brain structures in relation to other structures). Whichever name we use, this region sits below the knee-like bend in the corpus callosum and is strongly connected to the amygdala and the autonomic nervous system, both the up-regulating sympathetic branch and the down-regulating parasympathetic branch. This makes the ventral anterior cingulate a crucial player in the parenting brain, despite its small size. In a healthy parenting brain, this region turns on whenever the amygdala reacts to something potentially threatening or negative, including a child's behavior or negative facial expression (Heinz et al., 2005). By co-activating the ventral anterior cingulate along with the amygdala, the parent, without knowing it, is already beginning to regulate the negative reaction toward the child. In other words, if your brain doesn't co-activate your ventral anterior cingulate with your amygdala, it will be harder for you to control your negative reaction. This includes both an angry and a fearful reaction. In brain-imaging studies of patients with anxiety disorders and depression, the ventral anterior cingulate fails to activate when the amygdala is triggered, a brain pattern associated with poor emotion regulation.

So, this little bottom region of the anterior cingulate cortex is quite an important part of the parenting process. In essence, activation of the ventral anterior cingulate begins the process of regulating a potentially unparental reaction. This braking operation allows you, as a parent, to start moving upward in your brain into the middle and topmost regions of your prefrontal cortex, if needed, to regain your parental state of mind, to reconnect with your smart vagal engagement system, and to think about what you are doing.

The activity of the anterior cingulate now shifts upward from the bottom to the middle region and to the top, called the dorsal anterior cingulate. The middle region provides access to your middle prefrontal region to promote self-reflection and attunement to your child's feelings, while the dorsal anterior cingulate provides access to your highest prefrontal region, your dorsolateral prefrontal cortex, for reappraising your initial "take" on what's going on, for gaining a "higher," more objective understanding of the situation. Now, with the help of the anterior cingulate bridge, your brain is an open, flexible, reflective state that is conducive to a more mindful and sensitive way of relating to your child, regardless of the state of mind he or she is in. This is where you need to be in your brain when parenting gets challenging and the bottom-up system can't do the job of keeping your brain in a parental state. This is when you need to use your top-down state regulation system, your executive powers, to be "the adult in the room."

BOTTOM LINE: In parenting terms, the anterior cingulate bridge helps you to "feel and deal," to stay connected to your feelings and your child's feelings and to think at the same time—to be the "adult in the room."

Parental Self-Monitoring

In order to respond sensitively and contingently to a child's signals, parents have to utilize a brain system that evolved to monitor progress in staying on track with a goal or intention by detecting errors or deviations from the goal and making rapid corrections or adjustments in behavior to get back on track. In the domain of parent–child attunement, the parent has to use this self-monitoring, error-detecting, self-correction system in order to "stay attuned" to the child's inner states.

The neural system that supports this self-monitoring and error-detection process is a circuit that relies heavily on the functioning of the anterior cingulate. The anterior cingulate becomes active when a person becomes conscious of a conflict or disparity between a current goal or purpose and the immediate feedback about progress toward that goal. The greater the conflict, the greater the activation in the anterior cingulate. People who exhibit strong anterior cingulate activation shortly after making perceived mistakes are more likely to make adjustments in their attentiveness and actions following error detection. In a sense, the anterior cingulate is part of the brain's "uh-oh" system, alerting us that something is amiss and requires greater attention and more care.

This self-monitoring system is very important in parenting because it helps you to take in feedback from your child and use it to attune better to what is going on if what you are doing isn't helpful or effective. Indeed, recent research shows a strong correlation between activation of the anterior cingulate after making a mistake on a computer-based task and sensitivity to a child's feedback during parent–child interaction in the home (Fleming, Gonzalez, Afonso, & Lovic, 2008). This research suggests an important link between the ability to pay close attention to what you are doing—to be "mindful"—and the ability to attune to a child's needs.

The internal conflict resolution system develops in stages in the brain, and its development has been shown to depend, in part, on the kinds of experiences one has early in life. Also, individuals vary greatly in the size and functioning of the neural circuitry that supports internal conflict resolution. Research using brain imaging comparing extraverted to introverted people shows differences in patterns of activation in the anterior cingulate regions associated with self-monitoring, error detection, and conflict processing. Extraversion correlates with lower activity in the anterior cingulate, whereas introversion correlates with greater activation in this brain region during tasks that require sustained attention to one's own performance in relation to a specific goal.

Based on the growing research into the neural correlates of self-monitoring and internal conflict resolution, it seems likely that parents who exhibit poor attunement and low sensitivity to their children are "low activators" of the neural circuitry that supports self-monitoring, self-reflection, and reappraisal. This likelihood suggests that one of the goals of working with these parents would be to enhance the functioning of this self-monitoring system to facilitate greater reflectiveness and greater capacity to recover from disruptions in the parent-child relationship and to reconnect with the child.

BOTTOM LINE: In parenting terms, parental self-monitoring—your "uh-oh" system—alerts you that all is not well with your child or with the state of your relationship and prompts you to pay more attention to what is going on so you can respond more effectively, in a more attuned way.

Parental Attention: The Anterior Cingulate, the Executive Attention System, and Mindful Parenting

Intriguingly, the top part of the anterior cingulate, the dorsal anterior cingulate, is now known to be a crucial part of what neuroscientists Michael Posner and Mary Rothbart (2007) call the *executive attention system*, the system we use when we have to keep our attention focused in the face of distractions and competing impulses and habits. This brain circuitry is known to develop and improve with age; we begin to show an adult-like level of attentional control around the age of 17, on average. The executive attention system makes it possible to stay focused or to shift attention in a flexible way, as needed, to stay on task or to adapt to changing situations. This system also is highly variable among individuals and tends to be more developed in females than males.

Parents are likely to vary widely in the structure and functioning of this brain system. Whereas parents with an underactive executive attention system will have difficulty attending sufficiently to their children, parents with overly active systems are prone to worrying too much about their children and to being hypervigilant about their safety. Research shows that this part of the brain is overly active in people who are chronic worriers, including people with obsessive–compulsive disorder (OCD) who are constantly getting signals from this region that make them feel that something is wrong and needs their immediate attention. So, it is probably best to be "in the middle" with regard to this aspect of parental executive functioning. In a later chapter on parental reflection (Chapter 6), we present recent research that suggests that parents can improve their executive attention system with certain kinds of mindfulness practice.

BOTTOM LINE: In parenting terms, parental executive attention allows you to shift your attention in a highly flexible way in response to your child's changing needs and to changing circumstances.

When the Parent's Brain Engages with the Child's Brain: Meeting Oscar

Children are strongly motivated from birth to interact with adults, coming into the world equipped for social engagement. This means that the parent-child relationship is a reciprocal one from the start and that parents need to be responsive partners in this two-way dance.

Parent–Child Reciprocity: Comfort and Joy

Because infants are so dependent on our love, interest, and attention, they are born "wired" for engagement, ready from the get-go to capture our eyes and ears and hearts. Even newborns track our gaze and prefer that we look directly at them. Born knowing their mothers voice, they quickly start to associate that special sound with that special face. In turn, our brains are wired to be "captured" by our babies' charms. Indeed, we are wired to experience our babies as adorable and irresistible even when others might not find them so precious, especially when they are throwing up, crying, and soiling their diapers. This is nature's system of parent–child reciprocity, a mostly automatic, "bottom-up," neurobiological dance that links us to our kids much more powerfully than our intellectual powers alone could ever do. As parents, we need to be moved by our child's bids for attention; we need to be open and receptive as much as possible in order to reinforce the child's efforts to engage us and to strengthen the child's trust in us as communication partners. This engagement goes beyond the interactions based on distress and comfort that are associated with attachment security, expanding into the realm of sociability in which, as Colywn Trevarthen so beautifully describes, the parent becomes the child's "first companion." When the twin systems of atttachment and companionship are well joined, parents and children create a robust two-way system that encompasses both comfort and joy as well as all the other human experiences that make our lives rich and deep.

Children are limbic creatures, making their way in their new world through expressing their feelings and trying out all the ways to move and emote. They need to have the space in which to give their limbic systems a full workout. This is how they learn to trust their own emotions and to feel safe inside their own bodies. Indeed, it is through the use of this system, of this "affective core," that the child builds the brain power to regulate limbic drives. Too much restriction or a lack of sensitive parental co-regulation of the full range of a child's affective experiences leads to underdevelopment of the brain system devoted to self-regulation. What is self-regulation? We'll begin with what it is not: It is not suppression. Rather, it is the resilient capacity to "feel and deal," to experience a full range of affect, and to modulate all kinds of feelings effectively enough to trust oneself to be able to cope well with the full range of human experience and to be an emotionally trustworthy partner and parent.

Meeting Oscar

To help us understand this intriguing interplay between a child's developing brain and the parenting brain, let's meet Oscar. Oscar has just turned 1 year old at the time of this writing. He's going to

Photo 1.1. Oscar smiling.

help us illustrate how kids learn to feel safe with "attachment figures" and how they engage parents in powerful, almost irresistible ways. Oscar is in the care of two loving parents, his biological mother and father, who are wild about him and highly attuned to his changing states of mind and body. In this photo we see him ready for

connection with a magical gleam in his eye and even his lower lip, inviting us to come play. His wonderfully expressive face shows us in an instant, way too fast for conscious processing, that kids are wired for engagement. Infants seek out our faces and voices and poke us into smiling and tickling and playing as long as we can sustain the "game" by staying attuned to their feedback. If we are not too stressed out or distracted, we will respond in an instinctively positive way to a child's endearingly smiling face and invitation to connect. Seeing Oscar's smile causes specific "child-reading" regions of our brains to light up and send messages to our emotion-generating system, moving us to approach. This Parental Child Reading System is an interactive set of brain regions that enable the parent to perceive and respond to a child's nonverbal communication in a sensitive, attuned way during the key stage for attachment formation and then throughout the parent–child relationship. Our Parental Child Reading System is activated by merely glancing at Oscar's open, smiling face.

What's happening in your brain as you look at Oscar? Although you can't feel your brain working, you can get clues by paying close attention to what's happening in your own face as you interact with Oscar's. Do you feel a little crinkling of the muscles just below your eyes? Do your eyebrows go up a notch? Does you jaw drop a little as the left side of your face gets a little crooked, showing the strong activation of your approach system? You may be using your mirror neurons to emulate Oscar's smile (see Photo 1.2).

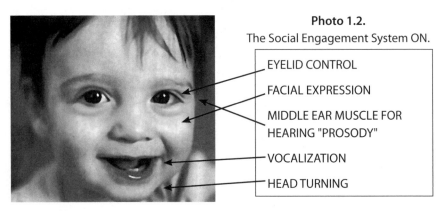

Photo 1.2.
The Social Engagement System ON.

EYELID CONTROL

FACIAL EXPRESSION

MIDDLE EAR MUSCLE FOR HEARING "PROSODY"

VOCALIZATION

HEAD TURNING

Oscar is actually using brain and body connections that are part of the social engagement system—the "smart" vagal circuitry described by Porges (2011). By turning his own social engagement system "on," Oscar invites us to do likewise, to become mutually engaged with him. Notice how the two sides of his face are expressing his readiness to connect somewhat differently, one side more strongly than the other. This reflects the difference between the limbic systems on the right and left.

Even though you don't know it, you probably just released some of that oxytocin into your limbic system, including into your amygdala. This release of oxytocin is part of the chemical dance that helps a parent to feel calm and loving when near the child. Oscar is also releasing oxytocin into his brain and body, helping him to feel safe and to stay in his engagement or approach system. Researchers have found that when parents and infants are engaged in a highly pleasurable, attuned interaction, both release oxytocin. In fact, intriguing research by Ruth Feldman and her colleagues shows that the parents with the highest levels of oxytocin during these moments of deep connection are the ones who report and demonstrate the strongest bonds with their babies (Feldman, Gordon, & Zagoory-Sharon, 2010).

Oxytocin is released through soothing kinds of physical contact, including hugs, caressing kinds of touch, and even massage. Oxytocin is also released when you hear the voice of a loved one, as when a college student hears his or her mother's voice on a cell phone or when a child hears his or her mother saying, "It's alright, everything will be alright" (Seltzer, Ziegler & Pollak, 2010). Because oxytocin can be released in multiple ways, even a depressed parent who has "flat affect"—does not express emotion in his or her face or voice—can stimulate the child's oxytocin system through touch, including the use of infant massage. And if the mother (or father) receives massage therapy, this good touch may help to trigger her oxytocin system and get the antistress, antidepressant effects of soothing touch that she has been missing as she and her child have "lost touch" with each other (Field, 2002).

Since it is also known that stress hormones can suppress the production of oxytocin and the functioning of the oxytocin system, stressed-out parents may have difficulty turning the oxytocin system on and getting the great benefits in terms of well-being and "felt" safety that oxytocin confers. When there is chronic conflict in parent–child relationships, both parent and child may be deprived of all the benefits of "good touch," leading to suppression of the oxytocin system in both. This oxytocin suppression is an important aspect of blocked care that makes it difficult to feel safe and warm and nurturing even when you want to experience these parental feelings. In a blocked relationship it is vital that the oxytocin system be revived to help restore good connections.

Because oxytocin has "stress-busting" effects, it is now thought to be a *neuroprotective* chemical that helps to keep the parent's brain healthy and free from the potentially damaging effects of stress hormones. This is probably one of the reasons that good relationships have been found to promote better health and longevity in both men and women. Good adult relationships and good parent–child relationships can be thought of as protection for the brains of both partners, making positive relationships literally "good medicine" (Gordon, Zagoory-Sharon, Leckman, & Feldman, 2010).

If you were stressed out a bit before you saw Oscar, you may be calmer now. You may have even shifted your internal state of mind from a drowsy state to a more engaged, more interested state that helps you to understand this material about brains that could otherwise be too dry, too unemotional. This is the natural power of the child's social engagement system: It helps to ensure that primary caregivers pay attention, experience pleasure, feel nurturing, and don't develop blocked care.

Another way in which good relationships help promote brain development is by triggering the release of so-called *brain growth factors*. The brain produces a number of chemicals that promote growth, a key one being something called *brain-derived neurotrophic factor,(neurotrophic* means growth-inducing). In good relationships, both partners produce more brain-derived neurotrophic factor, and this increased production, in turn, promotes the continuing development of both partners' brains (Roth, Lubin, Funk & Sweat, 2009). Brain-derived neurotrophic factor is active in regions of the brain that are crucial for good social and emotional functioning, especially the prefrontal cortex and the hippocampus (the structure that is so important for learning, memory, and stress regulation). Relationships that are safe and supportive appear to keep the brain-derived neurotrophic factor system activated, fostering growth in these key regions. In this way, good relationships help to build resilient brains.

In contrast, relationships that are chronically stressful and dysregulating to both parties are likely to suppress the activity of chemicals such as oxytocin and brain-derived neurotrophic factor in both. This growth-suppressing effect of poor interpersonal connections creates a scenario in which the relationship can become neurobiologically toxic, blocking brain growth and development and even producing the failure to thrive syndrome in children (Gerhardt, 2004; Perry, 1997). These growth-suppressing relational dynamics ramp up the stress and defense systems—a brain pattern that can lead to a variety of stress-based disorders, including depression, anxiety, and PTSD.

In essence, then, good relationships are neuroprotective and generative, mutually beneficial to both partners, while poor relationships are mutually dysregulating and growth-suppressing.

Below, we see Oscar again, but this time he's looking at us with a bit of wariness, illustrating the freeze response. Now his lower vagal system is "on," triggering immobilization with mild fear. Here, we see no crinkling of the muscles just below his eyes. This part of his face has gone flatter as he orients pretty intensely to our faces and tries to figure out whether it is safe or not to come close and engage us. His brow muscle is a little tense and his eyes are wide to take in as much as his brain can of what is going on. With his mouth open, he is actually also adjusting the muscle of his inner ear to hear the sounds we are making, to gauge our "prosody" to help him to know what state of mind we are in.

Photo 1.3. The freeze response.

Again, notice the difference between the two sides of Oscar's face. The right side (facing us), Oscar's left, clearly shows a fearful expression, whereas the left side (facing us) looks more neutral, maybe mildly apprehensive. Oscar's full face is displaying a combination of affect based on activity in the two sides of his brain. Since some aspects of facial expressions are orchestrated by the opposite side of the brain, the more fearful expression on Oscar's left side probably reflects the activation of his fear system on the right side of the brain, his right limbic system. He has shifted from his smart vagal social engagement system into a defensive state in which his attention has been grabbed by something that has set off at least a mild alarm reaction from his amygdala. Although he is not in full flight mode, he is in a mild freeze mode, much like the "deer in the headlights" reaction we see in our fellow creatures when they suddenly get very still as they orient to something they've just heard or seen and focus on it intently to figure out whether or not there is a real danger.

Here we are seeing the effects of Oscar's neuroception system as his amygdala does its job of trying to keep him safe by rapidly and unconsciously alerting him to stop playing and smiling and pay rapt attention to something in his environment that could be harmful. At this age, Oscar is not yet able to regulate his attention system by deciding to what he will or won't pay attention. Rather, his attention gets drawn to things using what is called his *orienting response*. This is an obligatory attention system, controlled largely by his amygdala and its reaction to all the things he senses in his environment and inside his own body. Later, as his brain matures, he will develop a "higher," more voluntary "executive attention system" that he can use to shift out of this obligatory, amygdala-driven way of attending to things. This higher attention system depends heavily on the development of the brain bridge we described earlier, wherein the anterior cingulate gets connected to the amygdala and gains control over the neuroceptive process, allowing the child to be less at the mercy of his amygdaloid moments.

It's not hard to imagine, looking at Oscar's face here, how a less fortunate child, living in a truly scary environment, could spend way too much time in a hypervigilant state about his safety and way too little time in carefree play, exploration, and joyful connection with primary caregivers. Having to use this freeze system a lot makes it stronger and easier to activate, setting the stage for chronic hypervigilance and difficulty relaxing around other people. Parents who grew up in unsafe environments tend to be hypervigilant about their safety and may have a hard time feeling safe enough to shift from defense into social engagement, even around their own children. You can see, then, how the development of a child's smart vagal, social engagement system is highly dependent on the kind of care he or she receives during this early stage of brain development and how this early brain sculpting process lays some of the foundations for parenting later in life.

Fortunately, Oscar lives in safety. His amygdala is not reacting to his parents. Instead, he can turn to them for comfort and for help with emotion regulation, using them as a secure base when he needs to do so. Then, when he's been comforted and has regained his equilibrium, he can engage his parents in joyful play or toddle off to explore that bug over in the corner, which he then eagerly tries to share with his startled parents. Seeing their looks of apprehension or disgust, he starts to shift from bug exploration to reconnecting with his parents and getting them to smile again so he will feel "in connection" with them. And so goes the dance of attunement, misattunement, and reattunement or relationship repair. This is the lovely parent–child dance that builds the child's brain while helping him or her learn to trust safe people and to count on their sensitive care, giving the child the luxury of spending lots of time exploring and learning, a luxury unavailable to children of stressed-out parents.

Photo 1.4

And now, in Photo 1.4, we see Oscar in clear distress, not feeling good about whatever is going on in the moment. Maybe he is seeing us for the first time and reacting to our "strangeness." He might next start looking for his mother. Here his brow is furrowed, his eyes are almost shutting, as if to avoid seeing something that is upsetting. He is ready to cry in distress to let someone special know that he needs comforting, that he needs to get back to his safe base. Don't worry, Oscar, Mom and Dad are right there and soon, you'll be smiling again (Photo 1.5).

Photo 1.5.
The Virtuous Cycle: Helping the child recover from distress and regain safety

Sensitive parental response that helps Oscar to recover from this stressed-out state and regain his sense of safety and well-being

When Oscar's parents respond in a timely, sensitive, attuned way to his distress, they are co-regulating his emotions and giving him the scaffolding he needs to transition out of distress back into a state of safety, well-being, and playful engagement. The daily repetitions of this good cycle in which parents help young children move from internal states of dysregulation back to more regulated states is known to promote brain development, both by protecting the brain from prolonged periods of distress and by stimulating the growth of connections in the child's brain that eventually give him or her more powers of self-regulation. In this positive cycle, we see the foundations of the brain capacity to be a good parent (Atzil, Hendler & Feldman, 2011).

The Child's Brain

In Photo 1.6, we use Oscar's different expressions to illustrate the process that Porges calls *neuroception*: the process by which our limbic system rapidly assesses for safety and threat and orchestrates our emotional and behavioral states accordingly.

Photo 1.6.
Oscar demonstrating neuroception.

NEUROCEPTION

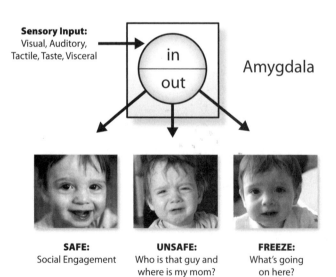

Thanks, Oscar, for helping us to understand the processes of social engagement, self-defense, neuroception, and secure attachment. And watch out for those bugs.

The Parent's Brain

The challenge for your parenting brain is to stay in safe mode even when your child is not in his or her safe mode. If you can keep your smart vagal approach system "on" when your child shifts into a defensive state of mind, you are much more likely to respond in a caring, helpful way that fosters his or her emotional development and strengthens his or her ability to regulate defensive, negative states. Your ability to keep your lid on and stay "parental" helps your child build those brain "muscles" he or she will need to do the same with those wonderful grandchildren you will have someday. This is why the health of your brain is so vital to creating a really positive, growthful cycle of good care in your family. Figure 1.10 below summarizes the top-down, bottom-up state regulation processes in the parental brain.

Figure 1.10. Putting It All Together.
The top-down and bottom-up state-regulation system in the parenting brain.

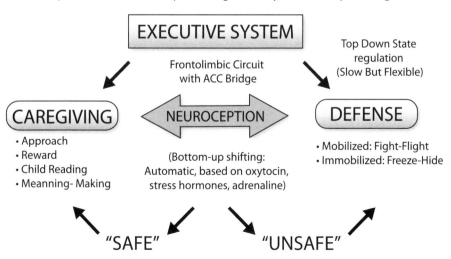

CHAPTER 2

The Five Domains of Parenting·

Human parenting involves several interrelated yet separate domains of functioning that together, constitute a robust, holistic approach to caregiving. Based on our reading of the neuroscientific research, we consider the five domains in Table 2.1 to comprise the core processes of effective parenting, each dependent upon the functioning of a particular brain circuit or system:

Table 2.1.
Domains of Effective Parenting

Parenting Domain	Parenting Process
1. Parental Approach System	The ability to feel safe and stay open and engaged while interacting closely with a child
2. Parental Reward System	The ability to experience parenting as pleasurable, satisfying, rewarding
3. Parental Child Reading System	The ability to understand, attune to, and empathize with a child
4. Parental Meaning-Making System	The ability to make sense of one's experiences as a parent, to create a coherent personal narrative about being a parent
5. Parental Executive System	The ability to regulate one's internal states, monitor the quality of the parent–child connection, and engage in timely, effective repair

The Parental Approach System

The Parental Approach System is the core motivational system supporting the caregiving process. This system has to work in order for a parent to feel safe enough to interact closely with a child. Research with animals reveals that this primary care system depends heavily on a mammalian brain circuit that links a part of the hypothalamus both to the body and to the emotion-generating limbic system. The key region in the hypothalamus is called the *medial preoptic area*, to which we were introduced in Chapter 1. Although the medial preoptic area is typically involved in sexual responding and mating, hormonal changes in mothers, triggered by pregnancy and the birth process, essentially shift the gears in the medial preoptic area from a nonparental to a parental configuration. This, in turn, signals the limbic system, especially the reward system, to become highly sensitive to the sensory experiences of interacting with a child. The priming of the medial preoptic area by the process of becoming a parent also calms the parent's amygdala, biasing the neuroception system we described earlier toward safety over self-defense. In effect, the priming of the medial preoptic area helps to deactivate the tendency to be wary about getting too close to another person. This is why the medial preoptic area also plays an important role in adult intimacy and in sexuality.

The medial preoptic area is a brain region that is rich in receptors for various hormones and chemicals called *peptides*. In terms of this process of shifting the medial preoptic area to support the parental state, the key chemicals appear to be estrogen, prolactin, and oxytocin. When estrogen is released during pregnancy in females, the stimulation of estrogen receptors in the medial preoptic area activates oxytocin and prolactin. While both of these chemicals are then circulated throughout the body, they are also both brain chemicals. Oxytocin travels to the limbic regions of the brain, especially the amygdala, as described in Chapter 1. Oxytocin acts as a calming, antianxiety agent in the brain, which helps to suppress the defense system that otherwise can be mobilized so rapidly by the amygdala. In this way, oxytocin plays a big part in helping a parent activate the social engagement, smart vagal system described by Porges. When oxytocin stimulates receptors in the output region that connects the amygdala to reflexive defense circuits in the brainstem, this circuit effectively blocks the defense system. Also, the brainstem region that is key to releasing basic defensive reactions of fight, flight, and freeze, called the *periaqueductal gray*, has oxytocin receptors that help to suppress the release of these "hard-wired" defensive behaviors in this region.

The approach system is more strongly connected to the left side of the brain than to the right. The threat/safety detecting neuro-ception system that we described in Chapter 1 is primarily a right-brain system. In a very real sense, the right brain is more involved in protecting us from harm and learning what to avoid in life and how to avoid these things, whereas the left brain is more involved in approaching things, either to interact with them in positive ways because they are good for us—or at least feel good—or to deal with them aggressively, forcefully, to get them out of our way (think *road rage*). Anger, then, perhaps surprisingly, has been found to be a left-brain emotion, along with joy, so both positive and negative "approach" emotions appear to be "left-lateralized," to use the scientific jargon.

Some people are wired to be more "lefties" or "righties," whereas others have a natural balance between these right- and left-brain systems. That is, some people are genetically inclined more toward harm avoidance than toward approaching and engaging with people and things in life. This difference is partly due to genes that influence the reactivity or sensitivity of the amygdala to novelty or uncertainty. This is why even shortly after birth, some infants light up to new experiences whereas others reflexively shy away and cry. Having a low set point for activating the amygdala's alarm system is part of the neurobiology of innate shyness (Kagan, 1994).

The right- and left-brain systems that support harm avoidance and approach are also learning and memory systems that perform these functions very early in life. So, if our early experiences are fraught with things that frighten us or cause us distress, our right-brain harm avoidance system learns to associate feeling afraid or stressed with those things that are sensed to be dangerous. In addition to this "associative learning," the approach–avoidance systems also engage in "instrumental learning," which is the kind of learning that connects *how* you got a reward or got hurt, physically or emotionally, with the experience of feeling rewarded or hurt.

For example, when a toddler touches an electrical outlet and gets yelled at by a parent, the child's right brain avoidance system makes a connection between the act of touching the outlet and the "pain" of hearing the parent's harsh voice. Then, the next time the child has the urge to touch the outlet, the memory of this connection between that action and being yelled at is triggered, helping the child avoid being yelled at again by suppressing the urge to touch the outlet. By combining the processes of associative and instrumental learning, infants learn a lot about how and when to approach or avoid their caregivers, long before they are able to "know" what they are learning. Instrumental learning becomes the "how" part of reward-based or fear-based memories to go along with the "what" part that we get from our associative learning.

For children exposed to insensitive caregiving, there are many opportunities for the harm avoidance learning system to do its thing, helping the children learn, both associatively and instrumentally, about surviving in an insecure environment. This is what neuroscientists call "attachment-based" learning. This process doesn't involve only serious conditions such as abuse or neglect; it extends to "smaller" and subtler areas. For example, infants become highly distressed when their mothers don't smile at them or engage with them or at least show some animation, some emotion, in their faces and voices—which is why maternal depression, which "flattens" the mother's facial expressions and voice, can be so disruptive to an infant's development and can trigger his or her very young alarm system.

One of the most memorable and difficult-to-watch experiments in the literature on parent–child interaction is Ed Tronick's (2007) "still-face experiment," a research model that briefly replicates maternal depression or neglect. In the still-face experiment, mothers of infants interact normally with them, in a highly engaged, playful way, until the experimenter asks them to put on a still face, to become immobile. Rapidly, the babies become stressed out, obviously disturbed and agitated by losing their sense of connection to their mother via her face, eye, and voice expressions, by losing their vital connection with their primary caregiver. Some of the babies even throw up. When the greatly relieved mothers are allowed to "come back to life," their babies quickly recover in their functioning and appear to come back to life, as well.

In physiological terms, the infants shift out of their smart vagal system into their defensive states, first the active defense of protest (sympathetic), then, into the most primitive state, the immobilized-with-fear state (lower vagal parasympathetic). The restoration of the mother's attention and positive affect quickly helps most of the babies to move back up this hierarchy in their nervous systems, shifting back into their smart vagal social engagement system with the mother's co-regulation or "scaffolding." Interestingly, babies with poorer vagal "tone," a measure of the functioning of the smart vagal system, take longer to recover from exposure to the mother's still face than do infants with better vagal tone. Differences in vagal tone in very young children are thought to be related to both genetic and environmental factors, including prenatal maternal stress (Porges, 2011). Watching this scenario is very moving and dramatically illustrates how powerful the mother's co-regulation is for the baby, how dependent the child is on the mother's "presentness."

Clearly, in order to develop the left-brain approach system for interacting comfortably with other people, the infant needs an interactive partner who consistently makes being close feel safe and often pleasurable. Infants such as those who spent the first year or more of their lives in large Russian or Romanian orphanages, with a large staff of shift workers and little (if any) nurturance or caring interaction— may have underdeveloped left-brain connections between the key prefrontal cortex regions— the orbitofrontal cortex and the lower anterior cingulate cortex—and the temporal lobe limbic regions, especially the amygdala and the hippocampus. For example, one recent brain-imaging study comparing the brains of a group of these kids with kids raised in homes shows this difference in a striking manner: Even an untrained eye can easily see the difference in the strength of the left-hemisphere frontolimbic connections between kids raised in home environments and the kids from the orphanages (Eluvathingal et al., 2006). This kind of research provides stark evidence that early environments quite literally sculpt children's brains in ways that reflect the nature of the care they receive. Although admittedly, children who spent up to 18 months or more in a warehouse-type orphanage represent an extreme case of lack of exposure to responsive care, their pattern of brain development should nevertheless send a message to all of us about the importance of sensitive parenting, especially during a stage when a child's brain is extremely prepared for—indeed, seeking—this brain-to-brain, two-person process.

The importance of the differences between left-brain and right-brain functioning for parenting is that parents who are righties—who have stronger harm avoidance systems than approach systems— are likely to find it more challenging to stay close to their children without becoming defensive than parents who, either genetically or due to early care, are lefties or at least have a balance of these two brain systems. If you are a righty, all is not lost, but you will probably have to work at overriding a natural tendency to move away from your child during certain kinds of interactions. You may need to practice "staying put" and going against this reflexive urge to draw back or to put up a self-protective boundary between you and your child when none is really needed. We discuss ways to deal with having an overactive right-brain harm avoidance system in later chapters.

The Parental Reward System

As we described above, when the Parental Approach System is activated, oxytocin is released and some of it travels to a region of the brainstem, called the *ventral tegmental area*, which regulates the release of dopamine. When oxytocin receptors on dopamine cells in the ventral tegmental area receive oxytocin, these cells release mine into several regions of the brain, including the prefrontal cortex and the reward center or nucleus accumbens. This is the region we described in Chapter 1 as playing a significant role in mediating parental joy. As you may recall, it is part of the motor or action system of the brain, and when it is triggered, we find ourselves highly motivated to approach things that led to reward in the past. This is the same brain region that is heavily involved in all kinds of "liking," craving, and even addictions. It is easy to see how the reward system contributes to connections of all kinds, including the bonds between parent and child.

In the parenting brain, then, oxytocin released from the medial preoptic area activates the dopamine neurons that feed dopamine into the reward system, leading to activation of the Parental Reward System (Fleming et al., 2008; Numan & Stolzenberg, 2008). The chain of events going from the estrogen activation of the medial preoptic area to the activation of the dopamine-driven reward system effectively links the Parental Approach System to the Parental Reward System. This interlocking system helps to ensure that parents keep parenting. Recent research on the father's brain suggests that prolactin and vasopressin may combine with oxytocin to promote similar brain changes that prepare fathers for parenting. Fathers, of course, have basically the same reward system in their brains as mothers, making the Parental Reward System a very important part of the paternal brain. Research suggests that mothers and fathers may tend to find somewhat different styles of interaction with kids rewarding, with fathers tending to prefer physically active forms of stimulation whereas mothers show a preference for quieter, calmer ways of connecting, on average (Gordon, Zagoory-Sharon, Leckman, & Feldman, 2010; Leuner, Glasper, & Gould, 2010).

In addition to being released into the nucleus accumbens, oxytocin and dopamine are also released into the lower regions of the prefrontal cortex, bringing these higher brain regions online and helping to orchestrate the approach and reward systems in a more top-down fashion. This sequence of brain activity effectively brings the emotion regulation system of the brain into play to help keep the parental approach and reward systems ON during interactions with the child. Importantly, as well, when these systems are ON, the parental brain constructs emotion-based memories, both associative and instrumental, of pleasurable interactions that help to motivate the parent to keep parenting. These are the kinds of memories that parents enjoy reflecting on later in the day and over the years, making the process of reflection warm and "friendly" rather than a process to be avoided. In this way, the Parental Approach and Reward Systems promote parental reflection.

The lower region of the prefrontal cortex, the orbital region, plays a key role in processing these rewarding experiences and creating positive parental memories. Meanwhile, a region we highlighted earlier, the anterior cingulate cortex, helps to deal with any conflicting emotions that may arise during close encounters with the child by activating the parental self-monitoring and conflict resolution system.

Recent brain-imaging studies of human parents show that the core mammalian circuitry linking the approach and reward systems is very much alive and well in our brains. In short, we deploy this core parental system for linking our approach and reward systems in a very automatic way to help ensure that we, much like our simpler mammalian cousins, are moved to engage in caregiving, to find it rewarding, and to regulate competing unparental feelings to keep the caregiving processs up and working.

Key to the functioning of the Parental Approach and Reward Systems is the functioning of the interlocking oxytocin and dopamine systems. Whereas oxytocin suppresses defensive reactions and promotes internal safety and trust, dopamine is key to all kinds of motivated behavior, from seeking food, to finding a mate, to taking care of others, to enjoying music and art, and even to experiencing pleasure from hard, productive work, including the harder aspects of parenting. Blocking either oxytocin or dopamine can shut down caregiving in animals. Dopamine supports what Jaak Panskepp (1998), a pioneer in the development of affective neuroscience, calls the "seeking system." Dopamine neurons learn to associate things and actions in life with rewards and then function as an anticipatory or reward-expectancy system, firing in the presence of stimuli that have come to predict reward based on prior experiences (Iversen, Iversen, Dunnett, & Bjorklund, 2010). In this way, the dopamine system serves a crucial function in sustaining reward-based behaviors, including all kinds of addictive behaviors as well as parental behavior, which some consider a lovely addiction to love (Marrazziti, 2009).

Different kinds of rewards in life compete for control of the dopamine system, which is why parental use of drugs can block the rewarding qualities of caregiving from gaining access to the reward system. Although overactivation of some of the dopamine receptors can lead to hyperactivity and even mania, suppression of the dopamine system is also a major factor in depression, now considered to be a stress-related disorder. In general, high levels of stress hormones can suppress both the oxytocin and dopamine systems in the parental brain, resulting in a major mechanism for the emergence of blocked care.

The Parental Reward System is an anticipation system related to a parent's expectations about how it will feel to interact with a child. The reward-driven dopamine system can "crash" when expectations of reward are violated. In other words, if a parent approaches a child with those dopamine cells firing away in anticipation of finding the interaction pleasurable, and then the interaction is just the opposite, the parent could very well experience a sudden shift in the brain from the approach–reward system into a defensive response, either anger or shame, or even fear, in some cases. This is basically what happens often in children when they are expecting to get a "reward" and suddenly get angry and frustrated when the reward is not forthcoming or gets delayed. We see this dopamine-crash effect as an important mechanism for the emergence of blocked parental care, especially when the parent has high expectations that parenting a child is going to be rewarding in some powerful and immediate ways.

Fortunately, human parents whose brains are relatively healthy have the capacity to activate the reward system not just from immediately rewarding experiences, but also from deferred rewards and from the process of doing a meaningful job well. This means that parents who can regulate their expectations and take pleasure in parenting a "difficult" child well could avoid the negative effects of challenging parent–child interactions and keep from developing blocked care. However, even for the most competent and confident parent, this is likely to be a challenge that may require continuing individual effort or turning to other adults for support, if the parent is to stay engaged and open with a child who does not provide much immediately rewarding feedback.

Both the approach and reward systems are under development early in life, and both are susceptible to the negative effects of unmanageable levels of stress. Exposure to parental stress hormones in utero and to stressed-out caregivers after birth can suppress the initial construction of both of these essential systems. This suppression appears to occur from the effects of stress hormones such as cortisol on the developing oxytocin and dopamine receptor systems. At the most fundamental level, stress hormones affect the expression of genes for the receptors of oxytocin and dopamine, and this gene expression determines the density or number of these receptors produced in the child's brain (Cushing & Kramer, 2005). Suppression of these genes by early childhood adversity, then, can lead to underdevelopment and underfunctioning of both the oxytocin and dopamine systems—in effect, suppressing the capacity for approaching others and for finding relationships rewarding. Early childhood stress is now known to be a risk factor for substance abuse and addiction, and the underlying neurobiology of this risk is thought to be highly related to the early suppression of the oxytocin and dopamine systems in children.

In addition to the effects of chronic stress on the approach and reward systems, acute unmanageable levels of stress at any time in life can suppress the functioning of these systems. These stress-induced impairments of the Parental Approach System and the Parental Reward Systems, then, can be a triggering mechanism for the development of blocked care. Figure 2.1 illustrates these two key systems that reinforce parental care of children.

Figure 2.1.
The Parental Approach and Rewards Systems

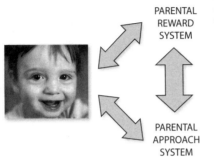

PARENTAL
REWARD
SYSTEM

(release of dopamine into the nucleus accumbens and the orbitofrontal cortex fosters pleasurable feelings and memories of "rewarding" interactions with the child)

PARENTAL
APPROACH
SYSTEM

(release of oxytocin in the MPOA and then in the medial amygdala inhibits defense, promotes approach)

The Parental Child-Reading System

In addition to being able to stay close to the child and experience parenting as rewarding, a parent needs to able to "read" a child's expressions and nonverbal cues. This involves a brain system dedicated in humans to reading, or deciphering the meaning of, facial expressions, tones of voice, gestures, and quality of touch to attune to what a child may be experiencing, intending, or thinking. This Parental Child-Reading System is linked to an interlocking system of brain regions that connects the processes of perceiving nonverbal signals, generating emotional and visceral reactions to these perceptions, and then tying these perceptual and affective processes to either defensive reactions or to the approach and reward systems that keep the parent in connection with the child. Problems with the Parental Child-Reading System, then, can throw the approach and reward systems off course.

In terms of brain anatomy, the child-reading process relies heavily on activity in temporal lobe regions that are dedicated to facial recognition and the detection of "biological movement," especially facial and eye movements, along with alterations in voice and body language. These people-processing regions feed their output into the limbic system for affective appraisal, for neuroception. The limbic system, especially the amygdala, filters this information and then shunts it either downward in the brain to basic brainstem defensive systems (i.e., fight, flight, and freeze) or upward to reward systems.

When this child-reading process activates the Parental Reward System, the parent can stay open to the child and continue to attune to the child's communication. If the neuroceptive process triggers a defensive reaction, the child-reading process can get shut down or short-circuited.

As with the approach and reward systems, the amygdala plays a key role in the child-reading system by filtering the parent's perceptions of the child's nonverbal communication to make a quick assessment as to the positive or negative nature of these signals. If the amygdala "detects" a threat, it sets off the defense system, possibly preempting further processing of what the child is intending or experiencing. In this way, an overly sensitive child-reading system that is biased to detect threat in the nonverbal communication of a child can suppress parental curiosity and reflection while engaging defensive reactions that the child then has to respond to—probably with his or her own defense system.

The Parental Child-Reading System is fundamental to the process of attuning to a child's inner states, to creating the kind of intersubjective, mind-to-mind communication we described in Chapter One. We can see the interplay of this child-reading system with the approach and reward systems because accurate child reading is clearly essential to sustaining an open approach to the child and experiencing parenting as pleasurable. The Parental Child-Reading System, then, feeds its processing of the child's communication into the other parental brain systems in ways that can either facilitate parent–child connections or impede them. Parents who have difficulty with the child-reading process will inevitably experience stress in trying to understand what a child is communicating nonverbally in addition to what is being conveyed in the literal meaning of the child's words.

Since nonverbal communication is processed much faster in the brain than the meaning of language, parents who can't read both streams of communication well are overly dependent on the explicit/ literal content of what a child says. Because we use nonverbal communication to color what we are saying and give it a twist, parents who either short-circuit the child-reading process by activating overly sensitized defensive reactions or who have a structural weakness in the brain regions dedicated to child reading will have problems with parenting and are at risk for blocked care.

As alluded to above, problems with the child-reading process can result either from a faulty perceptual system or from an overly sensitive limbic filtering system. Chronically stressed parents with an otherwise functional child-reading system overreact in a negative way to the child's nonverbal communication due to the overreactivity of the amygdala and other regions of the limbic system. Parents with either nonverbal processing problems (e.g., difficulty perceiving and using nonverbal aspects of communication such as facial expressions and tones of voice) or autism spectrum traits (e.g., difficulty with understanding other people's minds) have structural problems with child reading that can cause stress and lead to blocked care.

Parents differ widely from one another in their child-reading abilities, aside from the effects of stress on this system. Intriguingly, this process that is related to what neuroscientists call *mentalizing* and *theory of mind* is strongly connected with the ability to read emotions in other people's faces, especially from the region of the eyes (Frith & Frith, 2003). The research of Simon Baron-Cohen (2003) suggests that men and women, on average, differ in this ability, with women being better at it. Baron-Cohen relates this ability to what he calls the "E" brain, for empathy, which he contrasts with a stereotypically male brain that is "systemizing," leading to his shorthand: the "S" brain. Although males can have E brains and females, S brains, more females are likely to have inherently good empathy or "people-reading" skills. Baron-Cohen's research shows a link between people-reading skills and exposure to testosterone in fetal development, with higher exposure to testosterone being linked to lower empathy or higher systemizing abilities. Although this finding is still considered controversial (i.e., not sufficiently replicated to be generally accepted) among neuroscientists, there are clearly some important gender-related differences in this people-reading process that have implications for parenting.

Parents raised in highly stressful environments often develop an early bias toward detecting nonverbal signs of anger and fear in others

(Pollak, 2003). In the context of parent–child interactions, this "negativity bias" may be expressed in a hypervigilant style of processing a child's facial and vocal communication, leading to a tendency to feel that the child is being threatening or disrespectful—in short, to take the child's behavior personally. A parent with a highly sensitized system for detecting threat is at risk of reacting defensively to a child's nonverbal communication. Such premature defensiveness can short-circuit the parent's ability to find out what is going on in the child and lead to increased frustration and mutual defensiveness. Another important variable in determining whether or not the parent is able to engage in the open, curious, and reflective attitude of healthy childrearing practices is the response of the child. Just as with the parental approach and reward systems, the child-reading system maintains its active state the best when the child responds in a reciprocal manner—that is, when the child's approach and reward systems are also activated. Children have a "parent-reading" system in their brains, and when the child is feeling safe and has this system "on," it is easier for the parent to stay engaged in the child-reading process. When the child is not curious about the parent's inner life and is not working to make sense of the parent's behaviors and nonverbal communications, the parent is likely to have some difficulty maintaining an open, ongoing interest in his or her child. The parent is less likely to care why the child acted in a certain way, and the parent is more likely to move into a negative bias regarding the meaning of the child's nonverbal expressions.

There is a growing body of research that shows a link between people-reading abilities and oxytocin (Ross & Young, 2009; Guestella, Mitchell & Dadds, 2008). Researchers are investigating the potential for using oxytocin to enhance trust and the people-reading process, with some promising results, so far (Heinrichs, von Dawans, & Domes, 2009). In this line of research, inhaling oxytocin has been shown to improve performance on tests of reading emotions in faces (Guastella, Mitchell, & Matthews, 2008). Giving oxytocin to couples prior to therapy sessions improves trust and promotes more constructive, less defensive communication, at least in a research setting (Kosfeld,

Heinrichs, Fischbacher, & Fehr, 2005). People on the autism spectrum tend to have low levels of oxytocin; there is now some evidence that taking oxytocin may improve the nonverbal people-reading skills of some of these individuals (Andari, Duhamel, Zalla, Herbrecht, Leboyer, & Sirigu, 2010).

This line of research has very interesting implications for working with parents who have child-reading problems as well as the whole spectrum of caregivers that presents with blocked care symptoms. The possibility that boosting oxytocin levels in parents with blocked care could decrease their defensiveness, activate their approach systems, and improve their child-reading systems is quite intriguing. Since good relationships are the most natural way to boost oxytocin functioning (Gouin et al., 2010), the therapeutic relationship is clearly extremely important as a possible avenue to priming this key chemical system in the parenting brain.

The Parental Meaning-Making System

The ways in which parents construct meaning from their experiences with their children is another key domain of the parenting brain. The quality of our narratives—of the stories we tell ourselves about being parents, about the nature of our kids, and about our relationships—is determined by the functioning of our brains. In a healthy, well-connected and integrated brain, the meaning constructed tends to be nuanced, complex, and coherent, as described by Daniel Siegel (1999) and others. In contrast, stressed-out brains create stories that are polarized, told in black and white, stories of an *"either–or"* rather than a *"both–and"* nature. These more simplistic narratives are driven by the limbic regions that are devoted to defensive operations—those reaction systems that generate quick action, heated emotion, and unreflective thinking. Brain research (Baynes & Gazzaniga, 2000) reveals that we create narratives using our left hemispheres, with input from our right, so when our right-brain defense system is highly reactive, our left-brain narratives reflect this hypervigilant style of experiencing the world. Until you calm your defense system, which means calming your amygdala, it is difficult to construct more complex, positive, hopeful narratives. Our meaning making is intricately tied to our emotions and to our ability to link our emotional experience to our thinking.

Whereas stress-driven narratives tend to be simplistic stories, often having the flavor of victimhood or martyrdom—of me versus you—the human brain has a unique capacity to hold two seemingly opposing thoughts in mind and to create an integrating, "meta" concept based on a synthesis of these seeming opposites. This is called a *dialectical* process and it is the basis for a type of therapy for emotionally reactive people called *dialectical behavior therapy*. In this therapeutic approach, developed by Marsha Linehan (1993), self-soothing and mindfulness practices are taught to clients so that they can develop the capacity to calm their limbic systems and then activate the higher regions of their brains to create new levels of meaning and understanding. This is precisely the kind of process that attachment-focused therapy (Hughes, 2011) promotes, fostering safety and trust so that self-reflection and enriched meaning-making processes can be activated.

In order to create richer, more coherent narratives as a parent, we have to use the highest regions of the prefrontal cortex, the dorsolateral prefrontal cortex. The dorsolateral prefrontal cortex is the last part of the frontal lobe to mature, and it has a more complex structure than the lower regions of the prefrontal cortex. Because of this added structural complexity, this region can support more complex thinking, such as the kind of thinking involved in reappraising old ways of thinking and seeing things in a new light. Since the dorsolateral prefrontal cortex is the last part of the frontal cortex to mature and to become fully connected to other brain regions, the ability to engage in highly integrative thinking only comes online as the brain matures.

Since chronic stress suppresses the development of this higher region of the brain, adults who have been exposed to high levels of adversity may have underdeveloped dorsolateral prefrontal cortex regions and/or underdeveloped connections between this region and the rest of the brain. This underdevelopment would make it very difficult to "get above" the kind of polarized experiencing and thinking that characterize "hot cognitions" in a stressed-out brain.

The parental meaning-making system, then, is greatly influenced by parents' own histories, both their histories of brain development and their attachment histories. For example, if a mother's own parents experienced little enjoyment in her presence, if they took little interest in her nonverbal expressions or perceived her with a negative bias, or if they saw little meaning or value in playing, sharing, or communicating with her, this mother is likely to have difficulty experiencing meaning when she engages in these activities with her child. If as a child, this mother's thoughts, emotions, and wishes were not valued nearly as much as was obedience to the parents' directions, she will have difficulty experiencing positive meaning in coming to accept and understand her child's inner life, especially when her child disagrees with her own inner life.

Similarly, if the mother's childhood involved events with her parents that were too painful to be integrated into her own developing narrative, she is likely to have difficulty if her interactions with her child activate these poorly integrated memories. Examples might involve this mother's parents frequently or unpredictably reacting to her with rage and threats, or ignoring and isolating her as well as being disinterested in or rejecting her initiatives or deviations from their plans for her life.

In these situations, parents are not influenced by the uniqueness of their child and their reciprocal relationship as much as they are influenced by rigid, unintegrated memories from their past relationships with their own parents. In contrast, when parents have attachment histories characterized by both emotional intimacy with their own parents, combined with the freedom to develop their own autonomy, they are likely to have the same open, curious, and accepting relationship with their child. Parents with positive attachment histories typically find rich meaning in being a parent and in facilitating their child's development in all areas of his or her life.

It is important to note that difficulties in attachment history place us at risk of having similar difficulties in relationships with our own children. However, risk is not certitude, and if we have resolved these difficulties from our own history, the risk that we will react to our children as our parents did with us is even less (Wesselman, 1998).

Because our stories affect our emotions and our emotions affect our stories, there is a top-down, bottom-up interaction always in play between what we feel and what we believe. The top-down effects of our stories on our emotions can keep us stressed out and contribute to the development of blocked care. Narrative and cognitive therapists are quite familiar with the power of negative core beliefs to limit cognitive flexibility and the change that can come from that flexibility. In a brain-based model, we emphasize the continual interplay between meaning making and affect regulation and of the power of the dyadic relationship between therapist and parent to influence both processes. The therapist's ability to co-regulate a parent's affect can assist the parent in reappraising and re-editing old parental scripts as he or she gains greater ability to utilize higher brain regions and to engage both sides of the brain.

The Parental Executive System

Human parenting places great demands on such executive processes as emotion regulation, focused attention, and impulse control. These executive processes are known to be dependent on the functioning of our prefrontal cortex, the last part of the brain to mature. As described in Chapter 1, the executive system ties emotion regulation to the processes of self-reflection, empathy, and conflict resolution. The executive system also supports our ability to change our thinking and our behavior in light of new information. Our ability to change, based on our experiences as a parent, is one of the most important aspects of good parenting—and this ability rests squarely on the functioning of our prefrontal cortex.

The ability to learn from our experiences and make adaptive changes is connected to *cognitive flexibility*, the ability to change one's mind based on new information or changing circumstances. For example, parents need to have the cognitive flexibility to stop doing something that used to be adaptive but has now become upsetting to a child, as when a particular tone of voice or way of joking with a child "worked" when the child was younger but now simply irritates the child. In research, the ability to make this shift is called *reversal learning*, and it depends heavily upon the functioning of the lower region of the prefrontal cortex, the orbitofrontal cortex. When the orbitofrontal cortex is not working well for any reason, people have trouble changing their behavior even when they know, intellectually, that what they are persisting in doing is not getting the results they want. This perseverative behavior is seen both in people with damage to the orbitofrontal cortex and in stressed-out people whose orbito-frontal cortex is suppressed by stress hormones.

In addition to reversal learning, parents also need to be able to engage in a process that researchers call *attentional set shifting*. Set shifting is involved when we need to change the way we are looking at or understanding something. We use set shifting whenever we change our beliefs or our "framing" of a problem. In relation to parenting, an example of set shifting would be when a dad reflects on how he has been viewing his child a certain way, perhaps as "lazy," and then comes to see that his child has a learning problem that is causing what appeared to be "laziness." This change of viewpoints or beliefs about the child rests upon the parent's ability to engage the set shifting, reappraisal system of the brain—a process that depends heavily on the functioning of the highest region of the prefrontal cortex, the dorsolateral prefrontal cortex, which we discussed above in relation to meaning making.

When parents lack the cognitive flexibility that comes with brain maturation and freedom from too much stress, they are more at risk for the development of blocked care. This risk arises because their inflexibility inevitably disrupts their relationship with their children, creating unnecessary tensions and conflict. These parents are confronted with the repeatedly negative feedback from their children about the rigid way they are parenting. Parents who were exposed to high levels of adversity in early childhood or have experienced high levels of trauma earlier in life are likely to exhibit this kind of inflexible parenting due to compromised functioning of the executive brain system. Also, any time we become stressed out, we tend to become more inflexible in our dealings with our children, as we shut off the very regions of our big brains that could help us to avoid this rigidity.

The Parental Executive System also enables a parent to modulate the effects of problems in the functioning of the other parenting systems. For example, if a parent begins to experience disappointment when parenting is not as rewarding as expected, the executive system allows the parent to inhibit negative affect and reflect upon this experience. This "two-step" action of putting the brakes on a potentially disruptive emotional reaction and then thinking about the situation is rooted in the healthy capacity to activate the brain regions that can inhibit the limbic system and then the regions that support self-reflection and reappraisal. When the other four systems begin to shut down, leading to problems with parental motivation, empathy, and sense of purpose, the Parental Executive System enables parents to continue to act on their commitments to their children. The mature Parental Executive System helps a parent to stay in a parental state of mind and to keep the other parenting systems ON even when the process of parenting is stressful and does not feel good. By conferring cognitive flexibility and by modulating potential negative effects stemming from problems in any of the other parenting systems, the Parental Executive System provides the central orchestrating process for caregiving.

In addition to the various regions of the prefrontal cortex, the Parental Executive System depends heavily upon the functioning of the anterior cingulate cortex brain bridge we described in chapter one. When this system is well developed in a parent's brain, the parent is alerted by an internal error-detection signal from the anterior cingulate cortex if feedback from the child indicates that something is amiss or that what the parent is doing is not effective. When this system activates, the parent has the ability to put the brakes on and shift into a more attentive state of mind conducive to tuning in more deeply to the child and then making adjustments in the way he or she is interacting with the child. Figure 2.2 illustrates the interactive processes of the five parenting systems we have explored in this chapter.

Figure 2.2.
The Five Parenting Systems

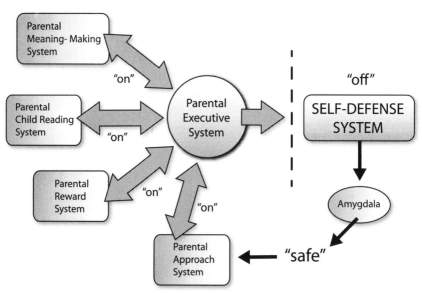

In the next chapter, we discuss how the dynamics of blocked care can interfere with the functioning of the Parental Executive System and disrupt a parent's ability to step back from unparental reactions, reflect, and reattune to the child.

CHAPTER 3

Blocked Care & How It Happens

At first, she was a great mom, spending all of her time caring for her babies. She fed them, kept them warm, cleaned the home, protected them from harm, and touched them in ways that made them feel calm and safe. If anything threatening came near them, she was ready to attack, to protect them with all she had, even to the death. Intriguingly, before she had her babies, she had no interest in being a parent. In fact, she found infants quite annoying, certainly not a source of pleasure. After she got pregnant and gave birth, however, everything changed and she was preoccupied with being close to them and taking care of them.

In fact, she found the process of mothering extremely rewarding, preferring it to all other rewarding things in life. With her attention now riveted on her babies, she could read their signals instantly and know what they needed. And if they somehow got separated from her and she heard their cries, she searched for them relentlessly until she found them and brought them home where she then gave them extra loving care.

> But then, something happened inside her, something she couldn't understand, and soon she stopped being this great caregiver. She let the home go to pot and resisted the attempts of her babies to get her attention and to let her know their needs. They began to lose weight, becoming frightened, hovering around her, not knowing what to do to bring back the mom they knew. Completely dependent on her care, they were now in deep trouble. Then, just in time to bring them back to life, she regained her motivation to be a mom and resumed all of the caring behaviors she had shown before. She emerged from her mysterious "blocked care" and with her nurturing powers restored, saved her little ones from sure death.

This poignant true story of parental love, lost and regained, captures the essence of blocked care. As you may have guessed, the mom here is not a human parent; she's a cute little white lab rat, one of the thousands who have taught us so much about ourselves and helped to improve our lives in so many ways. Yes, these little rodents tend to be great parents, dedicating themselves to the care of their young until their "kids" reach maturity after a long journey in rodent time of 20-some days. By the time their offspring reach maturity, the tired moms actually show a preference for other rewarding things in life over being with their now self-sufficient young adults. Sound a bit familiar?

The mom in our story stopped parenting for a while because those clever brain scientists temporarily "knocked out" the regions of her brain that are now known to be crucial to caregiving. Then, when they removed the block and restored the functioning of these key brain regions, she was able to parent again, regaining the core motivation she needed to override an otherwise natural aversion to infants. When these core brain regions devoted to parenting were turned back on, the mom regained her lovely obsession with caring for her babies, rediscovering the pleasures of being a mom. With her care system restored, she again became preoccupied with them in ways that allowed her to tolerate all of the stress and hard work involved in raising them to maturity.

In this vignette, the care system was knocked out by the scientists; in people, the core parenting system can be suppressed in a number of different ways. A dramatic example of this care-suppression process is seen in postpartum depression . Parents who develop postpartum depression find themselves unable to feel loving and empathic toward their children, despite having an intense desire to nurture them. Postpartum depression is not induced by parent–child interactions in the way that blocked care is, but rather is an internal process having something to do with the brain chemistry that normally primes the maternal brain for parenthood.

In general, depression and anxiety are care-suppressing conditions, affecting the parts of a parent's brain that are essential for experiencing nurturing feelings and caring about other people. Parents with closed-head brain injuries affecting the frontal lobes are likely to have problems maintaining good connections with their children. In addition, parents who are on the autism spectrum, including parents with Asperger disorder, often experience some difficulty with attunement and empathy as a result of the atypical functioning of the parts of the brain involved in "people processing" and nonverbal communication. However, in our model of blocked care, the primary source of interference with caregiving is unmanageable stress associated with the experiences of parenting and, in most cases, some aspects of the parent's own attachment history.

Types Of Blocked Care

Blocked care takes different forms, depending on the source and duration of the stress parents' experience. Below, we describe four types of blocked care:

1. chronic
2. acute
3. child specific
4. stage specific

Chronic Blocked Care

Rebecca spent the first 2 years of her life in the care of her mother and father. Her parents often argued and sometimes their arguing ended violently, with her mother being slapped and her father leaving home for days at a time. Before her first birthday, Rebecca had learned to suppress the terrible feelings that were triggered by her parents' angry voices and faces. All she had to do was freeze and shut off her mind, going numb as if she were playing dead. She learned to dissociate without even knowing she was doing so.

Her mother finally left her father and raised Rebecca herself, with the sporadic involvement of several different men who came and left over the years. At the age of 17, Rebecca met Billy and began having sex, which was the first time she had felt safe, for a little while, with another person. She soon got pregnant and the hormonal changes of the pregnancy also stirred feelings of love and warmth inside her that had long been suppressed. Billy was out of her life when her beautiful baby, Eric, was born. From the apartment she had been sharing with three friends, Rebecca moved back in with her mother.

At first, just after Eric was born, Rebecca felt a deep, all-encompassing love for him and a calmness she had never experienced before. But soon, when he would cry and flail his arms and legs, resisting her efforts to comfort him, she began to feel overwhelmed, angry, and stressed out. Her initial loving feelings began to erode, suppressed by her anger and a feeling of being trapped by parenthood. She began to tune out Eric when he sought her attention, using the old strategy from her early years of shutting out the world and numbing her feelings. Gradually, Eric stopped seeking her attention as much and turned, instead, to her mother (his grandmother), who became his "go to" caregiver. Sadly, despite all of Rebecca's initial expectations of giving and receiving unconditional love when Eric was born, her capacity for nurturing her son seemed to have disappeared. She had developed "blocked care."

Rebecca needed help from someone who could understand how well-meaning parents can lose their motivation to care for their children. She needed a therapist who could help her feel safe revealing her negative thoughts and feelings about Eric, someone with a deep understanding of the dynamics of blocked care and a roadmap for helping her recover her capacity to nurture Eric. Rebecca knew she wasn't "supposed" to feel the dark feelings she was experiencing about Eric and about being a parent, but she didn't know what to do with these feelings and the shame that lay just beneath the surface of her anger and resentment. She had never experienced being listened to and accepted without judgment and had no basis for trusting Jane, the home-based therapist who was assigned to her case when Eric's poor behavior at preschool drew the attention of family services.

When a parent has experienced unmanageable levels of stress beginning very early in life, blocked care stems from a combination of a poorly developed care system and an underdeveloped self-regulation system. In this scenario, the core caregiving domains of *approach*, *reward*, *child reading*, and *meaning making* are underdeveloped, making the basic caregiving process difficult to activate. Meanwhile, the top-down Parental Executive System is also underdeveloped, creating a dual-circuit problem that makes chronic blocked care particularly complex.

Rebecca's Brain

Let's look at how each of the five parenting systems may be affected in chronic blocked care. We will consider the effects on Rebecca's brain of growing up in adversity and then trying her best to parent Eric before she had a chance to develop the brainpower she needed.

THE PARENTAL APPROACH SYSTEM

Rebecca's early childhood forced her to play defense around her parents, overusing her right-brain harm avoidance system while having little chance to develop her social approach system. Her oxytocin system was not working well, due to both underdevelopment in childhood and her current stress. Instead of releasing this calming chemical when interacting with or even thinking about Eric, Rebecca was releasing stress hormones and activating her defense system, which kept her feeling insecure and uncomfortable around Eric and as a parent.

THE PARENTAL REWARD SYSTEM

Similar to the suppressing effects of stress on Rebecca's approach system, her reward system was underdeveloped due to the effects of early childhood adversity on the development of her dopamine system. Her reward system was geared toward immediate gratification due to spending her childhood in survival mode. Her need to find pleasure in "quick fixes" set her up for both hypersexuality and drug abuse, and she found herself caught up in brief sexual encounters, drinking, and pot smoking, unable to defer pleasure enough to find satisfaction in parenting Eric. As with many people exposed to adversity early in life, Rebecca had a heightened risk for addiction partly because of (1) underdevelopment in the prefrontal regions that could help her to regulate her impulses, and (2) partly because chronically high levels of stress hormones alter the sensitivity of dopamine receptors in the nucleus accumbens and orbital cortex—regions that are critically important to processing rewarding things in life (Winstanley, 2007). The more immediate activation of these brain regions by drugs and sex was blocking the naturally rewarding aspects of parenting. Plus, due to the tensions between Rebecca and Eric, many of his responses to her were now negative, defensive, and even aggressive, reinforcing her negative and defensive feelings towards him.

THE PARENTAL CHILD READING SYSTEM

In terms of her child-reading system, Rebecca had learned very early in childhood to be hypervigilant for facial expressions and tones of voice that signaled impending aggression, and this hypervigilant style caused her to react extremely rapidly to any "negativity" in Eric's nonverbal communication. She was quick to feel threatened by the least signs of anger in Eric's eyes or voice and would go into a preemptive state of defensiveness and anger herself, short-circuiting any further processing of Eric's experience in the moment. Thus, Rebecca did not read her son's unique nonverbal cues very well and did not really get to know him. Instead, her amygdala-driven hypersensitivity to the least signs of rejection from Eric was foreclosing the possibility of understanding her son.

THE PARENTAL MEANING-MAKING SYSTEM

Rebecca's meaning-making efforts, in her survival-based narrative about being a parent, were understandably quite negative. She had fixed beliefs that she was a bad mother and that Eric was an ungrateful child, essentially a story of victimhood in which she blamed both Eric and herself. Because her feelings of being a bad parent were intolerable to her, triggering deep shame, she rarely let herself think about her relationship with Eric, blocking any reappraisal of her strongly-held negative beliefs. Although her anger and resentment protected her from her shame and an underlying sadness about the deep misattunement in their relationship, these care-suppressing feelings also suppressed Rebecca's potential to change her mind about Eric, to see him in a new light.

THE PARENTAL EXECUTIVE SYSTEM

Finally, at the core of Rebecca's parenting problems was a poorly developed executive system due to the stress she had experienced in early childhood, during the sensitive period for constructing those all-important connections between her prefrontal cortex and her limbic system. A poorly developed executive system meant that she had little capacity to pull back from her initial defensive reactions to Eric, and reassess; instead, she would quickly lose her cool and have no effective way of putting on the brakes and recovering from these lapses in self-regulation. Also, Rebecca became a parent before her brain had fully matured, forcing her to try to deal with the challenges of raising Eric without the benefit of the prefrontal cortex power that comes with more neurobiological maturity.

Acute Blocked Care

Things were going well between Alicia and her 12-year-old daughter Tammy, until Alicia's mother died suddenly from a massive heart attack. Alicia's mother was her "rock," and losing her in this way was a huge shock to her, sending her spiraling into grief that took all her energy to manage. Her strong grief reaction quickly began to interfere with her parenting and her connection to Tammy, who was now a young teenager, already trying to weaken her dependency on Alicia. Alicia's lapses into extreme sadness took her further away from Tammy just at a time when Tammy both needed her and didn't want to need her. Alicia was experiencing an acute suppression of her motivation to parent.

Compared to Rebecca and the chronic blocked care she exhibited, Alicia had fairly well-developed systems for parenting Tammy and for finding pleasure in that role. Before her mother died, she was quite good at reading Tammy's communication; they shared thoughts and feelings and experienced being heard and understood.

Alicia's narrative about herself as a parent, before she developed acute blocked care, was generally positive. She thought of herself as a good and loving parent and of Tammy as a good kid. She connected her parenting to the way her mother had cared for her and saw herself as part of an intergenerational tradition of good mothering. In the aftermath of her mother's death, Alicia was struggling to regulate the intense feelings she was experiencing; much of the time, she found herself outside of her coping range. This acute reaction to extreme stress was temporarily suppressing her prefrontal functions while overactivating her limbic system. Although different in nature from the chronic blocked care scenario we see with Rebecca, Alicia is still in need of help to recover from the care-suppressing effects of the stress she is experiencing, a process that is putting her at risk for developing a more enduring type of blocked care.

Child-Specific Blocked Care

After years of trying to have their own child, Janet and Jim finally adopted Kim, an adorable Korean girl who had spent her first 2 years in foster care after her birth mother had given her up at birth. Janet and Jim were bursting with joy when they arrived home with Kim, eager to experience the rewards of being loving parents. It wasn't long, however, before they both began to experience extremely unsettling feelings of deep disappointment and an almost unspeakable sense of having been misled, almost duped. Kim rarely smiled at them and often went into a rage over the least little things. She resisted their hugs, but later would jump on them when they weren't looking and cling as if for dear life. Their expectations of what parenting was going to be like were being violated everyday, in multiple ways. By the time they had had Kim for a year, they were both feeling resentful and were having great difficulty feeling empathic toward their complicated daughter.

Janet and Jim were developing what we call *child-specific blocked care*. Although they were both caring people with good potential for parenting, their adopted child's lack of secure attachment behaviors and ongoing reciprocal interactions with them placed them at risk for gradually responding in a defensive manner that would create blocked care toward this child. This risk might have been reduced if they had been given preadoption education about the difficulties that their child might show in developing an attachment. It also might have been reduced if they had been more aware of their own attachment issues and had had a chance to work on any unresolved potential "hot buttons" from their own histories. However, because the Parental Reward System is such an important aspect of the natural parent–child bonding process, their child's poor response to their caregivng would still place them at some risk for developing child-specific blocked care. Their expectations were understandably not realistic about what it would be like to parent a child who had been forced to "play defense" early in life. Their caring feelings were eventually suppressed by the self-defensive feelings of rejection and anger they experienced from trying to parent a child who could not yet feel safe with them.

Under certain circumstances a parent may be able to provide very adequate care to one child while being unable to provide the same level of care to another child. This may occur:

- When one child is closely associated with an acute stressor from the parent's past so that the child's presence activates the defensive system called into play by that stressor. This might be the case if the child's appearance, temperament, behavior, or mannerisms remind the parent of someone else (e.g., his own parent or ex-partner).
- When one child consistently does not respond in a positive, reciprocal manner to the parent's caregiving behaviors. When these caregiving behaviors are ineffective, their failure is experienced as being extremely stressful, defensive systems are activated, and caregiving begins to shut down. There is a risk of this form of blocked care if the child manifests autistic features or if the child's attachment behaviors are inhibited or disorganized due to his or her history of trauma or loss. This may occur with a parent who is providing care for a foster or adopted child.

Child-specific blocked care might well become a source of extreme acute stress that could engender a more enduring, habitual form of blocked care if it goes on for an extended period of time. Although initially the parent may have been able to provide ongoing care to other children when his or her care for one child was a failure, eventually the stress of the child-specific blocked care places the parent at risk for acute blocked care for the other children as well.

Stage-Specific Blocked Care: Twos and Teens

Charlie had really enjoyed his relationship with his son Josh while Josh was an exuberant, playful preteen. They would wrestle together on the sofa, tickle each other, acting in many ways like "buddies." They shared similar interests in the outdoors and sports and often went off together for the day or talked into the night. Then, something changed; Josh entered puberty and didn't want to wrestle anymore. He was spending more time texting his friends and less time being interested in being around his dad. Charlie began to feel rejected and unappreciated—feelings he had had as a kid when he could not get his dad to pay attention to him. These feelings were growing now and making it hard for Charlie to like Josh anymore. They began to argue a lot, and Charlie found himself losing his temper in ways he hadn't when Josh was younger and playful. Charlie was struggling to stay parental following this shift from the little boy to the "tween" stage of Josh's development, and he was finding himself knee-deep in stage-specific blocked care.

Many parents are able to provide extensive care to their child when the child is engaged, receptive, and agreeable. These parents may have no trouble caring for their children when they exhibit a mellow and friendly temperament and seldom show any resistance to their guidance or directives. However, most children go through stages where they become more argumentative and independent for a time, and do not respond to their parents' caregiving behaviors. During these stages the child is not interested in a reciprocal relationship with his or her parents; rather, the child's focus is more on his or her independent activities and on peer relationships.

The "terrible twos" is one such common stage. Another is adolescence—or hopefully, more the *early* stage of adolescence, before the teenage brain starts to develop more prefrontal power, which then helps the teen start to emerge from the intensively egocentric stage of brain development that is normal during the earlier teenage years.

In early adolescence, the limbic system becomes much more active, driving emotionality, at the same time that the prefrontal cortex is not yet mature. As brain scientists like to say, this is like having a heavy foot on the gas pedal while your brakes don't work very well.

When the child becomes habitually oppositional to, or withdrawn from, the parent, the parent is at risk for experiencing stage-specific blocked care. The lack of reciprocity in the interactions is one factor. Another is the parent's intense experience of rejection, which is likely to trigger a defensive state within the parent. Many parents are at risk of entering such a state whenever they discipline their child. We often discipline our kids in ways very similar to the way our parents disciplined us. For many parents, their early experiences with being disciplined were likely to contain anger, threats, or a narrow behavioral focus with little openness to their own experience of being disciplined. Similarly, some parents have difficulty initiating relationship repair with their child following a conflict. When the relationship is not repaired, it is difficult for the parent to actively use all five domains of caregiving.

The Brain and Blocked Care: Stressed-Out Parenting

In parents who had to play defense much of their lives, their neuro-ceptive threat detection system (described in Chapter 1) is likely to *over*detect threats from other people. In chronic blocked care situations, the parents' amygdalas, especially on the right side of the brain, are likely to be enlarged and exquisitely sensitive to potential threats. This sensitivity causes the defense system to work overtime in an effort to keep them safe in the way this same system did when they were little children.

Even as the amygdala tends to grow and become more reactive from exposure to adversity, other regions of the brain that are essential to staying grounded and putting things into perspective tend to shrink from exposure to chronic or acutely excessive stress (Admon et al., 2009). These include regions of the prefrontal cortex and anterior cingulate cortex that are so vital both to keeping our lids on and to the capacity to see beyond our defensive reactions. This stress-induced brain suppression process also affects the hippocampus, that brain region that is essential for memory, learning new things, making new brain cells, and regulating stress (Fuchs & Flugge, 2003; Heim & Nemeroff, 2002).

As we've seen, the amygdala not only triggers the alarm system; it also helps to make memories, very enduring memories, of things in life that surprise us with their intensity, either positively or negatively. It does this by rapidly linking or associating previously emotionally neutral aspects of the environment with the physiological reactions of joy and pleasure or with the physiological states of self-defense, of fight, flight, or freeze. Simply being exposed again at any time in life to these reward-conditioned and threat-conditioned cues can reinstate both the pleasurable and defensive reactions we had earlier in life, before we are even aware of having been triggered by something. Once the right-brain defense system gets tuned to an unsafe environment, it tends to keep setting off the alarm system later in life when other people come close, causing frequent false alarms that make it difficult to stay connected and engaged with other people, even when trying to do so (Pollak, 2003).

False alarms are likely with this rapid, preconscious process because the quality of information to which the amygdala is responding initially is extremely rough, lacking in detail and in context. Although the amygdala soon receives more highly processed information both from sensory regions and from areas of the prefrontal cortex that are in close communication with it, the first appraisal system can short-circuit further processing and lock us into a survival-based state of mind and body.

Young children, by definition, are much more "amygdaloid" creatures than more mature people. However, we retain this quick appraisal and reaction system throughout life and at any age, we could have an amygdaloid, "limbic" moment if we encounter something very novel and very arousing, either positive or negative. We can also have these reactions when a strong memory of an experience from any time in our lives gets triggered. This is especially true of unresolved traumatic memories. When these memories are triggered, the amygdala on the right side of the brain becomes very active and can reinstate the pattern of brain and body arousal that took place during the actual traumatic event. Because the amygdala has so-called *back projections* to the areas that send it information, it can "revivify" a memory, bringing the sensory experience of that memory back to the level of intensity of the original occurrence (Vuilleumier, 2009).

This is the neurobiological process that gives rise to flashbacks and the sensory experience of not just recalling something, but of reliving it. Parents, then, who have unresolved memories of painful, frightening, or shaming experiences are prone to being triggered by their interactions with their children into unparental states of mind, during which they lose touch with what is really happening in the parent–child relationship in the moment. These parental "disappearances" or "out-of-the-blue" emotional reactions are inevitably upsetting to a child and can even be traumatizing.

Unfairly, then, parents who grow up in environments that are very stressful and that engender strong feelings of fear are likely to have more sensitive limbic alarm systems than parents who grow up in safety. Early childhood is a time when the limbic system is learning about the nature of interpersonal relationships. In this process it is also getting "tuned" to a certain level of reactivity or sensitivity to different kinds of social situations—and especially to the nonverbal communication that signals approachability or threat in others. Parents from unsafe childhoods are likely to experience limbic reactions to their children that are inconsistent with their intentions as parents. Implicit defensive reactions caused by limbic "false alarms" can make it very difficult for a parent to stay open, present, and attuned to a child in the moment. This is one of the most powerful reasons why we say that parental development begins in early childhood with the type of caregiving environment available to the parent-in-the-making.

Stress and the Prefrontal Cortex

When stressed out, parents do not use all of the prefrontal cortex. In particular, the middle and topmost regions are likely to shut down and be out of commission, whereas the lowest region, the orbital cortex, may function partially, especially the part of the right orbitofrontal cortex that responds to things that are threatening or punishing. The middle and upper regions of the prefrontal cortex turn on only when parents are emotionally regulated enough to step back and take a longer, slower, deeper look at what is going on, both within themselves and in their children (Banfield et al., 2004). In stressed-out survival-based brain mode—that is, in a state of *blocked care*, with the higher prefrontal regions suppressed—the vital functions of self-awareness and self-monitoring are offline, along with attunement to the child's thoughts and feelings, and the processes of conflict resolution and problem solving.

Early childhood adversity in the form of abuse and neglect can have a negative impact on the very regions of the brain that are so important for healthy social and emotional functioning (DeBellis, 2001). The affected regions, as seen in brain-imaging studies of adults who experienced abuse or neglect as children, include the prefrontal cortex, the hippocampus, the anterior cingulate cortex, and the corpus callosum (which connects the two sides of the brain and helps the right and left hemispheres "talk" to each other), as shown in Figure 3.1 (Teicher et al., 2003).

Figure 3.1.
Effects of early childhood adversity on the brain from a study of adults abused or neglected as children. ACC = anterior cingulate cortex; PFC = prefrontal cortex. Research from Teicher et al. (2003).

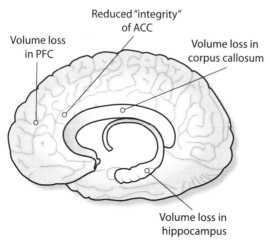

Parenting with a Stressed-Out Brain:
Effects on the Parent–Child Relationship

Unmanageable or chronic stress fosters a reactive style of parenting that is narrowly focused on the immediate behavior and most negative aspects of the child. Parenting in this inflexible, hyperfocused way inevitably suppresses openness and positive feelings between parent and child, the very qualities in a parent–child relationship that help to sustain emotional bonds and build strong connections. Stressed-out parenting stresses the child and tends to promote a runaway feedback loop that ramps up mutual defensiveness between the two.

One of the hallmarks of stressed-out parenting is a tendency to overreact to a child's nonverbal communication. Since our brains process nonverbal communication in the form of facial expressions, tones of voice, and gestures much faster than we consciously process the content of verbal communication, our reactions to each other's nonverbal signals begin before we even really understand the words we are hearing. Under stress, this implicit rapid appraisal process is likely to be biased toward the negative aspects of the other person's nonverbal expressions, easily triggering our defenses. The stressed-out parent, primed for detecting negativity in the child, reacts instantly to the child's eye movements or subtle changes in tone of voice.

When a stressed-out parent keeps reacting to a child's nonverbal "displays" of negative feelings, the parent–child interaction can get hijacked by mutual defensiveness. Reacting to each other's "nonverbals" blocks the interaction from becoming more open and from going deeper into a sharing of inner experiences. And, since nonverbal communication is largely automatic, taking a child's nonverbal expressions "personally" leads to misconstruing the child's real intentions while pushing the parent's "hot buttons." Quickly triggered into defensiveness, the parent goes no further in trying to understand the child; in turn, the child starts to give up on getting the parent to listen or understand. This is a recipe for blocked care.

Another feature of parenting under stress is the strong tendency to be judgmental, both toward the child and toward oneself. Under stress, the brain makes rapid appraisals and judgments about what is going on between parent and child. These rapid assessments, in turn, produce simplistic cognitions, black-and-white thoughts about child and self. This one-dimensional way of carving up experience is adaptive for survival-based living. Parents under too much stress feel like they are fighting for survival and, sadly, they experience their children as the threat to their well-being.

The stressed-out brain, needing to keep things simple, has no time for ambiguity, complexity, or uncertainty. Survival is all about rapid assessment and quick action, requiring the reduction of complexity and the narrowing of options. This is a job for the amygdala and the lower limbic system, not for the hippocampus, with its need to compare and contrast, or for those higher, uniquely human parts of the prefrontal cortex that would only gum up the works with subtlety and complexity.

Rejection and the Brain:
The Neurobiology of Taking Things Too Personally

Because parenting is such an emotional and visceral process, parents have a strong tendency to take their children's reactions to them personally, both the positive and the negative reactions. In brain terms, taking things personally is related to the activation of that lower stream in our brains, our limbic system, which is so tightly connected to our hearts and the rest of our bodies. When we react to anything in life that moves us strongly, this system is turned on, and when this system is on, we experience what is happening as highly personal, as happening *to us*, as being *about us*. This is why it is often difficult for us to deal with signs of rejection or invalidation when we are interacting with another person. Our first appraisal in these situations comes from our limbic system, not our higher, more objective and reflective regions of the brain. We can easily get captured in this "egocentric," personalizing part of our brain's reaction, especially if we are interacting with someone whose reactions to us really, really matter. For us as parents, the reactions we get from our children matter big time and are very likely to stir up our limbic systems, for better and for worse.

Recent studies using brain imaging show that the experience of feeling rejected activates the same pattern in the brain as feeling physical pain. In other words, emotional pain and physical pain are processed similarly in the brain (Ochsner et al., 2008). One of the key regions in the brain where social rejection registers is the anterior cingulate cortex, specifically the upper or dorsal region of the anterior cingulate cortex. This is also a key part of the brain involved in the suppression of painful feelings, both physical and emotional, and includes the dissociative process in which the dorsal anterior cingulate cortex is shut down, helping to create a scenario in which we feel no pain even as we are otherwise experiencing something that is "painful." This is the way a young child can turn off the emotional pain caused by a parent's hurtful, insensitive parenting. In this way, a child, and later a parent, can truly say, "I don't care."

Blocked care is likely to affect the parent's brain by activating this social rejection system centering around the activation of the dorsal anterior cingulate cortex, the part of the brain that helps to detect conflicts or errors between an intended or anticipated result of parents' attempts to care for children and children's responses to their parents. In other words, when parents approach children anticipating positive reactions and instead the children react nonverbally (and, perhaps, verbally) in a way that parents perceive as negative, the brains of these parents may activate this social rejection system. Parents might then respond to this emotionally painful experience much like they would to physical pain: by drawing away and becoming protective of themselves. Being rejected by one's child, even if the perception of rejection is a false alarm, is literally painful.

The activation of the social rejection system inevitably creates a visceral feeling that children's reactions are personal, much as if they had literally hit parents or done something to cause physical pain. This "gut reaction" registers in the insula, that part of the brain that receives input from the visceral parts of the body, including the heart, lungs, and stomach region. As discussed earlier in relation to parental empathy, the insula and the anterior cingulate cortex are strongly connected, so whenever the insula is activated by our visceral systems, whether positively or negatively, the effects register in the anterior cingulate cortex, giving rise to gut feelings. If parents get immersed in this initial gut reaction to their children's reactions, feelings of rejection are likely to become stronger and to affect the way the parents feel and think about those children.

Indeed, activation of the social rejection brain circuitry is likely to affect all of the basic parenting systems—approach, reward, child reading, and meaning making. In the throes of feeling rejected, all of these systems would be, at least temporarily, suppressed, basically going offline while the parent's self-defense system is online. In particular, the Parental Approach System and the Parental Reward System—the two brain systems that keep parents near their children and engaged in parenting—would be inhibited. Meanwhile, the Parental Child-Reading System—parents' system for attuning to their children's minds—would be highly constrained by their own defensive states of mind. This defensiveness would cause parents to perceive their children as being in a rejecting or ungrateful state of mind when this perception may be inaccurate or only a superficial reading of what the children are really experiencing. The meaning that parents construct while captured by this defensive reaction is likely to be negative and to further reinforce the immediately painful feelings of rejection. This meaning construction could be along the lines of "I'm a bad parent," "You're a bad kid," "This is pointless—I give up," etc. The risk that parents will experience social rejection when their children do not respond to their caregiving behaviors points to the importance of reciprocity in the parent–child relationship. In short, and as common sense tell us, it is much easier for parents to engage in ongoing caregiving behaviors when children respond in kind with warm, joyful engagement.

The key now is what happens with the Parental Executive System. Do the parents have the capacity to engage this system and start to regulate this "felt rejection" in a more productive way that can help them regain equilibrium and repair the connection with their children? If they are able to activate the Parental Executive System and regulate this powerful negative reaction, then they will be able to step back from taking their children's reactions personally and reappraise the situation—to take a "second look" at what is going on, to reflect upon their children's behavior and their own reactions to it. This is essentially a mindful response in contrast to a more automatic, reflexive, personalized response.

The Parental Executive System involves the top-down fronto-limbic circuitry we described in Chapter 1, those "vertical" connections that could enable a parent to turn on the self-regulating system at the same time that the feeling of rejection is kicking in. Failure to engage the Parental Executive System at this point will mean that parents' initial feelings of rejection, along with the automatic meaning that comes with it ("You don't love me," "You're ungrateful," etc.) will rule their brains and cause them to go into unregulated defensive responses. Blocked care is the result when the parental defense system is activated repeatedly, without the self-regulating help of the

Figure 3.2. Blocked Care

Failure of the Parental Executive System to regulate unparental reactions suppresses all parenting systems.

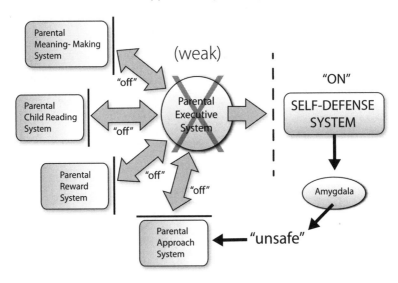

Parental Executive System. Figure 3.2 provides an illustration of this undesirable process.

Since blocked care involves the suppression of caring feelings, not permanent impairment of the potential for caring about a child, we see blocked care as a treatable condition. To us, this is the value of understanding the parental brain and how stress can suppress the caregiving process, making it seem to parents, and even to therapists, that the parents are simply uncaring and unempathic, when, in reality, their caring potential might very well be "awakened" or restored with sensitive, brain-based intervention. So next we turn to a discussion of understanding and assisting parents who have developed some type of blocked care.

CHAPTER 4

A Caregiving Formula

Playfulness, Acceptance, Curiosity, Empathy (PACE)

We have emphasized throughout this book that the parenting brain is designed to create an ongoing, open, reciprocally enjoyable relationship between parent and child, a heart-to-heart connection that goes far beyond managing the child's behavior. The five domains of parenting (approach, reward, child reading, meaning making, and executive), working in concert, foster a social engagement to facilitate the child's development by creating a deeply meaningful parent–child relationship. While this is all well and good, how does the science play out in real life? What are the characteristics of this open, engaged relationship that the parent can intentionally, mindfully bring to it? We'll take a closer look at these specific characteristics in this chapter.

Intersubjectivity is the term used by many theorists and researchers to refer to the reciprocal relationship between a parent and child. Within this mind-to-mind intersubjective rapport, both the parent and child are open to one another, receptive to and sharing each other's experience of self, other, and the world. Each accepts the influence of the other in the here and now. For example, when a father experiences his son's courage in handling a bully, the son is likely to become more aware of his courage by experiencing this aspect of himself through the mind and heart of his father. When the son responds to his father's experience of him with increased self-confidence and pride, the father, in turn, is likely to experience a renewed sense of satisfaction and competence himself. When a mother and her infant feel mutual joy in each other's presence, the infant experiences him- or herself as capable of eliciting Mom's joy, and the mother experiences herself as capable of eliciting her infant's joy. Through such reciprocal moments, each person becomes safely and deeply engaged with the other. The parent is better able to have a positive influence on her child's development and, in so doing, is positively influenced by the child's response (Hughes, 2006).

What can weaken these moments of healthy reciprocity? A need for self-protection and defensiveness. When either the parent or child shifts from openness to defense—often as a way to maintain psychological safety in the face of perceived evaluation by the other—the other is at risk of making a similar shift, and thereby jeopardizing the healthy reciprocal rapport. Mutual defensiveness moves parents and children away from intersubjective experience and joint influence and into a desire to gain control of the situation. To use Dan Siegel's language, there is a shift from a "we" interaction to a "me" versus "you" interaction (Siegel, 2010). But if parents can use their executive power to stay regulated and "parental," suppressing their own natural tendency to shift into defense in reaction to their child's defensiveness, then the child is less likely to linger in a defensive state of mind. Parents' ability to stay engaged and open helps the child recover faster from states of extreme emotion, distractible thoughts, and impulsive behaviors, and this recovery process helps to build the child's resilience and emotional competence at the same time that it strengthens his or her trust in the parents' ability to keep the relationship emotionally safe.

Parents, even those with blocked care, can improve their ability to stay parental, regulate their internal states, and promote intersubjectivity in their relationship with their children. In this chapter we present four key components of this process—playfulness, acceptance, curiosity, and empathy—and use the acronym *PACE* to refer to them as a unit. All four of these core components of intersubjectivity can be linked to one or more of the brain-based caregiving domains. The idea here is that through experiencing and practicing the processes of PACE, you can, in turn, strengthen your parental brain power.

Playfulness targets the components of intersubjectivity that mostly involve the Parental Approach and Reward Systems. *Acceptance*, a nonjudgmental attitude, also supports the approach system by helping to promote interpersonal safety and maintaining the parent's and child's mutual feeling of trust and connection. The nonjudgmental stance is made possible by the smart vagal system, the brain–heart circuit that forms the bedrock of open parenting. *Curiosity* links most directly to the child-reading and meaning-making systems, and *empathy* promotes the integration of all of the systems, connecting parental emotions with parental reflection and mindfulness. The four components of PACE function in an integrative manner, with considerable overlap, so that examples of one will often also involve qualities of the other three.

PACE applies equally to the parent–child relationship and to the therapist–parent relationship. The open and engaged stance that is crucial for effective parenting is just as vital to a strong therapeutic relationship. Without this openness, there can be no real trust and connection. At home, if a child approaches the parent in a defensive stance and the parent responds in an open, empathic, accepting way—that is, with PACE—the child will feel safer and the distress is more likely to diminish. In the therapist's office, if a parent approaches the therapist in a defensive stance and the therapist responds from a position of open acceptance of the parent's distress, the parent's defensiveness diminishes and he or she is more likely to be open to explore the problems that he or she is having with his or her child. Let's explore the components of PACE separately, looking at how they work in the parent–child relationship first, and then we'll give some examples for how they can play out in therapy.

Playfulness

Playfulness is a frequent reciprocal attitude that occurs between the parent and child. It represents the moment-to-moment, fully engaged interactions involving facial expressions, eye contact, voice prosody and rhythm, gestures, postures, and touch. Within this fully present intersubjective space, both parent and child experience deep joy, pleasure, and fascination with the other and with the shared activity.

It is not hard to see how playfulness engages the approach and reward systems of parents' brains. Indeed, playful interactions are known to stimulate the production of both opioids and dopamine, powerful chemicals that help to suppress pain and distress and promote feelings of enjoyment and pleasure (Panksepp, 1998, 2004). What an excellent prescription for helping a parent with blocked care begin to shift out of his or her defensive state and begin to experience some hope that things could be better! Blocked care is a stress-based condition, and stress suppresses playfulness in both animals and humans. Stress hormones literally block oxytocin and dopamine, the key brain chemicals for activating parents' approach and reward systems. Playfulness is potentially a "stress buster" that can reawaken these essential parenting processes. In a playful state, with the help of oxytocin, defenses are inhibited and there is little desire to pull away and withdraw from the interaction. The pleasure associated with being playful together taps the power of the reward system in both parent and child, generating a desire to spend more time together. Parenting your child within this enjoyable, reciprocal state is not a chore but a delight.

Play is also known to activate the higher regions of the brain, enhancing cognitive functioning (Panksepp, 2004; Pellis & Pellis, 2006). Because the dopamine that is stimulated by play enters the prefrontal regions, play enhances executive functions as well as the core approach and reward systems in both parent and child. Keeping playful interactions "alive" and fun actually requires a lot of attention to the play partner's nonverbal communication and the ability to make rapid adjustments in response to these cues, while also regulating emotional intensity to stay in the "right frequency" for sustaining this pleasurable connection. Panksepp and Burgdorf (2000) have shown, for example, that rats actually use a particular frequency of vocalizing to keep their play going with each other. Shifts in this frequency, much like changes in prosody in humans, can bring play to a halt instantly, along with a shift into freeze mode of mobilized defense.

In short, free play is actually a very creative process requiring a lot of people-reading and emotion regulation skills, a lot of "emotional intelligence." When playfulness is suppressed in a parent–child relationship, both parent and child are robbed of one of the most powerful processes for strengthening their connection and both partners' brains. The ability to play with a child strengthens the parent's ability to handle the unplayful aspects of the relationship—those interactions that require high levels of parental tolerance, patience, and self-control. The creative use of play by Eliana Gil (2006) to promote healing from trauma is a testament to the serious power of playfulness. Play, then, has the potential to strengthen a parent's approach, reward, child-reading, meaning-making, and executive systems, enhancing the integration of parental brain systems.

As playfulness emerges, it is characterized by:

1. An air of lightness, with a sense of relaxed, reciprocal enjoyment.
2. A sense of hope and increased confidence about the future.
3. A sense of unconditional acceptance of the other, regardless of any differences.
4. An awakening of the positive side of life, to offer a balance to the negative that characterizes their difficulties.
5. A reduction of shame for both.
6. An increased sense of trust and safety.
7. A confidence that one is liked by the other.
8. An increase in caregiving (and reduction of blocked care) for the parent and attachment behaviors for the child.

A central feature of playfulness is the sense of openness to possibility that it generates: Play can generate hope. The current situation, no matter how stressful it might be, is experienced as only one aspect of the overall relationship and the ongoing characteristics of the child's development. The lightness of play enables both parent and child to keep the current situation in perspective, and it facilitates an attitude of reflection. In this way, playfulness fosters the very sense of lightness that is conveyed in writings about mindfulness.

This playful attitude is most evident in the parent–infant relationship. But it is just as important—and is definitely attainable—in the parent's relationship with the older child. When playfulness is embedded into the ongoing parent–child relationship, it instills both parent and child with greater confidence about the depth and meaning of the relationship. Playfulness makes it clear implicitly, without words, that any conflict is manageable when experienced in the context of a robust, supportive relationship.

Example: Molly (the mother) has just told her 4-year-old son Ben that they cannot play outside any longer because it is time to get lunch ready. In anger, Ben shouts, "I don't love you!" This dialogue followed:

Molly: Oh, Ben, you are very angry with me!

Ben: And I don't love you!

Molly: Are you sure about that, Ben? Let me check. (*Molly bends down and touches Ben behind the ears, under his chin, his knees and elbows.*) Yes, Ben, your love for me is still in all those places on your body where it stays when you are angry with me. See, check out my ears. My love for you is still there when you are angry. And so is yours!

Ben: I don't see your love.

Molly: Oh, Ben, because you don't have Mama eyes, you can't see it. But you can hear it, here (*pulling him close*)—put you ear on my chest. You will hear my heart beating. My heart is beating now in a happy way because of my love for you.

Ben: It doesn't sound happy.

Molly: You can't hear its happiness? Must be too noisy outside. After lunch we'll snuggle on the couch, and it will be quiet and you will be able to tell that my heart is happy because of my love for you. You will hear it then.

Here playfulness immediately followed empathy for her son's distress and proved to be a gentle and light way of assisting him in managing his anger. It is important not to confuse playfulness with sarcasm nor to laugh or joke in response to a child's anger, which would dismiss the experience as not worth acknowledging or taking seriously. In this example Molly first acknowledged Ben's anger before moving into a lighter exchange over his denying that he loved her. In the next example the father first relates to his 12-year-old daughter's complaint with acceptance, curiosity and empathy, and only after she has been heard fully does he gently lead the relationship back to its foundations with the help of playfulness.

Stan: I'm really glad that you took the time to let me know that this was bothering you, Jenny. I thought something was on your mind and now I'm confident that we can work it out.

Jenny: I figured you didn't know how important it was for me to be able to see Sue this weekend. Now you know.

Stan: I do. And I think you know why I want you to come with us to Gran's house this weekend.

Jenny: I guess I do.

Stan: I should have approached you about it, but I dropped the ball. So thanks.

Jenny: I learned years ago that you're not perfect, Dad.

Stan: Not perfect but I've raised one great kid.

Jenny: Mostly because you have a great kid who doesn't need much help.

Stan: Mostly she doesn't need much help now because I did such a great job for 12 years.

Jenny: So now you're taking it easy?

Stan: Now, we're in a transition stage. Next, you'll be helping me put my socks on.

Jenny: OK. I'll do that for 12 years and then you're on your own. That's fair.

As playfulness begins to make its presence felt in the parent–child relationship, it helps to maintain the sense of safety for both parent and child. Its lightness and laughter convey confidence that the relationship is much stronger than are any conflicts.

How Playfulness Works in Therapy

When parents first see a therapist about problems they are having with their child, it's often hard for them to become immediately engaged in safely discussing their concerns. Feelings of discouragement, fear, anger, and shame may be on the surface. All of these emotional states are likely to lead a parent into a defensive state wherein a therapist's routine questions and suggestions may be experienced as critical judgments about the parent's caregiving behaviors. The open, reciprocal enjoyment and fascination that we just discussed in the parent–child relationship are not likely to be immediately present in the parent–therapist relationship. The therapist is wise not to try to force playfulness by minimizing the parent's negative emotional state, nor by telling jokes or pointing out the "silver lining." Early in the relationship it is wise for the therapist to stress the other three components of PACE and allow playfulness to gradually come alive once the parent's need for full acceptance, understanding, and empathy have been met. Playfulness needs to emerge naturally within the relationship as the parent's sense of safety with the therapist develops. In some sessions playfulness may never present itself. For this reason we sometimes speak of pACE (lower-case *p*) to indicate the prominence of the other three features, which are always present to some extent, whereas playfulness might not be. When playfulness does emerge, the parent is likely to be open and receptive to the therapist's perspective and suggestions regarding the parent's relationship with his or her child.

The following dialogue occurred in a parent's fourth session with his therapist. During the first three sessions, the parent, Robert, expressed a great deal of anger and discouragement over the many problems that exist in his relationship with his 13-year-old son Luke. On a number of occasions Robert expressed criticism toward the therapist, Cindy, for seeming to blame him for the conflicts with Luke. He had expressed the belief that Cindy really did not appreciate how hard he had worked to be a good father for his son. As Robert gradually entered the state of safe, social engagement in the session, the supportive and integrative role of playfulness gradually emerged.

Parent: So do you know what that little turkey said after all that I did for him to make it possible for him to attend the concert? He told me that he really didn't want to go very much but he was going because of all the work I put into it.

Therapist: Like he's going to the concert for you and not for himself! Why do you think he said that?

Parent: I don't know. Maybe the teenage way of saying "thanks"?

Therapist: *Teenage*, combined with *masculine*?

Parent: You're not saying anything about men and their lack of emotions or gratitude, are you?

Therapist: Certainly not older-than-teenager men!

Parent: Yeah, like my generation were so much better with feelings than males are now!

Therapist: Yes, I think that men have come quite a long way in handling and communicating about emotional things in their lives. I don't imagine that your father would have come to see a therapist if you and he had struggles like you do with Luke.

Parent: Believe me, if I challenged my father like Luke challenges me, I would have struggled a great deal. Not my father.

(*Therapist and parent now engage in a long discussion regarding the parent's difficulties with his father and how he wants more in his relationship with his son. This dialogue ends with this playful exchange.*)

Parent: Don't tell me that you are going to push me into that touchy-feely stuff with Luke.

Therapist: No, just enable your feminine side to naturally express itself.

Parent: Great! I got a feminine side now!

Therapist: OK, that may have been unfair. How about if we call it your affectionate side? Your caring side? Your love-for-your-son side?

Parent: Yeah, that's better. Just don't tell me to hug him in front of you.

Therapist: I'll turn my back.

Parent: You might have a long wait.

Therapist: Or not.

Parent: Yeah, just don't push it.

Therapist: I won't. I'll only nudge it a bit if I am sure that you are both feeling it. I would have to be sure that it would be successful.

Parent: I would like that.

As was true with playfulness in the parent–child relationship, it is also true in the therapist–parent relationship that playfulness conveys a sense of lightness, optimism, and confidence that whatever problems are being explored will be managed and the relationship will not be harmed.

Acceptance

When parents are with their infant, they tend to be unconditionally in love with him or her, accepting the baby as he or she is, with no strings attached. Parents do not evaluate the rightness or wrongness of their baby's behavior or judge him or her to be "good" or "bad." Evaluation exists only in so far as parents must determine the infant's immediate needs for nourishment, sleep, a diaper change, etc. Parents' primary attitude toward their infant is one of acceptance, not evaluation.

When infants—and later, children—experience acceptance from their parents they are likely to feel free to give expression to their feelings and desires, thoughts and perceptions, intentions and memories, safe in the knowledge that they will not be evaluated for aspects of their inner lives. As children mature, parents begin to evaluate their behavior, guiding and directing them toward engaging in behaviors that are safe and in the best interest of them (as children or adolescents) and others. Within the context of acceptance, this evaluation is purely behavioral and does not place either the relationships or the children in any psychological risk. Acceptance of children enables behavioral discipline to have an important, but limited, role in their development. The relationships with parents—the source of safety and intersubjective learning about self, other, and the world—remain the dominant influence that parents have on their children's development.

In this relational context, *correction* (i.e., discipline) is linked with *connection*, helping both parents and children to know that their relationships stay strong even when parents need to set limits and be firm. In a deeply accepting relationship, when the inevitable parent–child tensions arise, the relationship bends rather than breaks. Although there is inevitable misattunement (Tronick, 2007), the misattunement does not trigger intense fears of abandonment and rejection in a healthy parent–child relationship. Indeed, the relationship draws strength from both parties experiencing the natural cycle of attunement, misattunement, and repair (Siegel, 2005).

The important role of acceptance in children's development and in parent–child relationships is supported by Porges's (2011) polyvagal theory of neurological development, which we first explained in Chapter 1. Acceptance—seen as central to the experience of mindfulness—is facilitated through the activation of the smart vagal system, the brain–heart connections that promote openness, empathic listening, and attunement. As described in Chapter 1, this circuit involves connections between . . .

- The heart
- The anterior insula (the "visceral brain)

- The anterior cingulate cortex (that vital brain bridge, which reptiles don't have, that is so important for caring)
- The orbitofrontal cortex (that region of the prefrontal cortex vital to attachment-based learning)
- The medial prefrontal cortex (that region in the very front of our brains that we use for "self–other awareness," a region much expanded in comparison to our primate relatives)

This is the brain–heart circuitry that we use when are making a concerted effort to deeply understand another person's experience rather than judge him or her while planning our rebuttal. It is also the brain circuitry that has recently been shown by Michael Posner's group to be strengthened by certain kinds of practices that emphasize a focus on nonjudgmental attentiveness and empathy (Tang et al., 2010). Acceptance, then, facilitates the kind of nonjudgmental awareness that is crucial for the robust functioning of the Child-Reading and Meaning-Making Systems and for promoting mindful parenting.

When infants are in the open and alert state of consciousness—in their smart vagal state—they are open and receptive to their experience of the world and especially to their interaction with their parents. Infants' welcoming attitudes toward their experience of the world are present when they feel safe and have good "vagal tone." They are deeply interested in being engaged in the social world as experienced in their interactions with their parents.

Even as the smart vagal complex links parents' brains and hearts, promoting calmness and well-being, parents' acceptance of children links the children's vagal systems with the parents', promoting the development of the children's social engagement system, their heart–brain connections. This interpersonal, "intervagal" process, supported by the parents' capacity to stay engaged and accepting, enables parents to hold their children in their minds, hearts, and bodies with tenderness, awareness, and a deep sense of connectedness.

When children's lower vagal system—as opposed to the upper, smart vagal system—is activated, they lose connection with their parents, entering into a shutdown state. This defensive posture is thought by Porges (2011) to be frequently activated when children experience shame, when they feel judged and invalidated. This process of shutting down in shame is a growth-suppressing one that can promote a dissociative style of self-defense, creating a risk for later problems with intimacy and with parenting (Schore, 1994).

When parents experience acute or chronic conflict with their children, their overall experience of the parent–child relationship inevitably turns toward the children's behavior, and acceptance, along with playfulness, tend to be minimal. Parents then tend to become increasingly focused on behavioral problems, evaluating their children and communicating their displeasure regarding their behavior as well as the consequences that they deem necessary. At the same time, parents are likely to experience their children as evaluating them, being angry with them or disappointed in them as their parents. Both parents and children have moved unintentionally into a defensive posture with each other in which the capacity for caring about each other is suppressed, blocked. Neither is open to the experience of the other. The children are likely to rely on anger, defiance, or avoidant behaviors to try to influence their parents or minimize their influence in their (children's) lives. Parents are likely also to rely on anger, which can wrongly be used as a weapon parents come to depend on when they are actually feeling powerless. As issues of power and control become more important in these relationships than connection, discipline loses its meaning and effectiveness, becoming a battleground, an end in itself, isolated from concerns about the quality of the relationships. This kind of discipline is ineffectual over time, generating unwanted side effects such as submissiveness, withdrawal, secretiveness, or explicit acts of anger and defiance. One of the greatest challenges of parenting is blending limit setting with empathy, using discipline in the spirit of teaching, while keeping the parent–child relationship safe and intact. When parents are able to "correct in connection," they give their children wonderful opportunities to practice emotion regulation and, when appropriate, negotiation.

Example: Nancy (the mother) had just asked her 11-year-old daughter Tracy to put the laundry away before calling her friend. Tracy screamed at her mother and ran out of the room. Nancy then went to her daughter's room to discuss the incident with her.

Mom: You expressed a lot of anger at me, Tracy. What's up?

Daughter: You never seem to give me a break. It's always that I have to do what you want! What you want is more important than what I want!

Mom: So it seems to you that I'm always thinking of something that you should do for me and not just letting you do things that you want to do!

Daughter: Yeah! If not the laundry then the dishes, or the vacuuming, or watching my little brother, or . . . whatever. It's always a . . .

Mom: Like I forget that you're a kid! That I'm not interested in what you want. Only what you can do for me.

Daughter: That's how it seems to me, Mom!

Mom: Then I can understand why you got angry with me—if you think that I only think of you when I want your help, and when your helping me seems to you to be my main interest in you—not what will make you happy.

Daughter: It does seem that way, Mom—sometimes, anyway. Today I just had a really hard day at school.

Mom: Tell me about it. (*Tracy then gives a detailed account of some problems that she encountered at school.*) So you have had a hard day.

Daughter: Yeah, Mom, I have . . . but I guess I shouldn't have taken it out on you. I'm sorry.

Mom: Thanks, sweetie, for telling me what is going on.

Daughter: Sure, Mom, but I really want to talk with my friend about it. So how about if we stop talking so I can do the laundry now.

Here, by looking beyond her daughter's outburst and trying to determine the underlying feelings or emotions that led to it, the mother discovers what's on her child's mind, becoming more accepting in the process.

How Acceptance Works in Therapy

When parents enter the therapist's office due to ongoing problems with their children they may be experiencing blocked care toward their children. Relationship stress caused by behavioral problems tends to greatly reduce the activation of the five domains of the brain so central to providing ongoing care. Although they still may be able to engage their executive system in their interactions with their children, their ability to be with them and to enjoy the interaction—while being interested in them and their experience—is likely to be diminished. Parents' sense of the meaning of caregiving tends to move from the positive to the negative. Their evaluation of their children also tends toward a negative perspective of their motives, values, thoughts, and feelings. At the same time, they are likely to have developed a negative perception of themselves as parents. This perception places them at risk for an ongoing sense of shame and defensiveness. All of this may lead parents to assume that the therapist will be critical of them, and the parents may perhaps have one or more of the following thoughts:

"He [the therapist] thinks that it's all my fault!"
"He thinks that I'm a bad parent!"
"She [the therapist] thinks that I'm too hard on my son!"
"She thinks that I'm just being selfish!"
"He's blaming me for what happened!"
"He thinks that I'm too easy on my son!"
"She thinks that I don't love my daughter!"
"She thinks that I'm not trying very hard to be a good parent!"
"He thinks that I'm putting my own needs above those of my daughter!"
"She thinks that I'm just feeling sorry for myself!"
"She thinks that I'm not consistent [sensitive, caring, attentive] enough!"

When parents assume that the therapist is making these negative evaluations of them, they most certainly are not feeling safe. They are then not able to benefit from any ideas. They are not open to the therapist's experience of them as parents, assuming that it is negative and that experiencing such a judgment would be very painful. Judging themselves, they assume that the therapist is judging them. They do not believe that the therapist thinks that they are good parents who would benefit from a new childrearing idea to which they had not been exposed. Rather, they assume that any suggestion is intended to make up for their failure as parents.

A therapist's primary responsibility when meeting parents experiencing blocked care is to actively maintain and communicate an attitude of acceptance toward them and their efforts to raise their children. The therapist's acceptance of them comes from an assumption that they are good people, doing the best that they can, and that they love their children to the best of their ability to do so. The therapist's acceptance also comes from the assumption that parents' current angry, pessimistic, and possibly punitive attitude toward their children may well not be longstanding. It is impossible for the therapist to know with certainty how the parents behaved a month ago, a year ago, or immediately after their child's birth. Their caregiving behaviors in the past may well have been strong, positive, and consistent. If those qualities are not evident now, the therapist does not know why they are not and will not judge parents for any failure to provide ongoing care. As we discuss shortly, this foundation of acceptance leads to the equally important experience of curiosity and empathy for the parents who are now experiencing blocked care.

A therapist actively communicates acceptance by being entirely nonjudgmental regarding the parents' inner lives in relation to their children. Whatever they think, feel, wish, remember, perceive, intend, and value is accepted as it is. A therapist strongly holds the intention of *understanding* an individual's inner life, not evaluating it. The same is true, at least initially with regard to acceptance of the parents' behavior. Even if the therapist believes that the behavior would be hurtful to the children (e.g., one or both of the parents swear at the children), the therapist focuses first on understanding the meaning of the child's behavior, including how the parents view it, before deciding how to approach it.

If therapists approach all interactions with parents with the goal to suspend all judgments about what the parents are saying—to focus only on accepting and then trying to understand and to respond with empathy to the parents' emotional responses to what is being explored—then parents are likely to begin to feel safer, and they are then more likely to open up to therapists' experiences, including any possible recommendations. Therapists' acceptance of parents may in turn create an opening within the parents themselves to accept themselves and then safely explore a particular experience or event without shame. In so doing, therapists help parents reduce their instances of blocked care and re-engage in the process of caring for their children.

An Example of Acceptance (Curiosity and Empathy Embedded)

In this example, the mother, Debra has had continuing difficulties raising her 10-year-old son Raymond. Her own childhood was marked by much family conflict and a lack of emotional intimacy. Her son's defiance and perceived rejection of her has undermined her confidence and led to blocked care. This dialogue occurred in the first session with her therapist, Allison.

Therapist: So you've tried your best and now it seems hard to keep trying to make it better.

Parent: So you don't think I'm good enough, is that it? It's my fault!

Therapist: I am so sorry, Debra, if you experienced what I said as blaming you! I'm sorry that I wasn't better at saying what I was trying to say.

Parent: What are you trying to say?

Therapist: Simply that you are trying so hard, and it seems to be wearing you out! You give, give, give, and it seems that you are feeling that it isn't enough.

Parent: Why doesn't he understand that? Doesn't he know how much I love him?

Therapist: How painful that is when it seems that he doesn't respond to your love.

Parent: He doesn't! He thinks it's not good enough!

Therapist: Ah! And you're doing the best that you can!

Parent: And it's not good enough! Sometimes I don't want to try anymore! Sometimes . . . I don't love him. Sometimes, I hate him! There, are you happy now? Sometimes I hate my own son! How disgusting is that!

Therapist: Oh, Debra, how painful . . . how very painful that must be for you . . . to be aware that sometimes you feel hatred toward your son.

Parent: I hate my kid! Aren't you listening! Doesn't that tell you something! Maybe you won't admit it, but I know you agree with me! I'm a failure as a parent!

Therapist: Oh, Debra, again, I'm sorry that you experience me as judging you . . . as thinking that you're a poor parent but just not saying it.

Parent: So, I hate my kid and I'm a great parent! I don't buy that!

Therapist: And you love your kid, and have loved him, and haven't given up, and are here now trying to get some help for him, for yourself, and for your relationship. And you still love him, even when he seems to reject all of your efforts.

In this dialogue the therapist accepted the parent completely without arguing with her or telling her that she needed to think, feel, or do something differently. The therapist accepted Debra's perception of her as judging her. She accepted Debra saying that she hated her son. She accepted Debra expressing shame over her hatred. She accepted her discouragement and doubt without giving her false hope. And the therapist also found—and accepted—Debra's strength embedded in her pain and her continuous effort to "get it right."

If a therapist understands the dynamics of blocked care, it makes it easier to understand and accept parents' anger, shame, and lack of loving feelings for their children. If parents understand the nature of blocked care, it makes it easier for them to both understand and experience empathy for themselves for feeling hatred toward their children and for their "unparental" responses. When there is a lack of reciprocal positive experience in the parent–child relationship for a given period of time—a sustained lack of playfulness and joy in the relationship—it is particularly hard for parents to keep the core parenting systems—approach, reward, and child reading—"on." With these systems "down," parents must rely heavily on whatever executive powers of self-control they can summon to keep from becoming blatantly abusive or neglectful.

Debra, in the example above, was somehow able to refrain from abusing Raymond by exerting executive power to keep her brakes on her intensely negative feelings and impulses. In the midst of blocked care, this is often the best a parent can manage to do. And since stress, especially chronic stress, can suppress executive functioning, there is a high risk for abuse and neglect in the context of sustained blocked care. When parents experiencing chronic blocked care also have weak executive systems, for whatever reason, preventing outright abuse and neglect may be extremely difficult.

Curiosity

From the moment of birth, parents and infants are typically intensely fascinated with each other. The eyes of infants search for the eyes and faces of their parents, and when they find each other, they begin to gaze into each other's eyes in a way that is rarely replicated. The eye gaze reflects a deep interest in the other, a passion to discover the unique features of the other. Remember Oscar's gleaming eyes as he looked into his parents' eyes? Infants find what is unique about their parents—what distinguishes their parents from all others. Over time this preference for this unique adult develops into an attachment. At the same time the parents are discovering what is unique about their infant that distinguishes him or her from all other infants. What they discover, they treasure, value unconditionally, and fall in love with.

Professionals might be tempted to describe these acts of discovery as positive delusions, thinking that parents see what is not there. Or is it that parents see what is there, and the rest of us, who have not gazed so lovingly for so long at this infant, do not notice? Most likely, parents discover the unique spirit of this infant, something of greater value, the roots of which may grow into abilities that can one day be measured, seen by all. Herein lies the power of nature's loveliest obsession.

These acts of discovery are described here as curiosity wherein parents are fully immersed in getting to know their infant unconditionally. This is not a rational exercise but rather an act that fully engages parents reflectively, emotionally, spiritually, viscerally. As they get to know their infant, possibly more deeply than they have known anyone in their lives, their knowledge often has a profound impact on them. The word *love* may describe this impact. It is also known as a *parental bond*. At a core level, parents experience the infant as being a part of them, with their identities becoming interwoven for life. At the same time the infant's discovery of the parents has a profound impact on the infant's experience of him- or herself, others, and the nature of the world. This intersubjective experience between parents and infants involves all aspects of the parents' brain. It is an emotional experience characterized by playfulness and empathy and a reflective experience characterized by curiosity.

Curiosity rests upon the functioning of brain regions involved in the child-reading and meaning-making systems. Within parents' temporal lobes are regions dedicated to perceiving their children's facial expressions, voices, and movements, noticing subtle variations over time. In addition, the parents' mirror cells help them to subtly experience what their children are experiencing moment to moment. This combination of child-reading and mirroring processes helps parents tune in to the inner lives of their children—helps them to make sense of their children's emotions, thoughts, wishes, perceptions, interests, and intentions. Parents are actively making sense of their infant's expressions in the here and now as well as in the context of the past and future. Their ability to meet their infant's needs is enhanced through their curiosity about their baby. Parents who are in this open-minded, curious state tend to give positive meaning to whatever their children are expressing . However, this early positivity bias may shift into a negativity bias in the face of ongoing parental stress. Under stressful conditions, the input from the child-reading process gets filtered through the parents' amygdala in that rapid neuroceptive process we described in Chapter 1. When this information from the child-reading system reaches an amygdala that is mediating signals of threat, what was once seen as delightfully positive is in danger of now being seen negatively. When the amygdala is on high alert, it can bias the rapid neuroceptive process toward detecting threats over safety, making it very difficult for parents to distinguish between a real need to play defense and a false alarm. When parents become hyper-vigilant in this way, whether from chronic or acute stressors, their internal state regulation processes are impaired, and the parents then have great difficulty feeling safe enough to stay open, accepting, and curious toward their children. Their approach system, which is linked to the smart vagal system, gets suppressed in favor of self-defense. As they lose vagal tone, they shift out of their social engagement system into one of the two defensive systems, either mobilized fight–flight or immobilized fright. In these states, being curious and reflective are not options. The parents are now preoccupied with personal safety and are therefore taking very personally their children's negative facial expressions, body language, and tones of voice.

Curiosity aims to maintain the positive mind-set in which parents continue to be fascinated by their children and energized by their efforts to understand them. Their eyes gaze upon their children with love, which enables them to see their children's positive attributes and developing abilities while taking their problematic behavior in stride, as a natural part of being developmentally immature. Problems are vulnerabilities to be addressed and strengthened. Curiosity benefits from the release of brain chemicals such as oxytocin and dopamine, which help to keep the connections between higher and lower regions of the parenting brain open, supporting the integration of feelings and cognitive processes.

The meaning-making system, depending heavily on the upper regions of the prefrontal cortex (i.e., the medial prefrontal cortex and especially the dorsolateral prefrontal cortex), also can greatly reinforce the strength of parents' curiosity. Activating these regions of the brain, with the help of the anterior cingulate cortex (the "brain bridge"), enables parents to suspend the narrow, rapid judgment of the amygdala and to stay open to their own feelings and thoughts, including reflections based on their history and the traditions of parent–child relationships to which they were exposed in their childhoods. Some aspects of their history might not reassure them of their safety, and these signals would cause the amygdala to shift back into defense and close down the potentially constructive process of reflection. But if parents can stay open to the feelings triggered by these memories, they can resolve old wounds and clear their minds more for parenting. This process of reflection and reappraisal, made possible by areas of the prefrontal and anterior cingulate cortex inhibiting the defensive reactions of the amygdala and maintaining vagal tone, strengthens parents' capacity for "feeling and dealing" (Fosha, 2000), expanding the parental window for staying grounded and flexible enough to respond constructively to their children's behavior. Curiosity, when it trumps defensiveness, promotes openness to a widening range of experience and the integration of parents' narratives, whereby they blend past, present, and future into a coherent story. Thus, without curiosity a parent may react with anger and consequences to his or her child's tantrum. With curiosity, the parent pauses to make sense of the child's behaviors, considering the present circumstances as well as past, recent events and worries that the child may be having about the future. Only then does the parent decide how to respond to the child's behavior.

Curiosity enhances intersubjective experiences in the following ways:

1. Parents who are curious are fascinated with their children, wanting to know as much as possible about their developing selves.

2. Parents who are curious simply want to understand their children, long before they think about evaluating them.
3. These parents stay within a not-knowing mind-set, wherein they remain open to trying to grasp the meaning of their children's behaviors.
4. Curious parents inhibit their first reactions to their children's undesirable behavior (unless there is a perceived emergency) and wait until they make sense of that behavior before responding to it.
5. As they come to know their children, curious parents do so from the inside-out. The inner lives of their children (how the children feel about themselves) are of greatest interest to these parents, with their children's behaviors, successes, and failings seen within that context.

Example: Ken is the father of 15-year-old Kathleen who just started her second year on the high school debate team. She did well the first year and had been looking forward to being on the team again. Then she mentioned at dinner that she had decided not to join the team this year.

Dad: I had thought that you really enjoyed it last year and were planning to debate this year too. What made you decide not to?

Daughter: I don't know. Just want to do some other stuff, I guess.

Dad: So you're not sure yourself.

Daughter: Dad, I just don't want to! Isn't that enough! I shouldn't have to if I don't want to!

Dad: Sweetie, I'm sorry if I gave the impression that I'm annoyed with you or disappointed in your decision. I want you to do what you want to do. I'm just puzzled because just last week you said that you were looking forward to it.

Daughter: So, I changed my mind.

Dad: And my asking you about it seems pushy. I'm sorry because I don't mean to be pushing you.

Daughter: Then why do you keep asking?

Dad: Because I'm surprised, and if you are at all mixed up about your decision to change your mind, I want to give you the chance to talk about it.

Daughter: I do like it, Dad. I really do. It's just . . . I don't want to be a know-it-all.

Dad: A know-it-all?

Daughter: Yeah! Some of my friends were laughing about my being so smart my head might explode. They were making fun of me for always asking so many questions and having an opinion, and they said that the debate team was made for me. And they laughed some more.

Dad: Ah! That would have been hard. And these were your friends laughing.

Daughter: Yeah! Would they like me better if I agreed with them all the time? Or if I wasn't smart? It's not my fault I think about stuff and have opinions and like to discuss stuff.

Dad: No wonder you're not sure about debate. It seems almost like you have to choose between friends and being on the debate team.

Daughter: I know I don't, Dad, but it does feel that way sometimes. I just wish my friends would accept me the way I am. If I'm a nerd, then I'm a nerd.

Dad: Do you think you are?

Daughter: Maybe, but I'm a fun nerd who makes a good friend.

Dad: And a wonderful nerd who makes a most special daughter.

Daughter: Maybe I haven't decided yet about debating.

In this example, the dad expressed his curiosity about his daughter's decision to stop debating, not to get her to change her mind, but rather to help her clarify her reasons. She assumed that if he was surprised by her decision, he might be trying to change her mind or be ambivalent about her decision. However, he remained nonjudgmental about her decision throughout the discussion, facilitating her ability to make sense of the factors that were influencing her decision so that she could arrive at the decision from a deeper, more reflective inner space.

How Curiosity Works in Therapy

When parents who are experiencing blocked care seek therapy for their difficulties with their children, they most often have difficulty separating their judgment about their children's behavior from efforts to understand this behavior. They are not in a mind-set wherein they can safely explore the possible meanings of their children's behavior; they just want it to change. At this point, the behavior is most likely experienced as wrong or inappropriate and the reasons for the behavior are either considered irrelevant or they are assumed to reflect "bad" motives, wishes, thoughts, or feelings.

If the therapist tries to stress the value in understanding what the reasons might be, parents experiencing blocked care might assume that the therapist is seeking excuses for their children's behavior. If the therapist tries to understand the reasons for the parents' behaviors, parents might experience this focus as an effort to uncover something wrong with what they are doing and so blame them. When parents are stuck in a blocked care mode, their goal is often to ensure that the therapist agrees with them that their children's behavior is wrong and then to advise them regarding what they might do (specialized discipline) to correct the behavior. Anything else is likely to be experienced as being unsupportive.

If the therapist has been able to convey to the parents that their inner lives are completely accepted and that the therapist has a sense of urgency to simply *understand*—not *evaluate*—many parents may begin trying to understand as well. The therapist's reflective stance evokes the parents' reflection on their inner lives, their children's inner lives, and the meaning of the behavioral events that are occurring. Stepping back to look at themselves and their children with curiosity, they may well begin to experience a return of the caregiving behaviors that had become blocked.

Example: Ann has been experiencing blocked care in relationship to her 16-year-old son who has been increasingly noncommunicative with her over the past 2 years. When he does talk with her, it is mainly to ask her to do something for him or to criticize her parenting. She sought treatment for this problem with her son from the therapist, Bill.

Mom: I just want basic politeness! Is that asking too much? If I ask him a simple question, it seems that I deserve—anyone would deserve—an answer. And I get nothing except maybe he sighs and walks out of the room.

Therapist: That does seem like such a small request that you are making . . . and yet he doesn't give you a simple answer. Any sense of what that might be about?

Mom: What difference does it make? Are you looking for something that would justify what he is doing?

Therapist: Ann, I'm sorry if I implied to you that his behavior is OK and I want to justify it.

Mom: That's what it sounds like.

Therapist: Then I need to be clearer. I'm not searching for an excuse for his refusing to answer a simple question, just what the reason might be.

Mom: What's the difference between a reason and an excuse?

Therapist: With a reason, he is still accountable for his behavior. Finding a reason doesn't imply that you need to be OK about the behavior—just that you can make sense of it better.

Mom: Again, what does it matter?

Therapist: So you know how to respond in a way that's more effective. If your response isn't working, then maybe you're assuming a reason for his behavior that's not accurate.

Mom: I just want him to answer my question. I'm not after a hug or even a smile.

Therapist: Has he given you a smile or a hug in the past few months?

Mom: Are you kidding! I'm a servant to him. I'm acknowledged only when he wants something from me.

Therapist: What's that like?

Mom: What do you think it's like? Am I supposed to be OK about it?

Therapist: I'm sorry if I seemed to suggest that it shouldn't bother you. My sense was that it bothers you a lot, and I'd like to understand how it affects you.

Mom: It drives me wild. I'm his mother! He shouldn't treat me that way! He should treat me with more respect!

Therapist: Ah, it seems like he doesn't respect you!

Mom: Doesn't it seem that way to you?

Therapist: It could be a lack of respect, I don't know. That's why I'm trying to make sense of it . . . to know what it means. If it is because he doesn't respect you, what would that mean to you? (*The therapist and mother continue to explore possible meanings of her son's behaviors and their conflicts, with the mother more engaged in making sense of the behaviors.*) And an even greater fear seems to be that he may not share your dream. You worry that he may not want a close relationship with his mom that lasts a lifetime.

Mom: Why doesn't he?

Therapist: How are you sure that he doesn't?

Mom: He doesn't talk to me!

Therapist: And again I ask why . . . what might his reason be . . . what if it's not disrespect? What, for example, if he thought that you were not proud of him . . . that you were unhappy with the young man that he's becoming? What if he still shares the same dream that you do but senses that you don't have that dream any more?

Mom: Why would he? Wait . . . he said a few weeks ago that I just want him to accomplish things so that I can brag to my friends and neighbors about him. That I'm really not interested in what he likes or wants for himself. But he's wrong! I don't think that.

Therapist: Ah . . . Ann. He says that he experiences you as being dissatisfied with who he is. That what he wants, who he is, is not good enough for you.

Mom: But that's not true.

Therapist: Ann, please, I'm not saying that I believe his experience to be what you feel about him. I'm saying that if that is his experience, then it is easier to understand why he avoids you now. Maybe he hides his experience that you are disappointed behind his ignoring of you or being angry with you.

Mom: Why would he experience me that way when I don't feel that way?

Therapist: I don't know. Any ideas?

(*The therapist and parent continue to explore the possible meaning of the son's behaviors. Each new possibility opens the parent to possible options that might suggest ways to reduce the conflict and deepen their relationship.*)

In this dialogue, the therapist repeatedly brought Ann back to exploring her own experience, so that she could understand it more deeply and gradually become open to wondering about her son's behavior. Without curiosity, the meaning of the behavior will not enter awareness, for either the parents or the children. With safe, accepting, nonjudgmental curiosity, parents' brains stay open enough to make better sense of the behavioral events that are the source of the problem. When the focus is only on evaluating and trying to control behaviors, the parents who are experiencing blocked care, with their brains in survival mode, are not likely to awaken their range of caregiving behaviors. Unless the children experience their parents' care again, the children are not likely to openly address the behavioral conflicts. If the children do address them—with nonjudgmental curiosity—any changes that result are likely to be short-lived if the parents are not equally involved.

Empathy

Empathy is the other side of playfulness. When infants are in a relaxed, open, and engaged state of mind with parents, the enthusiastic, joyful,

129

and affectionate interactions dominate, conveying a sense of delightful playfulness between them. When infants are in distress, they begin to feel unsafe and shift into a defensive state without the happy engagement that they were just experiencing. Their interactions with their parents are now characterized by "comfort seeking," "goal-directed" behaviors (Cassidy & Shaver, 2008). When parents experience their infant's distress and respond with empathy, communicating the experience of being with the infant in the distress, the infant's attachment behaviors have been effective in getting the parents' attention and activating their empathy. The infant turns to the parents for safety, wanting the parents to end the distress. Empathy conveys to the infant that the parents are aware of his or her distress, will not leave him or her alone, and will help him or her to manage even if the distress does not stop. The parents' ongoing, emotionally regulated presence helps the infant to recover from the stressful state and to regain equilibrium. The infant's frightening, possibly very painful, emotions are likely to be more manageable when the parents are present and conveying empathy for their baby's difficult time.

When engaging in playfulness, the parents and infant regulate and enhance the experience of positive emotions together. With empathy, the parents and infant regulate and reduce the experience of negative emotions together. These two processes, one centering around joy, the other, comfort, strengthen each other, creating a more robust relationship that can handle the full range of human experience without breaking.

Empathy involves regions of the right brain (Schore, 2003) that enable parents and infants to be in synch, right brain to right brain, and so manage together any intense emotions that are emerging. The orbitofrontal cortex, insula, and anterior cingulate cortex, especially on the right side, are all involved in parents' experiences of empathy for their children. The insula helps parents to have an intuitive, bottom-up sense of their children's inner lives by receiving and transmitting input from the heart, lungs, and gut (visceral system) to the orbitofrontal cortex and anterior cingulate cortex—all of which may resonate with children's bodily expressions. As you may remember from our earlier discussion of parental warmth and empathy, the orbitofrontal cortex, anterior cingulate cortex, and insula contain those special von Economo cells—present only in certain mammals—which provide a heightened awareness of the emotions of self and others. Mirror neurons also contribute to empathy by feeding output into the anterior cingulate cortex, where the conscious awareness of empathic feelings begins to emerge. When the anterior cingulate cortex detects something "amiss" with children, it sets off that "uh-oh" reaction that alerts parents to be even more attentive to them. Finally, empathy combines with *mentalization*, a more left-brain, cognitive way of understanding children's experiences as parents' brains connect the intuitive, bottom-up way of attuning to their children's immediate experience with the higher-brain processes involved in thinking about their children's "minds."

This is the Parental Child-Reading System in full gear, promoting both a reflective process whereby parents understand their children's experience, as well as an emotional component whereby parents sense their children's emotional states and intentions. It is not surprising that empathy, broadly conceived, contains both features, activating the orbitofrontal–insula–anterior cingulate system that serves as a bridge to parents' higher awareness and meaning-making functions. When parents' empathy systems are "on," the smart vagal system is "on," helping to keep parents in this open, engaged, empathic state of mind. In this state, parents, without knowing it, have one "foot" on the amygdala as a brake on the self-defense system. Children then experience parents as tuned in, as "getting it," and are with them, hopefully conveying confidence that they will go through it together and manage it successfully.

Example:
Boy [6 years old]: I want to play!
Mom: I know you do! It is so hard for you now that you have to go to bed!

Boy: No! I want to play some more!

Mom: I know you do, Son, I know. You don't like having to go to bed now!

Boy: No! I don't want to go to bed!

Mom: It is hard to stop playing! It really is. We'll have to find an especially nice book to read in bed. That might help.

In this example the primary response of the mother is empathy for her son's anger over having to go to bed. Redirecting his thinking to reading a book will be much more effective after the mother first acknowledges his wish to not go to bed.

Example:

Girl [9 years old]: I can't do anything right! I'm so stupid!

Dad: You're trying so much and you can't get it! That is so hard!

Girl: I can't do anything right!

Dad: Oh, sweetie, it must feel awful for you when it seems that you can't do anything right!

Girl: I can't, and I'll never change!

Dad: I'm sorry that it seems that way to you now, honey. I'm sorry (*giving her a hug*).

In this example the father does not try to change his daughter's mind about her abilities. By expressing his empathy for her distress about her inability to do something and her associated view of herself, he helps her to regulate her negative emotion. Because her emotion remains moderate and not extreme, her own reflective abilities will enable her to see the big picture and remember her overall abilities and successes. Trying to convince her that she has more abilities than she now feels is likely to meet resistance and be less likely to influence her and help her to manage her distress. After she experiences his empathy, she is likely to be open to his calmly reflecting about some of her recent successes—ones that at this moment she does not seem to recall.

How Empathy Works in Therapy

When parents are experiencing blocked care, they are likely to experience little empathy for their children. As they are not able to maintain a positive, reciprocal, and satisfying relationship with their children, parents' approach and reward systems get suppressed, and they eventually begin to focus on behavior from a judgmental, critical stance. When this approach does not lead to success, they most likely become increasingly defensive themselves, experiencing failure and both resentment toward their children and shame and doubt toward themselves. Parental empathy, in contrast, requires an open receptivity to experiencing their children's distress. Under intense stress, this openness is out the window. Despite good intentions, parents now find it extremely hard to experience their children in this manner. Their focus is mostly on self-protective behaviors and a singular goal: to change their children's behavior.

As was the case with the other features of PACE, when parents are experiencing blocked care, they are unlikely to be able to experience the therapist's empathy for them. They are not receptive to the therapist's experience because they are anticipating his or her judgment and so they steel themselves with a distant, cautious attitude. Not feeling safe, they overlook or are skeptical of the therapist's experience of empathy for their parenting problems. Their defensive attitude serves the purpose of protecting them from experiencing the vulnerability that arises from the failures that they are experiencing as parents. Empathy invites them to become vulnerable, and they may, understandably, resist that invitation. At this stage in the therapist–parent relationship, the parents' threat detection system— their amygdala-driven vigilance system—is still on high alert, ready to detect the least signs of judgment and invalidation from the therapist. Since the amygdala is so sensitive to nonverbal communication—the raising of an eyebrow, the shift in gaze, the subtle change in the therapist's tone of voice—it is quite a challenge for parents to feel safe with the therapist. They are getting many "false alarms" even as the therapist seeks to create a safe atmosphere.

If the therapist does not experience and convey empathy, but rather adopts a rational, problem-solving approach when parents are experiencing blocked care, the parents are likely to experience the therapist as pulling away and becoming judgmental. Many parents may basically decide to leave therapy at this early juncture. To preclude this unwanted development, the therapist must gently and persistently convey an empathic attitude even though many parents will mistrust it initially and find it difficult to tolerate. If parents become dismissive of the therapist's empathy, the therapist needs to accept that response and then be curious about it, without judgment. If parents express disbelief regarding the therapist's experience of empathy, the therapist again accepts their response and then wonders about the source of their disbelief. Through acceptance and curiosity, the therapist is able to slowly and gently convey safety to parents as they experience his or her empathy. (As was indicated earlier, the components of PACE are often very interwoven aspects of one, unified, intersubjective experience.)

As parents experience the therapist's empathy, they gradually become able to regulate whatever emotions emerge that are associated with the problems between them and their children. These emotions may include fear, sadness, anger, or shame. As they are able to remain regulated in response to these emotions, parents become more able to safely explore the events that they are facing with their children. In short, their reflective functioning is engaged and exercised. At the same time they are able to begin to have greater empathy for themselves and eventually to experience empathy for their children. Their brains are opening up pathways to higher functions, beginning to lift the blockage that has been suppressing these functions (including the capacity for empathy. To borrow a phrase from a leading trauma-focused therapist, the relationship with the therapist is starting to awaken the parents' prefrontal cortex (Ogden, Minton, & Pain, 2006).

Example: In this dialogue the mother, Linda, is feeling overwhelmed with the repeated arguments—often followed by defiance—that she is experiencing with her 11-year-old daughter Julie. Linda has begun to avoid contact with her daughter, focusing on maintaining the rules and routines of the house and interacting with Julie primarily when she is not doing what she should be doing. Julie, however, seeks Linda out to challenge the rules and express her displeasure with Linda's judgments. Linda does not experience any sense of the joy and satisfaction that she had hoped for when her daughter approached adolescence. The therapist, Jim, focuses on experiencing and communicating empathy for her distress.

Mom: She just won't leave me alone. Complain, complain, complain, that's all that she does.

Therapist: So you want a break from the conflicts and she seeks you out. You just want some peace!

Mom: So I tell her to leave me alone, and we'll talk about it later. She keeps talking so I leave the room . . . and she follows me!

Therapist: It's like you're being trapped in your own home! No way to just relax a bit, take a deep breath and then try to figure out a way to approach it. No way to just take a break!

Mom: So what should I do? Put a lock on the door? She'd probably stand on the other side and start kicking it! She'd make me open the door to stop what she is doing!

Therapist: Again, how hard! Like you're not safe in your own home . . . with your own child. What a sense of feeling trapped . . . and hopeless that must create.

Mom: So what should I do?

Therapist: Before I try to come up with any ideas, could we stay a bit longer with the impact that this situation with your daughter is having on you?

Mom: I know the impact that it is having on me! It's driving me crazy! I just want to know what to do about it! That would help me a lot more than talking about how hard it is!

Therapist: So you are becoming frustrated with me now that I haven't given you any suggestions about this.

Mom: Yes! That's why I asked to see you! I want practical ideas about what to do to make things better with Julie!

Therapist: My fear, Linda, is that if I gave you some suggestions now, they might not work. And that would be so unfair to you . . . another thing you tried that failed. I fear that you would only become more discouraged.

Mom: So if you're not going to tell me what to do, why am I seeing you?

Therapist: Right now I want to know you better. I want to know how this very, very, hard time in your life is affecting you, as a parent, as a partner, and as a person. I want to "get it," at least in a small way, what it is like for you now.

Mom: It's worse than anything I've ever had to face in my life! I dread getting up in the morning! There! Is that what you want!

(*The dialogue continues during which the therapist does not give the advice that the mother is asking for, rather laying a foundation of empathy that is necessary before any advice will have a chance of success.*)

Therapist: I believe that if I don't convince you that I understand, that I really know about this hardest experience that you've ever had in your life, than nothing I say will give you any confidence that it will make things better.

Mom: Maybe you'll never get it.

Therapist: Please give me a chance. Help me to understand how hard this is for you now!

Mom: I've been her mother for 11 years. My life has centered around her! I held her when she was an infant! And played with her all the time when she was 2 and 3 and 4. And showed her how to become a young girl! Sometimes I loved her so much I would start to cry. I have never experienced what it was like to love a person like I loved her. And she loved me back! She loved me back! She was so happy to be with me! She brought things to me! She wanted me to carry her and snuggle with her in bed! And now she doesn't! Now she doesn't! I'm some stranger to her! I'm somebody that she doesn't even like! (*Begins to cry.*)

Therapist: Love so strong that it made you cry. Love that you never experienced before. And now it seems that it's over . . . that Anne does not want your love and does not love you. How painful that must be for you . . . how painful.

(*Slowly the therapist and mother begin to explore the pain of her daughter's rejection. As the mother expresses her distress more openly, she begins to feel uncomfortable with her vulnerable feelings.*)

Mom: You don't think that I'm just feeling sorry for myself.

Therapist: Just feeling sorry for yourself? You are grieving the loss of that most special relationship that you had with Julie for years. And you are experiencing the terror of thinking that it might be gone forever. And you worry that your grief and terror suggest that you are weak?

Mom: I should be stronger.

Therapist: I see you as being very strong to face this pain, to trust me with it, to show your vulnerability—facing the hardest thing that you've ever had to face in your life—I see your strength. Stronger than pretending that it does not bother you. Pretending that you can parent without feeling anything. Without being vulnerable. Without feeling love anymore.

Mom: You spoke of terror. That is the most terrifying thing of all. I might some day stop loving Julie. I would not want to live if that happens.

Therapist: As I said . . . you are so brave to face this terror . . . and all the pain that it carries . . . and you do it . . . because of the immensity of your love for your daughter.

Mom: What if I can't do it anymore?

Therapist: Because of the mother that you are, I don't think that you will stop loving her and caring for her. Maybe you won't feel close to her, you might really feel disconnected,

> but the core of love will still be there. And at some point in the future—we don't know when—at some point the feelings will get stronger again too. You'll feel that intense love again.
>
> *Mom*: Do you mean that?
>
> *Therapist*: I mean that.

In this example, the therapist patiently and persistently tries to experience and communicate empathy for Linda so that she can experience more fully the pain and confusion that she feels about the increasing distance and conflicts in her relationship with her daughter. The therapist is convinced that if he presents behavioral strategies to Linda at this point, she will probably not be motivated to try them for any period of time if they do not show immediate signs of producing results. Also, the therapist is unlikely to be able to give her any appropriate strategy because he does not know what is creating the conflicts and distance between Linda and her daughter. Through allowing herself to experience the therapist's empathy for her pain, Linda is more likely to find the strength to experience the pain again—now with him experiencing it with her. This is likely to increase her readiness to work to make sense of the conflicts—again, with his active presence—through an open curiosity about their meaning. Throughout this process, Linda is more likely to be able to accept whatever emotions and thoughts emerge, rather than focusing on what either she or her daughter *should* think, feel, or do. Now she is using her parental brain much more fully than before, getting ready to begin the task of reconnecting with her child.

Affective–Reflective Dialogue

In presenting the four components (PACE) of intersubjective experience we have repeatedly demonstrated them through dialogue. In stressing the relationship between parents and children, we have emphasized the central role of communication in conveying safety and fostering new learning and so that the relationship then develops in a deeper and more comprehensive manner. *Communication* is much more than "just talking," which may simply involve lectures and information giving. Communication has nonverbal and verbal components that contain the whats and the hows: *what* is being communicated and *how* it is being communicated. In conversation between parents and children, the deepest, most personal meanings are conveyed nonverbally, through voice prosody (modulations and rhythms), facial expressions, eye gaze that repeatedly makes fleeting contact and then looks away, as well as gestures and movements.

The kind of communication that we are describing involves the utilization, development, and integration of the five parental brain systems. It facilitates both emotional regulation and reflective functioning within parents and children. It involves the components of PACE, usually with more than one of them at a time. We call this way of communicating *affective–reflective dialogue*. With practice, it becomes a remarkably effective way to improve the parent–child relationship by developing and strengthening the interacting brains of parents and children.

The affective–reflective dialogue that we are describing can be found in the various examples of dialogue throughout this chapter. In our experience, affective–reflective dialogue (with the embedded components of PACE) is the most direct means for activating and maintaining the functioning of the social engagement system. The smart vagal system that supports and enables the kind of open and engaged parenting that we have highly valued throughout this book is given robust support by affective–reflective dialogue. Within this specialized dialogue our emotions are allowed to influence our thinking, and our thinking is allowed to influence our emotion. Within this form of communication we are likely to approach (the Parental Approach System) and enjoy (Parental Reward System) being with the other person. We are more able to express clearly and understand more fully the emotional meanings being conveyed by each other. We both read each other better (Parental Child-Reading System) and are more able to experience the ongoing relationship as having deep and rich meaning (Parental Meaning-Making System).

Finally, within such dialogue we are more likely to be fully present to each other, open and balanced in a state that might be described as intersubjective mindfulness, a state that links our highest brain powers with our bottom- up affective core. This linkage allows us to experience what is unique about the other and the situation and to be able to initiate a flexible, "best-fit," response to the other, using our executive capacities, as needed, to stay in the "right" state of mind (Parental Executive System).

When we are communicating via an affective–reflective dialogue there is a strong storytelling flavor to our conversation. That is, we are not giving a lecture or dispensing information. We are communicating meanings—emotional, social, historical—that express our inner lives and enable us, feeling safe, to be open and receptive to the inner life of the other. Within this dialogue voices are rhythmic and modulated, fully expressive of the subtle, unique meanings of self and other in ways that the words themselves cannot convey. With such rich voice tones and inflections, with heightened affective emphases and soft states of wondering, we are more likely to remain interested in each other and the conversation itself. Such dialogues hold the attention of both participants while each safely explores the inner world of the other. In such dialogues your children are more open to your clear—gentle or strong—influence and you are more open to being influenced by your children's expression of their experiences of their world (including the world that they share with you). This degree of open engagement is less likely to occur when you are giving a lecture.

The qualities of PACE are frequently present within affective–reflective dialogue. There is often a quality of enjoyment—quiet or exuberant—in the sharing of one's experience with your children, even when there are differences. There is an overriding sense of acceptance of the experience of your children, even when you disagree with their behavior. You assign priority to understanding—deeply and fully—the meaning of your children's thoughts, emotions, wishes, and behaviors, and you place much less emphasis on evaluating their behaviors. You are truly interested in your children and their world, and your curiosity about them results from being fascinated by who they are and who they are becoming. Finally, you are likely to be able to experience their experience emotionally to the degree that they feel "felt," as Dan Siegel so beautifully describes this aspect of interpersonal neurobiology (Siegel, 1999). This is empathy. When you experience empathy for your children, your interactions are guided by compassion and understanding much more than by power and authority. When your children experience your empathy, they will be much more likely to accept your perspective and guidance, knowing that you "get it" and truly have their best interests in your mind and heart.

Summary

Working hard to engage all components of PACE brings all of the five systems of brain-based parenting into a more real-world realm. By practicing PACE and affective–reflective dialogue, parents can gain more intentional control over how their brains work. In moments of stress and frustration, when the amygdala and limbic system want to "go it alone," practicing PACE will help you move away from defensiveness and blocked care and utilize the systems that regulate your emotional responses and allow you to reflect on what is transpiring to get you back on track.

This good news is even better when you consider that as you practice PACE and involve all of the five parental systems in the brain, they all begin to become stronger and more integrated. As is true for other parts of the body, when you use your brain it improves in both structure and function. It is not simply a matter of "use it or lose it." A more apt phrase is "use it to improve it." We believe that PACE and affective–reflective dialogue will do that. In the next two chapters we will explore further the twin components of *emotion regulation* and *reflective functioning*.

CHAPTER 5

Mastering Emotional Regulation

When Peter was born, his father, Jim, was ecstatic. Driving home from the birth, he went the wrong way on one-way streets, totally immersed in the powerful emotions of becoming a dad. His love for Peter was instantaneous and total. Now Peter was 13 and pushing all the limits in his unending quest for manhood and independence. One night, after Jim came home from his long day at the office, he and Peter got into a heated argument and Peter ended up, in total frustration, yelling, "You just don't get it. You suck as a dad." Jim, usually mild-mannered, felt a surge of anger that quickly escalated into rage. Peter ran upstairs and Jim, fists clenched, chased him up to his bedroom. But when he saw Peter cowering in fear on the edge of his bed, his anger immediately dissipated. He had seen Peter frightened before, but he had never been the cause of his son's fear. As they hugged each other, both began to cry.

Parenting is a deeply emotional process. Our love for our children permeates our thoughts, wishes, motivations, worries, dreams, fantasies, and actions for years and years and years. Often love is in the foreground of our experience as it mingles with joy and enthusiasm, excitement and pride, tenderness and compassion. The meaning we create in this loving state of mind is positive and hopeful. Yet, at other times, the emotional tone of our love lies in the background as the stress of parenting generates other natural emotions, including anger, disgust, fear, sadness, and shame. The meaning we create in these states of emotion is very different from the meaning constructed in a caring state of mind. Parenting takes us places emotionally that we may never have traveled before, truly one of the precious gifts our children give us. Each emotional state we enter brings with it different action tendencies and ways of thinking, different ways of making sense of our experiences with our kids. As a brain scientist would say, meaning making is "state specific"—that is, meaning making is linked to the state of mind we are in at the time we assign a meaning. Our feelings and our thoughts are tightly interconnected.

Our children need us to be moved by them, both when in their presence and when thinking of them when apart. The goal of emotion regulation is not to block feelings so that we can raise our children with cool reason alone. The goal is to raise our kids with "warm reason," with *emotion-informed reason* (Damasio, 1996). Thankfully, our brains are designed for translating our feelings into thoughts to help us make good decisions—decisions influenced by our empathy and intuition. The more we are able to stay open to our experiences as a parent, the better our brains get at linking emotional and cognitive processes, at integrating affective and reflective functions.

It's not an exaggeration to say that the biggest challenge for us as parents is to regulate our emotions, to feel the intensity of the full range of human feelings without breaking the connection with, or hurting, our children. This capacity to feel things deeply while staying grounded and aware enough to keep from doing and saying things that could seriously harm the parent–child relationship is hard enough with a mature, healthy brain. Indeed, this capacity to use good judgment in hot moments is the hallmark of a mature brain. The lack of brain maturation is why adolescents, who are so good at "cool cognition"—knowing exactly what they should do in hot situations—often fail to put this knowledge into practice when they are actually in the hot situation. In addition, because stress can suppress this capacity for handling hot moments well, having a stressed-out brain is a risk factor for developing blocked care.

Because stress leads directly to impediments in functioning, it is important to learn to manage your stress and to keep your brain healthy. It's also important to work at improving your capacity to handle hot situations, to "feel and deal," the essence of emotional intelligence (EQ). You can actually raise your "EQ" by putting effort into improving your self-control and practicing reflection. The good news is that by practicing emotion regulation, you can change your brain and actually strengthen the regions and connections that you use to put your brakes on, step back from your autopilot reactions, and reflect on what is going on. (This conscious effort to improve brain functioning is called *self-directed neuroplasticity*.) This braking power depends heavily on your executive system, which in turn depends heavily on your prefrontal cortex.

The prefrontal cortex is central to both emotion regulation (the focus of this chapter) and reflective functioning (the focus of the next chapter). The lower regions of the prefrontal cortex are instrumental in the regulation of emotions that are emerging from the limbic system, whereas the upper regions of the prefrontal cortex are instrumental in reflective functioning. Both upper and lower regions of the prefrontal cortex work in conjunction with the anterior cingulate cortex (or just *anterior cingulate* for short) that lies adjacent to the prefrontal cortex in your brain. As you may recall, the anterior cingulate serves as a brain bridge between the lower and upper regions of the prefrontal cortex, especially when we are emotionally challenged and experiencing conflicting feelings and impulses toward our children. In performing this vital self-monitoring and bridging function, your anterior cingulate helps you to pay more attention to your child and to connect your emotions with your thinking. Figure 5.1 illustrates these key connections between the basic emotional processes of caregiving and the Parental Executive System.

Figure 5.1. Integrating Parents' Emotion and Thinking Functions.
The anterior cingulate bridge links the core parental emotions to higher cognitive, reflective processes, moving up the prefrontal cortex.

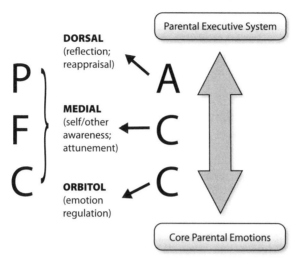

The Parental Executive System, rooted in the frontolimbic system, provides top-down modulation of your nervous system, helping you to regulate your limbic system *from above*, so to speak, rather than from your more reactive amygdala. This top-down modulation enables you to remain on the "high road" even when you are experiencing intense feelings, triggered by your child's "amygdaloid" moments or by other sources of stress in your life (Siegel & Hartzell, 2003). By using your executive abilities, you are able to reduce or manage your emotional intensity sufficiently to focus on what needs to be accomplished. You can think about your child's needs and, if necessary, put aside what you "feel like doing" in order to do what's best for your kid. Emotion regulation, then, isn't an end in itself; it's a step in a multistep dance of "staying parental" when we are experiencing inevitable conflicts between our parental and our unparental reactions and motivations.

Emotion regulation, in relation to parenting, is all about maximizing the ability to stay in the open-minded state associated with our smart vagal system and to recover effectively from defensive reactions. We use our Parental Executive System, which is directly linked to that smart vagal system, to help us accomplish this goal. All of our emotions, from joy to anger, activate our autonomic nervous system in some way, changing the level of arousal in our brains and bodies to help us enact that particular feeling. We are moved emotionally in order to move physically, and we are moved by our movement. We jump for joy, run in fear, assert ourselves in anger, and shrink into ourselves when sad. Meanwhile, our brains automatically adjust our level of vigilance either upward, by releasing norepinephrine, an adrenaline-like chemical, or downward, by releasing opioids, serotonin, GABA (gamma-aminobutyric acid), and other inhibitory substances. In an immature brain, the amygdala tends to run this show, promoting rapid shifts in arousal as a child's emotions shift.

The more developed the brain, the more these changes in arousal are orchestrated by the prefrontal regions and the anterior cingulate. When this frontolimbic system is well developed and functioning optimally, we have much more flexibility in the way we manage our emotions and regulate our internal states. Using our executive brains, we are able to stay more grounded as parents and to spend more of our time in the smart vagal social engagement system than in the defensive systems. The smart vagal system enables us to adjust our level of arousal flexibly to support emotion regulation by adjusting our heart rate, our breathing, hearing, facial expressions, voice quality, and pattern of brain arousal (Porges, 2011).

When parents who seek treatment for their parenting difficulties are experiencing blocked care, they are often also experiencing strong negative emotions associated with childrearing and having difficulty regulating these emotions. Such parents are likely to find themselves reacting with intense anger, or perhaps fear, to their children's "misbehaviors," especially those that are repeated and seemingly impervious to parents' equally repeated directives and oft-stated wishes. These parents often avoid their children, wanting to escape to some emotionally safe place, some island of "peace and quiet," to get away, either physically or psychologically. In brain terms, the parenting systems that help a parent stay close and engaged, the approach and reward systems, are shut down, robbing the parent of emotional safety as well as positive experiences. In this state of mind, it is even hard for a parent to think about parenting, to focus at all on the child, without triggering negative feelings. This hypersensitivity, in turn, makes it unlikely that the parent will choose to spend time quietly reflecting about the relationship and how to make it better. Discouragement and even despair may have set in, blocking caring feelings along with some of the pain of not having those caring feelings. In a very important sense, blocked care is protective of the parent, impeding self-awareness and warding off feelings of failure and rejection.

Most significantly, parents in a state of blocked care are defending against the experience of shame with regard to their parental functioning. They may well have high parental ideals and know that they are not meeting them. With shame and the other negative emotions come greater avoidance of child-care situations, less pleasure, less interest, and a loss of meaning in being a parent that may once have served to keep them parenting. Blocked care leads to even more blocked care, and parental shame may be buried beneath other emotions, especially anger.

Before we explore the negative emotions that we parents need to learn to regulate and integrate, let's first consider attunement, which describes how our brains are designed to work in combination with another person's brain in order to be better able to regulate emerging intense emotions.

Attunement

Attunement is that aspect of open, intersubjective experience that involves emotions, their expression, and their regulation. When parents are attuned with their children's emotional states, they are also very likely to communicate that they want to share these experiences with their children. Attunement is at the heart of the reciprocal relationship between the parent and child that facilitates both caregiving and attachment behaviors as well as the experiences of mutual joy and delight. As we have mentioned with regard to the five parenting systems in the brain, this reciprocity of affect, awareness, and motivation is most helpful for maintaining the ongoing activation of these parenting systems. Such reciprocity promotes full utilization of the brain system that gives rise to empathy and effective child reading (or mentalization). Without frequent, or at least periodic, *reciprocal* activity between parent and child—without the child actively seeking and responding positively to parental care some of the time—the parent is at greater risk for developing blocked care. When the parent and child experience each other within attuned affect their relationship is recharged so that it can stay strong regardless of the routine stresses inherent in daily family living. Each moment of such attuned affect facilitates the brain's development and promotes attachment and bonding. Remember, it's in these moments of attunement that both parent and child are most likely to release oxytocin and to feel "in sync" with one another (Feldman, Gordon, Schneiderman, et al., 2010) while also producing growth-enhancing brain chemicals. Attunement builds the relationship by enhancing the functioning of each partner's brain.

With attunement, parents are also able to co-regulate children's emotions and their expression, enabling young children to develop the psychological ability to "self-regulate." Infants are not able to regulate their emotions; they have no emotional thermostat. Their emotions start and stop suddenly, are big and then disappear, with no apparent transitional phase. Their emotions can be extremely intense, expressed fully in their whole body, whether they are experiencing distress or joyful excitement. These expressions—if shown in an older child—might resemble rage, terror, or despair, highly dysregulating feeling states.

Along with co-regulating children's emotion, attuned parents are also able to understand children's experiences more deeply. This understanding is from the inside, out (Siegel & Hartzell, 2003). Parents' nonverbal, bodily experiences, in synch with the resonating qualities of children's bodily affective expressions, lead parents to intuitively sense what children are experiencing. Attunement facilitates empathy for children, activating the anterior insula, the anterior cingulate, those unique von Economo cells, and the mirroring system we told you about earlier in the book.

We know that a person—whether infant, child, teenager, or adult—is experiencing an emotion by how the emotion is manifested or expressed in the person's body. We readily observe anger in a person's eyes, face, voice, gestures, or posture. We define the bodily expression of an emotion as *affect*. Dan Stern (2000) defined attunement as "the intersubjective sharing of affect" (p. 141). He said that we could measure affect via six of its features: intensity, rhythm, beat, contour, duration, and shape. For our purposes, we consider rhythm and intensity and we focus mostly on the voice.

When we speak, the emotional content of our communication is conveyed primarily by how we say the words and only secondarily by the actual words. The nonverbal component of speech is known as *voice prosody* and refers to the modulations of tone and intensity, latencies and rhythms of vocal expression. Remember, too, that prosody is connected to the smart vagal system, which has a direct impact on the way we use our voices to express emotion. Our prosody is connected to the regulation of heart rate and breathing.

When parents match the prosody of their infants—the affective expression of infants' emotions—without necessarily having the emotions themselves—infants are much more able to regulate those emotions. This is true as long as parents are themselves regulated. If parents match the emotion instead of the intensity of the affect— as when parents respond to infants' anger with anger—infants may become even more upset. Infants' emotions can cause dysregulation—extremely intense, seemingly uncontrollable and inconsolable feelings—when they experience the emotion alone. But when their parents match their affective expressions of the emotion, infants are likely to be able to regulate the emotion and prevent it from becoming extreme.

When infants are in distress, the parents tend to be more animated, matching the movements of their infants' bodies, creating a joint rhythm to those movements, while showing a voice cadence, pitch, and rhythm that are close to infants' vocal expressions. The parents are actually using their good vagal tone, flexibly adjusting their heart rate and the intensity of their affect, to help infants recover from having lost their vagal tone. This matching increases the likelihood that infants will calm down and remain more regulated than if parents were very calm when the infant was not. By such affective matching, infants experience the parents being safely with them, heart to heart, breath to breath, assisting them in managing whatever the emotion is. In this "intervagal" state of connection, infants' emotions need not be frightening and overwhelming. The same is true for a toddler.

Example:

Toddler: (*Screaming and shouting in an intense, repetitive manner*) No! No! No!

Parent: You are angry with me! You're saying, "No! No! No! I want to go outside now, Daddy, and you won't let me! I'm angry with you, Daddy!"

Toddler: (*Points at the door, yelling*) Out! Out!

Parent: I know you want to go out now, Son, I really do (*using same rhythm and intensity as the child's voice*). Not now, Son, not now! Oh, this is hard for you! This is hard!

Toddler: (*Openly cries while holding up his arms to be picked up and hugged.*)

Matching of the affective expression of the toddler's emotion in this way conveys empathy for his emotion and helps the emotion to remain regulated, run its course, and end in a quieter state, often with the child accepting comfort. This is attunement. If the parent becomes angry himself in response to the child's anger, the situation is likely to escalate, with the child either becoming more distressed, with increased anger or moving into an immobilized defensive state of anxious vigilance. If the parent remains calm (which certainly is better than anger but not as helpful as matching the affect) the child often does not experience empathy, but rather the parent's acceptance of the child's emotion and assumption that the child can manage it on his or her own. The same is true for an older child.

Example:

Girl (14 years old): You guys treat me like a baby! I'm 14 and ought to be able to decide this myself.

Mom: No wonder you're mad! You don't think that I treat you like you're 14!

Girl: You don't! You think that I'm still a child!

Mom: And you want more freedom for yourself! I get that! You want to have more of the choices in your own life!

Girl: If you got it, then you would let me have it!

Mom: I hear you, Honey! It's hard! How much are you ready for! You say more and I say less! That is hard.

Often when parents simply acknowledge the different perceptions and thoughts, while matching the affective expression of children's emotions, the children (even teenagers!) feel understood and are more likely to be able to accept parents' decisions. In addition, when parents focus on communicating understanding of the children's experiences through matching the affective expression of their emotions, parents are likely to remain regulated rather than to react with intense emotion themselves. The same policy of using affective matching to convey attunement and regulate intensity is true when only positive emotions are involved.

Example:

Boy: (11 years old, running into the house) Mom, Jake's parents asked me to go to Disneyworld with Jake and them! They want me to go with them!

Mom: Oh, Sam! Wow! You thought that they might and they did! That's great, Sam!

Boy: This is the happiest day of my life! I can't wait! I can't wait to go!

Mom: How excited you are! You are happy! And I'm so happy with you! Wonderful!

Children need assistance in regulating positive emotions just as they need help in regulating negative ones. When children are excited and parents are not present to experience it with them, the excitement might become more intense, be hard to regulate, and turn into anxiety. Children who have experienced neglect or abuse often have difficulty regulating the experience of joy, happiness, or love.

The attuned response of parents is central in assisting children to regulate their emotions—negative or positive. In turn, the attuned response of a partner, friend, or therapist can greatly assist a parent in regulating the emotions that emerge during the activities of parenting.

Shame

Failing as a parent is a most shaming experience. When adults become parents, they most often place their parental role at, or near, the center of their identities. They might be able to accept their lack of progress in learning to Salsa or play racketball, but they will find it much more difficult to tolerate their lack of success as a parent. Because shame is an extremely unpleasant emotion that may cause great inner turmoil, parents may well avoid it by focusing on their children's behavior and avoiding the possibility that the problems are emerging from within their *relationship*. To acknowledge that they may have contributed to the difficulties would likely elicit feelings of shame. It may be easier to believe that the children are simply being impulsive, self-centered, rude, or disrespectful—all on their own.

Shame is a blocking emotion that is often part of the dynamics of blocked care. In a shame state, the upper regions of the brain involved in self–other awareness are shut down, suppressing any reflection or engagement with one's own feelings. As the emotion of shame decreases, parents are more likely to be able to face other negative emotions that they have toward their children, as well as mistakes that they may have made in their parental interactions. As their shame decreases, parents are likely to experience greater empathy for themselves, which will open them to experience greater empathy for their children. Parents' ability to feel sad about the state of their relationship with their children is often a sign that their capacity to care about their children is beginning to re-emerge as shame and anger begin to dissipate.

Example of unregulated shame:

Parent: (*After 8-year-old child spills juice on the carpet*) Don't be so clumsy! You've just ruined that carpet, and it's going to cost a lot of money to clean it!

Child: (*Withdraws from parent, lowers his head, and seems ready to cry.*)

Parent: (*Feeling shame over the intensity of his angry expression and his very critical comments, but voice still intense*) OK, I'm sorry that I yelled at you! But if you would just be more careful, these things wouldn't happen. You have to try harder!

In this example the parent tries to repair his relationship with his child when he thought that he was too harsh in his reaction, but his shame made it hard for him to truly acknowledge his responsibility for managing his response to his child's behavior. He still blamed the child, indicating that the child was at least partly responsible for the parent's behavior.

Same example, but this time with the parent identifying, managing, and reducing his shame:

Parent: (*After 8-year-old child spills juice on the carpet*) Don't be so clumsy! You've just ruined that carpet, and it's going to cost a lot of money to clean it!

Child: (*Withdraws from parent, lowers his head, and seems ready to cry.*)

Parent: (*Begins to experience shame over the intensity of his angry expression and his very critical comments, but he is able to regulate the shame; voice now lower and gentle.*) I'm sorry, Son, I really am. I know that you didn't mean that, and I should not have yelled at you that way and called you clumsy. You didn't deserve that! I spill things too and I'm a lot older than you. I made a mistake in yelling at you like that! I promise to try harder to handle my anger better. (*Goes to the child and offers comfort.*)

When parents are able to accept their mistakes, they are likely to remain in the social engagement system and be open to their children and whatever they need to do to repair their relationship with them. Shame is likely to move parents into a self-protective stance generating either mobilized defenses (fight or flight) or immobilized defense (freezing in fear). In either of these defensive states, parents can't access the higher functions provided by the prefrontal cortex and anterior cingulate, which would enable parents to accept both themselves and their children. Parents are also not likely to access the positive reward-based memories stored in the orbital region that had been generated during past successful interactions with their children. Whenever they can acknowledge their mistakes by shifting out of defense into the open parental state, parents are likely to experience empathy for how their children are affected by their criticism and blame and be less likely to make the same mistake again. Through parents' modeling of this process of owning and repairing mistakes, children, too, will increase their ability to face their mistakes and repair any damage that they have done to the relationship.

Anger and Rage

The degree of anger toward children that parents sometimes experience is often as intense as parents experience toward anyone in the course of their lives. This makes sense when you consider how important your child is to you and how much is at stake in this relationship. When your child reminds you of unresolved, difficult aspects of your own childhood (many of us were raised with habitual, and often unpredictable, anger), you are at risk of experiencing more intense anger than you otherwise would in response to the present situation. Or when your child is not responding to your caregiving or actively rejects what you are offering, it's easy to understand why you may react in a defensive, "low-road" manner. At these times, it is extremely challenging to be able to accept a child's experience or even be interested in understanding it.

When parents experience habitual underlying anger toward one of their children, or frequent periods of acute, intense, anger, most likely parents are also experiencing blocked care. Anger often reflects the underlying shame of experiencing yourself as a failure in being able to connect with, and influence, your child. Anger may reflect the shame we felt as children with our own parents. In response to shame, parents may find themselves avoiding their children, feeling little pleasure in the relationship, losing interest in their children's experiences, and failing to find meaning or purpose in childrearing. Angry parents become progressively more impulsive and reactive rather than reflective and flexible in dealing with their children.

And, since anger tends to beget anger, a parent's anger is likely to elicit angry feelings in the child, along with an impulse to retaliate, to go on the attack. Since children are often acutely aware of the power differential between themselves and their parents, especially with their fathers, they may move away or "freeze" instead of act on their anger, while waiting for parents' anger to be spent. Children's reactions to their parents' anger will most certainly reduce the children's willingness to rely on their parents over time, while moving the children into an habitually defensive and solitary position. Chronic anger or frequent episodes of poorly regulated anger can easily impair all five of the parenting systems: suppressing the approach and reward systems, constricting the child-reading process, fostering "me versus you" kinds of parental beliefs, and degrading executive functions.

Example of unregulated anger:
Dad: (*Noticing his 12-year-old son talking on his cell phone an hour after he told him to cut the grass before doing anything else, and the grass is still not cut*) I thought I told you to cut the grass!

Don't you ever do what I say? When will you ever start acting responsibly? Now turn that off and cut the grass!

Son: Sorry, Dad, just a minute while I finish talking to Jake.

Dad: Weren't you listening to me! (*Now screaming, coming to his son and grabbing his arm.*) Now get out there!

Son: Leave me alone! (*Jumps up and moves away from his dad.*) This is so stupid! Like the grass can't wait another hour!

Dad: The issue is, you didn't do what I told you to do! Now *move*!

Son: Great! I had to get a stupid drill sergeant for a father!

Dad: Don't you talk to me like that! You just lost your phone for the rest of the day! Keep talking and you'll lose it for a week!

Son: (*Running from the room*) Cut the grass yourself!

In this example, the father reacted immediately with anger, without any effort to first understand why the grass was not cut. If his son routinely did not do what he was told, the father might first explore that pattern with his son rather than increasing his anger and giving consequences. If his son's failure to do his chore was unusual, then the father definitely might first wonder what was happening before responding. In any case his angry reaction prevented any chance for an open dialogue and for a resolution that might avoid power struggles. Such reactions are likely to create a relationship that increasingly consists of demands and either compliance or opposition. An even greater danger is that the anger will escalate and cause deeper damage to the relationship, making it more difficult to repair.

Pausing to breathe and put your emotional brakes on before acting on your anger is the first step to being able to regulate your response. This braking requires an active prefrontal cortex that is able to inhibit a tendency toward self-defense that might be emerging from the amygdala's "first take" on the situation. By using your prefrontal brakes, you may then be more receptive to alternative ways of understanding the behavior as you move up the ladder to your higher brain regions, enabling you to be curious and even empathic, rather than just self-righteously angry.

Example of regulated anger:

Dad: (*Noticing his 12-year-old son talking on his cell phone an hour after he told him to cut the grass before doing anything else, and the grass is still not cut*) Son, I notice that the grass is not cut yet. What's going on?

Son: Sorry, Dad, just a minute while I finish talking with Jake.

Dad: OK, finish it up with Jake and then come into the kitchen before doing the grass. (*Son comes into the kitchen 2 minutes later.*) You had an hour son, and I told you it's gonna rain later, and I really want the grass to be cut before we go on our vacation tomorrow morning. It's important to me.

Son: I meant to talk with Jake for just a short time but we got talking and I forgot.

Dad: I hear you son, we all forget sometimes. I'm noticing, though, lately that you've done that a number of times. Like you are taking your family responsibilities for granted and focusing mostly on the other things in your life. Would you agree?

Son: I guess. There's just so much time in the day, with school, my friends, soccer, music.

Dad: I'm glad that you have such a full life, Son, I really am. And I'll be happy to talk with you about how to organize your time better. Forgetting your part in the family is not the way to handle it though.

Son: I know, Dad. I'm sorry. Could we talk about it more after I cut the grass? It's going to start to rain soon and I want to get it done. (*Places his hand on his dad's shoulder and smiles before running outside.*)

Discipline—which literally means *teaching*—does not require intense anger, and certainly not yelling, to be effective. In fact, it is more effective when the parent is able to keep a threat to the relationship out of discipline itself. If parents do not experience their children's acts as threats to the relationship, then their children are not likely to experience a threat either. Discipline with PACE, rather than with anger, tends to keep parents and children focused on the problem itself and its solution, rather than creating additional stress to their relationship.

Fear and Terror

Often when parents do not feel safe in relation to their children, they are in the state of fear. Parents' fear might be activated by children's verbal, emotional, or even physical attacks on them. This fear might be a response to the difficulty that parents have in controlling their emerging rage or hatred toward their children and their terror that they might even attack their children. Another possible cause of parental fear might relate to a sense of impending failure in parenting abilities. Even if parents' fears are unrelated to children but due to other factors—separation and loss through the death of a loved one, the need to relocate, divorce, or parents' own childhood histories— the pervasion of fear will have a profoundly negative impact on their ability to provide consistent caregiving for their children.

In fear, parents are unlikely to engage with their children socially or emotionally; nor are they likely to enjoy their children's presence. Instead, these parents are primed to defend themselves, *not* to be engaged with their children in open, reciprocal dialogues and activities. These parents will not focus on understanding their children but rather on what they as parents might do to control behavior—either their parental behavior or their children's behavior or both. Parents dominated by fear will not be open to their children's experiences or to any deeper meaning or value of whatever interactions they are having with their child. These parents will not be able to co-create new meanings with their children because they are consumed with the need to re-enact the meaning of highly stressful events from their own childhood relationships with their parents or from other highly stressful relationships. One mother who sought treatment for her ongoing intense conflict with her adolescent son described herself as having a panic attack whenever her son came home from school. Fear generates a defensive, self-protective stance rather than an open, engaged one.

Fear activates parents'own attachment behaviors (efforts to seek care from others) rather than their caregiving behaviors. When parents are in a state of fear (unless it is fear *for* their children), they are focused on finding someone to take care of them, rather than providing for their children. Their own needs for safety dominate their feelings, thoughts, and actions. If the source of their fear is their children, they will try to avoid those children. If parents seek help from a therapist as this time, their fear may activate their attachment behaviors in therapy and so aid the treatment. However, if parents are unable to feel safe again, for whatever reason, they are not likely to be in a position to provide safety for their children.

Here are some ideas for regulating fear and preventing terror:

1. In a safe setting, reflect on the fear, wondering about its origins, associations, settings, and history. This requires that you bring to mind the social–emotional memories of experiences that are present within the prefrontal cortex, using them as a guide in making sense of, and regulating, similar experiences in the present. This activity will prove to be more successful if you are able to accept and have empathy for yourself and your emotional experiences. As you engage in this process, you are actually practicing staying in your open, smart vagal state— just where you want to be in order to parent your child more empathically and effectively.

2. Consider ways of managing fear, including traumatic events, with the aid of self-help readings, such as *8 Keys to Safe Trauma Recovery* (Rothschild, 2010).

3. Reflect on fears associated with being a parent and your relationship with your child. Try to see any connections with your own childhood and explore ways to deactivate any emotional reactions associated with your past. Anticipate conflict situations with your child and consider alternative ways of managing them. Simply adding consequences for your child's behaviors are not likely to be effective. Working out rewards and punishments will engage only a small part of your thinking brain (as

well as a small part of your child's) and be much less effective than engaging the entire prefrontal cortex and related areas that emerged in human brains for managing our complex social–emotional relationships.

4. Consider discussing your fears with a good friend so that you do not feel so alone and are able to experience another perspective. Be aware of what you want from your friend and let him or her know. Most often this means allowing yourself to experience comfort and support from your friend (activating your attachment behaviors), as your friend engages in caregiving for you. Through receiving care from your friend, you will be more able to provide care to your child. Good connections release those good brain chemicals, such as oxytocin, that help you feel better and safer.

5. Remember that when you are fearful, you are not likely to be able to engage in ongoing caregiving behaviors. Ask for another adult to help out.

6. Your child knows that you are experiencing fear (or that something is wrong), so acknowledge it without asking him or her for help. The information is likely to reassure the child that the reality isn't nearly as bad as the fantasy might be. Make the child aware of what he or she might expect while you manage it.

7. Seek professional assistance if the fears prove to be too difficult to handle through your own efforts. Remember that simply learning concrete skills with which to manage your child's behavior are not likely to address the complex social–emotional needs of either you or your child.

Sadness and Despair

When parents experience despair, they have little energy and even less motivation to do anything, so the day-to-day responsibility of caring for children may seem like moving a mountain. Sadness that borders on, or is part of, depression tends to shut down the thinking brain, making parenting an ordeal. For parenting to activate children's minds and foster their zest for life, the many tasks and routines involved in it need to be a frequent source of meaning, satisfaction, and joy. Parenting is meant to be an approach process that triggers our reward system, whereas sadness is a state in which both the approach and reward systems are "off." Although parents' sadness can activate a comforting, approach response from a caring adult (if there is such a person in the picture), it can also induce "parentified" caretaking behavior in children, potentially leading to role reversal and robbing the child of developmental energy. When caregiving is so hard that each small action seems like an overwhelming challenge and any reciprocal interaction seems like an endless chore, then parenting has lost its ability to empower children with the impetus to develop and discover who they are becoming and who they can be in the world.

Such despair could be caused by external factors in parents' past, present, or perceived future, but here we are focusing on the sadness and despair that are elicited by the daily responsibilities of parenting itself. When the needs and wants of children prove to be overwhelming to parents, they are experiencing blocked care. They have no desire to be with their children, and there is no pleasure in the necessary interactions. Their children hold little interest for them, and the children are seldom in their awareness other than as a perceived obligation. Whereas other aspects of parents' lives—a career, hobby, or activity with a friend—may hold meaning for them, the activity of parenting their children does not. Although the parents' executive system may be able to manage the practical activities of parenting much of the time, the energy of these activities does not contain the reciprocal joy and interest that enables children to develop fully. In this case the parents' executive system is not receiving the support that it needs from the other four systems to function well.

Such sadness and despair in response to parenting may well arise from a similar lack of joy and meaning parents experienced with their own parents. These unhappy parents may know the mechanics of parenting from observing others and reading books, but they do not experience the positive meaning and emotions often associated with parenting because they did not experience it firsthand with their own parents. Perhaps idealizing parenting, these parents "know" what they should be doing to parent their children well, but they are not be able to experience the day-to-day rewards of parenting that make the dreams come true. It's like knowing that you have to eat, but having no appetite or ability to taste your food. Eating becomes a chore rather than a source of pleasure.

Such sadness may also occur when parents hold narrow views of how their children should be developing, or what their children should be like. When their children do not meet these expectations, these parents may begin to lose interest in them and to experience parenting as an exercise in failure. Such sadness and despair may well be grounded in shame that is based on a vague awareness of failing to meet their children's basic needs.

Parenting-related sadness and despair may also be child-specific. These parents are successful in attaining deeply meaningful, reciprocal relationships with their other children but not with this one. This one child may have rejected their efforts to bond with him or her, refusing to express attachment needs, or may have a temperament and interests greatly at odds with parents' preferred way of living. This may happen when a child is adopted and, due to prior interpersonal trauma, neglect, and loss of attachment relationships does not express any love or affection for his or her adoptive parents. This may also happen when the child has special needs that make parenting him or her significantly less rewarding and more difficult.

When parents are angry or frightened during interactions with their children, there still are active relationships, however defensive and stressful they are. When parents are sad, withdrawn, and in despair when in the presence of their children, however, the relationships begin to wither and both parents and children are left isolated and often without spirit. If the activity of parenting holds no meaning for parents, it eventually comes to hold little or no meaning for their children. These children—who in the past initiated activity with their parents and later were alert to possible opportunities for interactions with their parents—are now indifferent to such possibilities and stop thinking about them. As children turn less to their parents for caregiving, the parents' caregiving behaviors are harder to activate and sustain.

Many parents realize, at some point, that they do not have a deeply meaningful relationship with their children, though they had wished for one years ago. They often believe that it is too late to change. These parents, as noted, often had childhoods that lacked close relationships with their parents, and they don't know what it would feel like to have such a relationship. They just know that the sense of emptiness that they felt when they were young has now followed them into their relationships with their own children.

For such parents it is important to remember that, just as they most likely wished that it could have been different with their own parents—a wish that lasted for years and may still be present—so too do their children have a similar wish. These parents need to become aware that if they truly are sorry for not actively parenting their children, and if they apologize and commit to changing those relationships, there is a good chance that their children will forgive them and work to develop the relationship too. Children can recover from blocked care, too, meaning that they are likely to be ready to remove the block and forgive when they have a reason to hope that it might be different, and that their parents are truly remorseful and ready to work at it. The need for connection is extremely powerful and even when blocked, still retains much of its potential for expression if the environment becomes safer. The specific ideas mentioned with regard to fear and terror may also be of help for parents struggling with sadness and despair.

Emotion Regulation in the Therapy Room

Seeking therapy because of difficulties in raising their child is in itself a very emotional decision for parents to make. Acknowledging that you need help with your child can cause shame and fear that you will be judged unfairly by the therapist. At the same time, when parents do seek professional help, they often are already feeling strong emotions—anger, fear, shame, and despair—in response to the daily problems that they are facing with their children. As a result, it is important that the therapist first attend to the emotions that parents bring with them to the treatment session. These emotions need to be accepted, understood, and met with empathy, before the parents are likely to be ready to begin to openly reflect on their concerns with their child. From there, they might begin to re-engage in the quality of caregiving that is proposed in this book.

Attunement in Therapy

The attunement of the therapist for a parent's emotion is equally as important and beneficial for the parent as it is for the child when the parent is attuned with the child's emotion. When the therapist is attuned with a parent's emotion, conveyed through empathy, especially when the therapist is matching the affect, a parent often experiences this empathy and feels understood (or "felt") by the therapist. This empathy leads to the experience of safety and to the activation of the social engagement system. With safety and the therapist's active, nonjudgmental presence, the parent is better able to go more deeply into the story of the problem, while developing its meaning in a more coherent and comprehensive manner. Felt safety and the therapist's co-regulating empathy are brain-opening processes that can help parents gain access to little-used and very likely underdeveloped parts of their brains that must be "awakened" in order to recover from blocked care.

The attuned responsiveness of the therapist to the parent's story is evident in the therapist's gentle rhythmic movements that are synchronized with the cadence of the parent's voice, or the therapist's vocal utterances ("Ah! . . . yes . . . I see") that are in step with the phrasing of the parent, or the subtle changes in the therapist's facial expressions that match the parent's small movements or gestures. (These aspects of a therapist's response must be organic and natural, not contrived or forced.) Attunement is also evident when the rhythm and intensity of the therapist's verbal response is essentially the same as the preceding verbal expression of the parent. Not only are these attuned responses crucial for a parent's sense of safety; they also help the parent to feel safe through the therapist's ability to co-regulate the emotion that the parent is experiencing. The intense emotions of a parent are much less likely to become extreme when the therapist matches the parent's affective expression than when the therapist remains calm and detached or especially when the therapist is frustrated and judgmental.

Attuned interactions between the parent and therapist—as was true between a parent and child—demonstrate clearly the two-way, reciprocal nature of brain functioning. The ability of one individual to influence another individual in a relationship is likely to be significant when the brains of the two individuals are functioning in a synchronized, harmonious manner. This influence is likely to be much less impactful when one person is giving another a lecture, even when the lecture is "psychoeducational" and well intended. In joint states of attunement, the co-regulation of emotion is likely. In such states intersubjective experiences are created where the experience of each individual is able to influence—deepen and facilitate coherence within—the experience of the other. As in the parent–child relationship, this kind of "intervagal" synchrony between a therapist and a parent is extremely beneficial. In this kind of interaction, the therapist's smart vagal system, tightly connected to the right brain (Schore, 2003), helps parents to shift out of the more primitive defensive parts of their nervous systems into their own smart vagal system—the system that evolved the latest to support social engagement and empathic, reciprocal connections. This is the "royal road" to unblocking blocked care. In this process, we see the power of PACE to activate the healing effects of interpersonal neurobiology, to create a "*we*" state of mind rather than the "me versus you" state that parents typically bring to therapy (Siegel, 2010).

Another way of discussing this process is to say that the caring, attuned attitude of the therapist, employing the five parental systems described in this book, fosters the activation of all of these systems in parents. The therapist's use of his or her own approach, reward,

"parent-reading," meaning-making, and executive systems stimulates the activation of these underused, blocked systems in parents,
enabling them to discover or rediscover their potential for empathy
and awakening the integrated systems of the parenting brain.

In the following example, the parent (John) is expressing anger to
the therapist (Rachel) over the deceptive behavior of his 15-year-old
son.

Parent: Why doesn't he just ask for what he wants instead of
trying to get it by going around my back! I get so tired of
his sneaky behavior!

Therapist: (*As John becomes more agitated, he moves his arms forcefully
and Rachel—without being aware of it—leans forward and
back in time with his arm movements, and her voice carries
the same intensity as his.*) Why! Why! You just wish he
would be more open with you!

Parent: Yes! Treat me with some respect and I'll treat him with
some respect!

Therapist: (*Her face and voice reflect his level of intensity.*) If he'd just
talk with you—directly—it would make it much easier to
work something out together!

Parent: Why can't he see that?

Therapist: Why can't he see that? What an important question! If he
did, you two could work together! You'd be closer—father
and son—something you so want. And instead, his going
around your back moves you further apart! And you want
to be closer!

Parent: I want to be his father! Not some policeman trying to
catch him doing something wrong!

Therapist: And you are his father! . . . Though now it doesn't feel like
you want it to feel.

Parent: No, it doesn't! I want him to trust me! We might not
always agree! I want him to just trust me! To know that
I'll work it out with him. We'll be together and handle it.

Therapist: (*John's movements and voice are now more subdued, showing much more sadness than anger. Again, Rachel is matching his bodily expressions of this sadness.*) That's what you want the most, isn't it? To be together. To talk openly and handle any differences that might come up . . . because you're his dad . . . and he trusts you and wants to be close to you too.

Following such an attuned interaction between the parent and therapist, the parent would most likely be ready to explore with his son—with PACE and the guidance of the therapist—his son's deceptive behaviors along with his own wish that they were better able to work things out between them, each being open to the experience of the other in resolving the conflict. With the therapist first expressing PACE for John's experience of his son's behavior, including being attuned to the emotional impact of that behavior on him, John is more open to maintaining the same attitude toward his son. He would be more open to accepting and exploring the reasons for his son's behaviors and less judgmental. Through experiencing the therapist's caring attitude, John would be more likely to reduce his experience of blocked care for his son. In turn, his son would be more likely to open up to his father's engaged communications and more likely to respond with a similar cooperative intention.

Shame in Therapy

When parents enter therapy in a state of blocked care, they are likely to be experiencing shame, which makes them even more likely to assume a self-protective, defensive stance. They are probably viewing the source of the problem as existing within the child and are seeking advice as to how best to change, manage, or control that child's behaviors. These parents need the attention of the therapist to stay on the child, not on them.

In relating with parents who are experiencing shame, the therapist needs to maintain an attitude of *radical acceptance* (Brach, 2003) of their perceptions, thoughts, emotions, and wishes. Such acceptance of parents' inner lives by the therapist enables parents to gradually acknowledge some of their own behaviors toward the child, without denying or minimizing them. Such acceptance gradually increases parents' trust in the therapist and allows them to share more of their inner lives. The therapist may first focus on the child's behaviors and related discipline, allowing parents to experience the therapist's understanding of how hard it is to raise a child with these symptoms. At this point there is no effort to discuss the cause of the symptoms, but rather to communicate that parenting a child who shows such behaviors must be extremely difficult. During this exploration the therapist focuses with curiosity and empathy on how parents experience those stressful situations for such a long period of time. What is being established is that regardless of the cause, being a parent in this situation would be very difficult.

With a voice that conveys deep empathy, the therapist might make one or more of the following comments:

"How hard that must be . . . day after day."

"How do you keep going . . . every day seems to be so stressful?"

"I bet that you never imagined when you became a parent that you would be having such hard times with your child."

"When you try so hard and nothing seems to work, do you get discouraged? Does it ever feel hopeless?"

"So sometimes you find yourself really disliking your child. What a difficult experience that must be for you."

Such comments, expressed with compassion and gentleness, convey to parents that they deeply love their child, truly do not want the current situation to be happening, and would do whatever necessary to repair their relationship with their child. "Whatever necessary," in the context of the therapist's acceptance and empathy, eventually begins to include parents' own experience of blocked care and its associated behaviors. As parents begin to feel safe in response to the therapist's acceptance and empathy, they may begin to acknowledge their shame with statements such as the following:

"I guess that I'm just not a good parent. I've tried but I think I'm just not good at it."

"Maybe I never should have become a parent . . . some people just aren't cut out for it, and I'm beginning to think I'm one of them."

"I've never felt like such a failure . . . never have I ever felt like I do now as a parent."

In response to hearing such comments, the therapist is tempted to reassure parents that they are not the failure that they experience themselves to be. The therapst may want to say:

"Oh, you are a good parent! We all make mistakes sometimes."

"You made a mistake. Don't take it so hard."

"For everything you've done wrong, you've done dozens of things right as a parent."

Such statements are efforts to reduce parents' pain caused by the pervasive shame that they are experiencing. The therapist may also make such statements because he or she is uncomfortable with their pain and is trying to "fix the problem." Or the parents' shame is eliciting shame within the therapist. If the parents are so inadequate as parents—and the therapist has treated them for a while—where does that leave the therapist? Not very confident in his or her ability.

A much more therapeutic response to parents' expression of shame is one of further acceptance and empathy, followed closely by curiosity (PACE, though in this case the playfulness is likely to be inappropriate, so *pACE*). PACE enables the therapist to experience parents' shame and to communicate this understanding with compassion, not judgment. This compassion enables parents and therapist to regulate the shame together, explore it, and gradually reduce it, along with the parents' harsh judgments about themselves. The following sequence reflects this approach to parental shame:

Parent: I really am a failure as a parent.

Therapist: Ah! That must be so hard for you to believe . . . and to say to me.

Parent: It's no picnic.

Therapist: No, it's more like a nightmare! You love your daughter so much and to feel like you're failing her must be so painful for you.

Parent: I just can't do anything right!

Therapist: So it seems like now when you think that you've not responded the best way with her, you think that it says something about you as a person . . . not just a mistake that you've made. Has it seemed like that to you for a long time?

Parent: Like, forever . . . no, I guess that's not true. When she was little . . . before she started school . . . I used to think that I was doing a good job! Like I was a good parent. But since then, it seems like every year, every month, it gets worse. And now I think that it must be me.

As the emotion of shame decreases, parents are likely to begin to face other negative emotions. Within an openness with the therapist that enables them to be co-regulated as well, parents begin to take a more reflective stance toward the difficulties that they and their child are experiencing. As the shame decreases, parents are likely to begin to communicate more clearly about the anger, fear, or sadness that occurs frequently during the parenting that takes place throughout the day. As parents accept the presence of these emotions and are confident that the therapist will accept them as well, they experience a freedom to explore the emotions with nonjudgmental curiosity. From this new perspective, parents are more likely to begin to experience empathy for both themselves and their child. The therapist is taking the lead in extending the qualities of PACE to parents, but the parents are now able to extend those PACE qualities to themselves, with their brains more open and more connected.

Anger in Therapy

Since children's anger is likely to be more intense and out of control than parents' anger, and since children's anger is often the presenting problem, there is a danger that the therapist will focus on children's anger without even being aware of the parents' anger toward their children. Also, parents may acknowledge their own anger, but then indicate that the child "started it," so the parents' anger is justified and would not be present if the child had not misbehaved so much. There is a danger that the therapist will agree with that reasoning and work with the child on anger management skills without being aware of the reciprocal nature of the anger that is present. The therapist may think that the child's anger is unreasonable and that the parents' anger is reasonable and so focus on the problem as if it existed within the child alone.

Another, equally limited perception is that parents' anger is unreasonable and thus creating the child's anger, whether it be reasonable or unreasonable. In this case the parents are perceived as being punitive and the solution is to focus on their habitual anger with the same psychoeducational, anger management focus, this time directed toward the parents. In each of these two perspectives the therapist first judges which—parents or child—caused the problem by having unreasonable anger. The belief is that this person(s) needs anger management and then the presenting problem will dissipate. That belief often leads to disappointment and treatment failure.

Most likely a more productive therapeutic approach is not to focus so much on "who started it" but rather on the ongoing reciprocal process that is generating anger and distance and leading to decreased attachment and blocked care. What should be the lovely functioning of the dyadic brains of parent(s) and child has become the separate functioning of isolated brains operating on the "low road" in reactive, defensive ways.

In working with the parents first and not each parent and child dyad, the therapist focuses on the parents' experiences of blocked care with an attitude of PACE, not evaluation. The therapist is not seeking the cause or the blame for the parent–child conflicts and the distance; rather, the therapist is seeking to help the parents to become more fully aware of their experiences with their child. If the therapist is successful, the parents will gradually incorporate the PACE qualities and will—either quickly or over time—reduce their negative evaluations of their child. When parents feel safe, their social engagement systems are likely to become active, and they will become much more openly engaged in the complex brain processes involved in regulating their emotions and making sense of the current situation with their child.

Therapists need to be aware of the possibility that parents' anger will trigger their own angry response—though it may be communicated entirely nonverbally. Therapists may experience parents as being punitive and then adopt the goal of protecting their children from that attitude. This is likely to lead to negative evaluations of parents' anger by therapists, and to a cycle of anger–defensiveness between parents and therapists that reflect the same cycle that exists between parents and children.

Following are two parallel examples of the therapist responding to the parent's anger toward her child. In the first, the therapist evaluates the parent's anger, and this judgment leads to a defensive tone in the ongoing dialogue. In the second, the therapist responds with attunement to the anger along with the attitudes of PACE and a resulting open, reciprocal, dialogue.

The parent, Betty, expresses to the therapist, Mark, her persistent anger toward her daughter and her daughter's negative, irritable, behaviors toward her.

Version 1

Betty: I just don't like her anymore! She is such a little brat most of the time! I don't call her that to her face, but I certainly think it!

Mark: That's kind of strong, isn't it! Her behavior is certainly challenging, and I can understand your getting angry at her. Do you really mean it, that you think that she's a brat and you don't like her?

Betty: I do mean it! She's been acting that way for so long, I don't have patience with it anymore! I just want it to stop and I just get tired of being around her when she's this way.

Mark: I fear that you might be becoming as negative as she is. If that's the case, she certainly will not be able to change her attitude. How about if we begin by working on your anger and then if you can become more caring, it will be easier to work on her anger.

Betty: So it's my fault! I'm to blame for her crappy attitude!

Mark: I'm not saying you're to blame for her attitude. I'm saying that if we can reduce your anger, we'll be able to change her attitude more quickly.

Betty: Well, I don't particularly care like doing all the work and my being responsible for her becoming civil with me. I'd like to see her assuming some responsibility for her behavior.

Mark: I agree with you that she has to become responsible for her own behavior. I'm just saying that you need to better control your anger before she is likely to do that.

Betty: And I'm saying that there would not be a problem with my anger if she acted in a respectful manner.

Mark: I'm not after who started the problem. I'm just saying that as the parent, you need to take the first step to solving it.

Betty: Maybe I don't feel like being the parent anymore.

Mark: Then I can't help you. And I can't help her.

Betty: I guess you can't. (*She gets up to leave.*)

Version 2

Betty: I just don't like her anymore! She is such a little brat most of the time! I don't call her that to her face, but I certainly think it!

Mark: Oh my, Betty! How hard it seems like it is for you now! How hard! (*Mark leans forward and speaks with the same rhythm and intensity as Betty does.*)

Betty: This is not what I thought that being a parent would be like!

Mark: Of course, not! When she was tiny you must have felt so close to her . . . and her to you, and you would never have imagined that your relationship would ever lead to such conflict and lack of closeness.

Betty: I never did. No, I never did. I wanted so much to have a relationship with her that was different from the relationship I had with my mother. And now I think of her as a brat! And I don't even like my own daughter!

Mark: How painful that is for you! You so much want to be close with her again . . . like you two were in years past.

Betty: If she just wouldn't be such a brat! There, I said it again. I'm so angry with her.

(*After some further exploration of the mother's anger and perceptions of her relationship with her daughter, the following dialogue occurs.*)

Betty: It is so important to me. I don't want it to be like this between us!

Mark: I can feel how important it is to you, Betty. How important it is. Could you tell me . . . you mentioned earlier that you want a relationship with your daughter that is different from the relationship you had with your mother. Could you tell me what it was like with your mother?

Betty: I was never close to her! But she didn't seem to care. But I care for my daughter!

Mark: I know you do, Betty, I know. And that's what makes it so painful . . . you do care! Please tell me more about your relationship with your mom. There might be some connection between how hard it was to be close to her and how hard it now is to be close to your daughter.

In this second version, Mark's attuned responsiveness, permeated with PACE, enables Betty to move out of her angry stance, access her sadness, and not move into a defensive mode when Mark wonders about the connection between Betty's past relationship with her mother and her current relationship with her daughter. Feeling safe with Mark, she trusts him that such exploration might improve her relationship with her daughter. Not feeling judged for her anger nor for her daughter's problems, she is able to trust Mark's guidance to begin to understand possible factors in her problems with her daughter along with ways to improve the relationship. Also, feeling safe with Mark, she is likely to be able to become aware of the problems that constrained her relationship with her mother, while being able to regulate any negative emotions that are associated with that relationship.

Sometimes parents will acknowledge that their anger toward their children is similar to their own parents' anger toward them. However they will then add that their parents' anger was justified because they were doing something wrong, and these younger parents will add that *their* parents' anger never hurt them in any way. It tends not to be productive to suggest that their parents' anger was *not* justified or that it *did* hurt them. A more helpful discussion is to ask if their parents' anger may have made it hard to be close to them, hard to communicate with them. Would these younger parents like to have had a closer relationship with their own parents, and do they want a closer relationship with their children than they have or had with their parents? Younger parents are likely to see how their parents' anger did constrain open communication with them, regardless of whether or not it was justified.

Fear in Therapy

When frightened parents enter therapy, they are likely to be in a state similar to that of an adult who is experiencing PTSD. Ignoring this fear and instead telling parents what to do to manage their children's behavior (which is creating the fear) is likely to be counterproductive. Whether the fear is associated with the parent–child problems or is due to something external to the children, it must be addressed and treated before the focus can turn directly to repairing the parent–child relationship. If the fear is related to the problems in the relationship, then addressing the fear is likely to be the first step in attending to the relationship itself. Parents need to feel safe before they are able to openly explore their fears about their children and their relationships with them. Parenting well requires internal safety.

PACE is ideally suited to address parents' fears. The therapist's accepting, nonjudgmental presence is likely to enable parents to feel safe enough to begin to explore the experience of fear itself. The therapist co-regulates the emerging fear, ensuring that it is not too much for the parents to manage. Within co-regulation, the therapist's attuned presence creates empathy, which further enables the parents to experience support in facing any terror that emerges in their minds. From there, curiosity enables parents to break down the behavioral difficulties, their sources and deeper meanings in the conflicts, and ruptures to the relationship. Exploration that does not entail evaluation but only acceptance and understanding generates safety. When the problems make sense at a deeper level, generally an avenue opens for approaching the situation, which in itself contains hope. This hope further reduces the fear and the need for parents to rely on the therapist for support. When the children join the parents in the treatment at a later date, the parents are likely to be ready to provide care for their children, using all five of the brain-based systems that we have been describing in this book.

When parents are in a state of fear (or the other negative emotional states), it is crucial that the therapist not move prematurely into evaluations and recommendations for behavioral change. The parents are unlikely to have the emotional energy needed to see the recommendations through in day-to-day living. Or if the parents are able to meet the behavioral expectations set by the therapist, there is a great risk that they will not be able to maintain the openly engaged, intersubjective presence that would facilitate a positive response from the children. If instead parents are in a somber, goal-directed, job-focused stance, the children will most likely react with a protective and defensive action that will provoke reciprocal negative reactions from the parents. Early behavioral changes need to be successful if they are to generate confidence and hope regarding their continued success. The safe, not the frightened, parent will be in the best position to achieve such success.

Example: The parent, Cathy, is quite agitated, expressing her very stressful day-to-day interactions with her daughter. Her therapist, Danielle, matches her affect, conveying that she understands and experiences, to some extent, her great distress, leading Cathy into a dialogue wherein she is able to attain greater emotion regulation and begin to reflect more openly on her situation.

Mom:	(*Ten minutes into a nonstop explosion of words that seemed to have no end in sight and in which Cathy seemed to be unaware of Danielle's presence and responsiveness*.) It is just endless! I dread the days! I dread the hours and the minutes (very agitated, talking quickly and with much intensity)! When will it stop? How do I keep going on like this? What am I supposed to do? Why just this morning before she left for school . . .
Therapist:	Cathy, Cathy, Cathy! I want to understand this. I want to know what you are going through. You seem to be SO overwhelmed with what is happening at home with your daughter. Your daughter! And it seems to you that it is just never going to end!
Mom:	Yes, I want to tell you when she got up and left for school . . . she ignored the breakfast that I had prepared for her. She grabbed a soda and a handful of crackers . . . didn't say a word to me . . . and ran out the door . . .
Therapist:	(*interrupting her account*) Didn't say a word to you! How hard that must have been!
Mom:	So I shouted out at her when she was heading down the walk, "I am your mother, you know!" And she yelled, "So what!" I can't stand it! She is so . . .
Therapist:	(*interrupting again*) When you tried to connect with her and she ignored you and then replied and you felt so hurt . . .
Mom:	She is so spiteful! All day I looked at the clock, fearing the moment that I'd hear her walking in the door. Something I think . . .

Therapist: In your own home. Waiting in fear for your daughter's return . . .

Mom: You keep interrupting me!

Therapist: I know and I'm sorry. I just want to understand what you are going through and you have such a need to tell me so much . . . so fast that I'm afraid that if I don't jump into the conversation, I'll miss understanding you.

(*As the parent continues to express how overwhelmed she is, the therapist continues to work to help her to focus on making sense of what is happening.*)

Mom: I just don't understand (*a much slower rhythm, followed by tears*) . . . why she treats me this way. I love her so much. Why doesn't she love me too?

Therapist: Oh, Cathy, oh, Cathy. You do! You truly do love her! So painful! So frightening to not know if she'll return your love . . . or if she'll attack you.

Mom: I want to know why.

Therapist: Yes, you do. You have to know why! If only you could understand. Then maybe you'd know what to do . . . what you could do about it.

Mom: Do you know why she does this?

Therapist: No, I don't, Cathy. That's what we need to understand. We'll talk and that will help. And then we'll get her to come here with you and we'll listen to her. And maybe then we'll start to understand what is going on inside your daughter to lead to her behavior toward you. Once we understand, maybe we will know how we can help her to stop.

Mom: (*a few minutes of silence and then a small smile*) Stopping would be good!

Therapist: (*Smiling in return*) Yes it would. Yes it would. And, Cathy, I love your smile. It gives me more confidence. Your smile will lead you . . . out of your dread . . . your terror . . . and it will help you to find your strength again. We can do this . . . together.

Mom: Don't expect me to smile all the time.

Therapist: No worries, Cathy. I am fine with your fear, your anger, your discouragement too. Wherever you are, I'll join you there and we'll begin there.

Sometimes parents are in such distress that they talk constantly at the therapist without being able to experience the therapist's empathy and understanding. Through such constant talking parents might be able to avoid experiencing the terror that comes from daily life with their children. This becomes a monologue that is not therapeutic and only leads to increased frustration and isolation for the parents. In these situations, the therapist needs to match parents' agitated expressions with quick, animated dialogue, even breaking into the monologue if necessary in order to begin a dialogue that will enable the parents to experience the therapist's acceptance and empathy. From there, with the therapist now co-regulating parents' emotional experience through matching its affective expression, the therapist is more able to elicit a more reflective stance within parents. Although the parents' stance may be judgmental initially and focused solely on change, with patience, the therapist is often able to help the parents first to simply understand and accept the current situation, with open curiosity toward their children's behavior.

Despair in Therapy

When parents do not experience the desire to have closer relationships with their children or when they are in despair about ever having such a relationship or being able to be a positive influence in their children's lives, therapists are likely to create only further disappointment and failure if they encourage these parent to do things with their children or to communicate with them more often. Such parents do not have the will to do so, the reason for doing so, or the satisfaction that might maintain their motivation when the going gets difficult. As is the case with parents who habitually experience the other negative emotions with regard to parenting, if therapists adopt an attitude of PACE, they may eventually be able to activate parents' wishes and hopes to find a way to become more engaged in parenting.

The following example concerns a parent, Dave, and his therapist, Ron. Dave manifests a passive and withdrawn manner in the session and expresses little hope that his relationship with his daughter will ever be different.

Dad: I'm here because I should be . . . I don't particularly want to be and . . . I really don't expect anything to change with me and Janet.

Therapist: Ah, Dave . . . you seem to feel such little hope . . . such little hope that things might improve with you and Janet. What's that like?

Dad: Well . . . maybe it used to bother me . . . but it really doesn't much anymore . . . I think . . . I think . . . it's probably just too late.

Therapist: Too late?

Dad: Yeah . . . I think I tried before to be a better dad . . . I remember giving it some effort . . . but that never led anywhere . . . and now . . . Janet doesn't seem to care much if I'm there or not . . . I don't know if she ever did, really. When I was watching her she always wanted her mother . . . I guess she knew then I wasn't much of a father . . . and I don't see that changing.

Therapist: I sense . . . as you talk, Dave . . . maybe it doesn't actively bother you, as you said . . . but I sense a deep sadness . . . a deep wish that it might have been different . . . that you and Janet could have found a way to be close . . . father and daughter.

Dad: Maybe you're right. Maybe . . . but what good is it now to talk about it?

Therapist: I don't know, Dave. I don't know. But would you be willing to just allow yourself to feel that sadness for a little bit.

Dad: (*After 2 or 3 minutes*) It's not a good feeling . . . It's not something I'd like to do often.

Therapist: No, I guess not. Such sadness . . . and I sense it is pretty strong . . . almost a despair . . . must be pretty painful when you allow it to be and do not distract yourself from it . . . I wonder, Dave, if you would stay in that sadness and let yourself imagine you and Janet having a wonderful father–daughter relationship . . . What would it be? What do you imagine?

Dad: (*After a few minutes*) I imagine us walking by the lake . . . I imagine her telling me about the medal she got in swimming and my holding it up and beaming with pride . . . and giving her a hug. I imagine her sitting with me and watching a funny movie on TV. . . and laughing . . . looking at each other and smiling. I imagine . . . I imagine . . . (*tearing up*) doing something with her . . . working on a puzzle at the dining room table . . . working on a damn puzzle . . . something . . . that I always wanted to do with my dad (*actively crying*) and never did. That's what I imagine.

Therapist: Dave . . . Dave, your sadness is covering so much pain . . . so much pain.

Dad: Yes, it does. But since it's never going to change . . . I don't have much choice but to bury the pain. There is really no reason to hope anymore.

Therapist: Yet you want desperately to experience hope.

Dad: That would only lead to more pain. I fear hoping again.

Therapist: And if Janet knew what you've just told me?

Dad: I don't think she'd care now. I think she's given up hope too.

Therapist: When did you first give up hope with your dad?

Dad: (*A sudden burst of tears, with difficulty talking*) I still hope.

Therapist: And maybe Janet does too.

Dad: Why would she? I've not been much of a dad.

Therapist: Why do you still hope with your dad?

Dad: Because he's my dad.

Therapist: And you're Janet's dad.

Dad: I don't know what to do.

Therapist: We'll work it out. It will be hard. I need to get to know you. And help you to get to know yourself. The parts of you that your dad never saw . . . I'll be with you. And at some point we'll invite your daughter here . . . so that she can see those parts too . . . and then we'll see what she wants to do . . . a scary moment for sure. And then we'll see if your hope becomes stronger. I think it will. Please trust me, I do believe it will. But we'll have to see together.

This example demonstrates that often at the beginning of treatment, the therapist's primary goal is to simply engender some hope in parents that things might be different, that they may be able to develop a more meaningful relationship with their children.

Summary

There is nothing more important in the parenting brain than for parents to be able to identify, regulate, and express their emotional lives when they are relating with their children. Trying to eliminate emotion while relying on reasoning alone is not a viable option. The brain works poorly when emotion and reflection do not work together. The social–emotional world of the human family involves a very complex reality that requires the rich processes of the prefrontal cortex, anterior cingulate, insula, etc., to be integrated with, to guide, and to regulate the immediate self-protective reaction tendencies of the amygdala and limbic system. Children also need to experience their parents' emotional connections with them. They especially need to experience the pleasure, warmth, and excitement that come with the joy and commitment of parental love. They need to experience this positive connection the most when the stress and strain of family life are generating anger, fear, sadness, and shame.

When emotion is accepted and regulated, then the events—both internal and external—of your life can be explored openly, accepted, and understood. Regulated emotion creates sufficient safety to enable parents to make sense of the daily activity involved in being parents and to reflect on these activities in a manner that leads to more satisfying and successful family life.

CHAPTER 6

Making Sense & Reflective Functioning

When your emotions are regulated, you are ready to experience the activation and integration of all aspects of the brain, including your various cognitive abilities. Within this integrated functioning, you are best able to make sense of the present situation, including its associations with the past and future. The emotional meaning of an event contributes to its cognitive meaning and together they enable you to decide on the best possible, unique, response to the situation. These decisions involve what is known as your reflective functioning and are the subject of this chapter.

Making Sense

How many of us parents have found ourselves yelling at our children over having done something that they should not have done (tracking mud over the kitchen floor) only to find out that someone else (maybe even our partners) did that and our children were innocent? Or we yelled at our children for doing something that we saw them do (going to their friend's house down the street before cutting the grass) only to find out that they acted for a reason of which we approved (their friend's parent asked to borrow a rake). All of us would say that we should know why our children did something before evaluating what they did, but too often we evaluate before knowing—before we make *good* sense of what they did. Too often our anger preempts our deeper understanding. Not only is that embarrassing for us when there really was no reason for the anger, but it also is detrimental to our relationships with our children—who assume (and often rightfully so) that we make negative assumptions about their behavior before really understanding what their behavior is all about. We certainly don't appreciate it when our friends or colleagues do it to us.

Parents are best able to make sense of a given event or behavior when they can maintain an open, curious attitude of "What's that about?", holding back the quick reaction system, before responding to the event. Why react in anger to a child's behavior before first knowing what the behavior means?—unless anger is necessary to put an immediate stop to behavior that is truly dangerous and/or hurtful to self or other. When parents do believe that a consequence is necessary for a certain behavior, it is still crucial to make sense of the behavior in order to know the most appropriate consequence. Making good sense is the gold standard of the kind of enriched, integrative brain processing wherein emotion and cognition—with the help of that anterior cingulate bridge we discussed previously—are robustly linked.

Making good sense of your child's behavior, as well as your own, is a multistep process that is easier said then done. It takes more brain power and brain time to make really useful sense because our quick appraisal system—the one that can trigger our reactions in less than a 10th of a second—easily preempts our slower, higher thought processes and can commit us to judgment and action before we've even begun to use the higher parts of our brains to figure out what's really going on. We all tend to respond more quickly, with less use of our big prefrontal cortex, in very familiar relationships, such as the ones we have with our children and spouses/partners, than we do in most other relationships in our lives. Familiarity fosters a shorthand way of using our brains that is highly automatic, often literally *thoughtless*, typically not *careful* (full of care). We just don't use our brakes as readily at home as we do outside of home where we tend to be more careful and vigilant about the way we respond to people.

Although our home-based ways of using our brains with each other is efficient and can save a lot of energy, changing these patterns when change is needed takes a lot of mindful effort and care: Change requires the use of our executive capacity, the brain power we experience when we access the highest, most uniquely human parts of our brains. We need to access these higher brain regions in order to slow things down, practice the emotion regulation processes described in the last chapter, and spend more time thinking, reflecting, and being curious about what is going on in our relationship with our children. Trying to change well-worn patterns of parental behavior and meaning making is not a task to be taken lightly. Let's take a look at the process of meaning making and how it relates to the way you are using your brain—to the brain state you are in when you are trying to make sense of your kids' behavior.

Meaning and Your Brain: Three States, Three Kinds of Meaning

The meaning we derive from our experiences depends on how we are using our brains, both at the time of the experience and later, when we are reviewing or reflecting on that experience (if we get to that point of taking a second or third look). We make different meaning or sense of things depending on which of three states we are in, as described in Chapter 1 and based on Porges's (2011) polyvagal model of our nervous system: (1) the open-minded, socially engaged state; (2) the mobilized defensive state of fight or flight; and (3) the immobilized-with-fear state. Let's look at the three kinds of meaning that these states produce.

- *Open-minded meaning (smart vagal system "on")*: "Something is going on here that I need to understand. This isn't the 'same old, same old' that my child is showing me. I'll hold back my urge to react and spend a little time being curious here."

- *Mobilized defensive meaning (sympathetic fight–flight system "on")*: "My child is disrespecting me and I'm not going to stand for it. I need to defend my role as parent and show him who's in charge here!"
- *Immobilized defensive meaning (lower, more primitive vagal system "on")*: "Oh no! This is really bad. Nothing I can do. I'm dying here! I'm not really here and this isn't really happening!"

The meaning we make determines the action we take. And, in a circular fashion, the action we take affects the meaning we make and our relationship with our child. In our open-minded state, we don't go with our fastest, first appraisal reaction because this is the work of that neuroception process we described in Chapter 1, the process wherein our right-brain amygdala can put a spin on what's going on in much less time than it takes for us to really think about what's going on. Remember, your amygdala on the right side of your brain can detect a "possible threat" in about 100 milliseconds, a 10th of a second. In most dealings with your child you can probably afford to take another 300–500 milliseconds to process the situation a bit more before you really need to do something.

So, in open mind, I let these "first responder" moments pass, maybe noticing them, calling them what they are ("false alarms," etc.), and keeping my mind open to process the information more fully before I go to "output," to action—kind of like waiting to send that e-mail I wrote in the heat of the moment and giving myself more time to reflect on what is really going on and what would be best to do about it before hitting that *Send* button). This is why we put the chapter on emotion regulation before this one on making sense. You have to use your brakes on your "quick responder" system to allow both the emotional moment and the impulse to act on that emotion pass if you are going to give your big thinking brain, your prefrontal cortex, time to do more work and make better sense of what is going on. Hopefully, only a few moments in life actually require that we act within less than half a second to deal effectively with a situation.

Making better sense of your child's behavior may involve a shift in your perspective on parenting, especially if you have been parenting with a stressed-out brain. Remember how stress can make you "simplistic," reacting with one of your quick self-defense systems and using mostly reflexive reactions to your child, rather than more thoughtful responses based on more reflection? If you have been accustomed to making sense of your child's behavior using your defense systems, as described above, you are used to making sense very quickly and automatically, without really using your big brain as fully as you could if you could slow down and give yourself the luxury of more time, more brain time, to construct better, more useful meaning. So, making better sense may mean a shift in your approach from a mostly behavioral focus to a relationship focus, a focus on understanding your child's behavior more before you decide how to respond. This involves using more of your parenting brain and less of your defensive, stressed-out brain.

The fact that you are reading these words means that you are already at least considering making some changes in how you are going about being a parent. You are brave enough to be willing to rethink your role as a parent, and this is a huge step, one that already represents a change in the way you are using your brain. If you are giving this book a chance to change your mind about some things you haven't questioned before, you are already cooking with gas; you have already activated your prefrontal cortex, awakening your powers of reflection.

The shift in thinking about parenting that we are proposing represents a shift from judging and reacting to your child's behavior to understanding his or her mind better. The best way to deepen that understanding is for you to have a more open and engaged relationship with your child, to open your brain and heart and ears to your child in ways that maybe you haven't been able to do in a very long time, or maybe have never been able to do. Based on our clinical experience, our understanding of the parenting brain, and the growing body of research about what kids need from us in order to thrive and not just survive, we believe that making the shift from a behavioral perspective to a relational perspective can change the way you feel about your children, strengthen your connections with them, and help them learn the things you've been trying to teach them.

To make this shift in your parenting, we want to help you turn on the highest regions of your brain, the parts in the middle and near the top of your frontal lobe, the regions called the middle prefrontal cortex and the dorsolateral prefrontal cortex. These are the most uniquely human regions of your brain, and if you've been stressed out for a while, you may not have been using them very much. You may have been using the lower region of your prefrontal cortex, your orbital region just above your eyes, to react to your child's behavior, to put the brakes on some of your frustration or resentment, and to try to figure out what rewards and consequences would work better to change his or her behavior. But you have probably not been moving up much higher in your big brain to those regions of your prefrontal cortex that lie above the orbital region: your middle prefrontal cortex, which can help you attune more deeply to your child's mind (to *mentalize*) and your dorsolateral prefrontal cortex, the topmost region that can help you think more deeply about your relationship with your child and come up with ideas and plans about how to really make it better (Fonagy, Gergely, Jurist & Target, 2002).

This kind of attunement, reflection, and "relational thinking" is pretty heavy lifting in brain terms and requires the use of these more complex regions of your brain, the last ones to mature and the first to shut down on you when you are experiencing too much stress. You need to wake up these higher regions in order to shift your mind from thinking about your child in a "me versus him" mode to a "we" mode (Siegel, 2010) of "we're in this together." When you start to make this shift and literally to "change your mind" about your relationship with your child—now understanding his behavior within the context of your relationship—you are getting ready to do the essential attachment-focused work with your child that can repair your relationship, help you to really get to know him or her, and get on with your lives together in a much more fulfilling way.

Making sense of your children's behavior, and your own, is not simply a cognitive process consisting of accumulating the facts associated with a behavioral event and then, in the fashion of a judge, deciding what happened, what were the mitigating circumstances, and what is the most appropriate consequence. Such knowledge is limited and does not extend our awareness into the human realities of our children's experiences and our relationships with them. The value of emotion regulation that we discussed in the last chapter is not simply to prevent our emotions from becoming dysregulated. The value is to increase the depth and scope of our minds, broadening our awareness to include an awareness of our children in relationship with us, the attuned awareness of our children's inner lives, and an openness to understanding them without judgment. Making better, richer sense includes "walking a mile" in our children's shoes in order to experience empathy for their experience.

For these reasons, the more cognitive regions of the prefrontal cortex need the input from the deeper regions of our brains, our affective core. This is where that anterior cingulate brain bridge needs to do its thing, linking your lower limbic system (your emotional brain) to your higher thinking brain system, so that you can "feel and deal" effectively. (The prefrontal cortex also needs the help of your insula, your visceral brain, which gives you an intuitive sense of a situation in order to attune more deeply and immediately to your children's states.)

Thus, emotion regulation, once it is established, has not completed its job. It is not inactive during the more cognitive process of making sense. This is really an interpersonal neurobiological process that begins with affect regulation and progresses to a linking of affect regulation with better meaning making, with cognitive processes that are being "informed" by regulated emotion and their affective expression. This is an integrative process that gets to the place that cognitive–behavioral interventions are intended to go. But this brain-based intervention model does it more effectively by incorporating the way the brain works: by honoring the limbic system and its contribution to intersubjective learning when it is both regulated and available to provide intuitive and empathic awareness of our children's worlds.

The effective regulation of our emotions represents the first step in a multistep process of creating new ways of viewing and understanding the parenting process. Once established, emotion regulation pathways create a readiness for integrative functioning within your brain as well as better connections with your children's brains (i.e., *interpersonal neurobiology*). With regulated affect, you can more readily activate the core parenting systems that we have been stressing. If parents become engaged in trying to make sense of their children's functioning, they will experience the desire to approach their children and get closer to them via an engaged dialogue (Parental Approach System) and to enjoy the interaction more (Parental Reward System). They are also likely to have a deeper interest in their children (Parental Child-Reading System and mentalization) and to see the deeper meanings in their interactions and in whatever behaviors are occurring (Parental Meaning-Making System). With regulated affect, the integrative functioning of the brain (Parental Executive System) is more effective, with all areas of the prefrontal cortex becoming involved, often with the aid of the anterior cingulate.

When you start relating to your children in this open-minded way, you will have different kinds of experiences with them than you have when you are stressed out. These new experiences of being curious and listening more empathically to children will give you "new food for thought," new information with which to create new meaning. So the quality of meaning you make depends both on your state of mind and on the kinds of interactions you are having with your child, the kind of material you have to work with when you create your narrative or "story" about being a parent. When your child is feeling more liked, seen, and heard—feeling safer to come close to you and share more of his or her inner self with you, to be "more real"—you will accumulate some great raw material for editing your old, more negative story about being a parent. By learning more about who your child really is, and is becoming, you expand your mind—you literally create more pathways in your brain—for holding your child in your thoughts and "playing" with those thoughts of him or her. Slowing down the way you use your brain in your relationship with your child allows for some good "slow-cooked" meaning, a more creative and satisfying kind of storytelling. Now you and your child are able to openly communicate with each other in a manner that makes you both receptive to being influenced by the thoughts and wishes of the other. Your mutually regulated emotional states foster slower, deeper, richer "co-construction" of meaning, the kind of meaning making that stimulates reflection and makes you want to revisit the events of the day and savor at least some of them. Now it feels safer to revisit these places in your mind and put them in your mental workspace, your "working memory," to reappraise them and to integrate them into your autobiographical memory system, your memories of living in connection with your child through joyful times and harder times.

Reflective Functioning

Parents (and children too) are best able to make sense of a situation when they engage in reflective functioning. This is a unique form of mental activity wherein the focus is on the inner life of self and other. Such a broad cognitive focus is the most successful when it occurs within the open, intersubjective space that we have been describing. Seeing the big picture entails making sense of current events and behaviors in the context of the family history and goals and the interrelated and independent stories of all members of the family. In understanding the inner lives of self and other, the whole brain needs to be functioning and integrative. Imagine that an eight-year-old boy steals from his mother on the second day of school, after getting into trouble for fighting with his sister, shortly before his mother leaves on a business trip. To know the meaning of his stealing, it might well be necessary to have an understanding of his relationships with both of his parents and his sister, his school history, his history of fighting and stealing, and how he acted in the past when he was separated from his mother.

Also, the emotional tone of the understanding contributes to its deeper meaning. In order to understand another's inner life, it is crucial that a person be aware of, and responsive to, the nonverbal communications of the other. This awareness, which is outside of one's conscious focus, often emerges from the attuned, resonating, nonverbal, reciprocal communications that occur rapidly between one person and the other. Affective–reflective dialogue, described in the last chapter, is ideally suited for facilitating reflective functioning for both parents and children.

Reflective functioning in relation to yourself as a parent requires an openness toward, and acceptance of, your parent-related memories, thoughts, emotions, intentions, wishes, perceptions, judgments, and values. When aspects of your inner life are associated with shame or terror, rage or despair, it is unlikely that you will direct your attention to them. To the extent that parents or children are able to be aware of and accept their inner lives, they will have a greater sense of safety and be more likely to understand the meaning of their specific thoughts, emotions, and wishes. They will understand how these relate to their history as well as the present situation. With good reflective functioning, parents will be likely to understand why they reacted with anger toward their child when he or she did something that usually does not bother them.

Reflective functioning in relation to your children requires the same open space, or acceptance, of whatever features of their inner lives are being expressed by their behavior. A distinction to note: Although the *behavior* might be evaluated, the *inner life* features that influenced the behavior are not. Such acceptance of the inner lives of your children is certainly enhanced through love and, in turn, facilitates the deepening of your love for them. When parents do not experience an active love for their children any longer, their ability to reflect on them and their behavior will tend to be restricted to a negative, evaluative stance that does not include their children's perspectives.

Reflective functioning rests squarely on the foundation of emotional safety, both yours with your own thoughts and feelings, and your children's with being near you. When you feel safe enough to fully explore your own inner life and the impact that an event is having on you, then the full, richer meaning of that event is more likely to be understood.

Reflective functioning might include questions such as the following:

- Why did my son [daughter] do that?
- What did he want to accomplish?
- Is that important to him? If so, why?
- What does he think about what he did?
- Does his behavior mean anything with regard to how he sees our relationship?
- Did he see any negative consequences to what he did? If so, why did he still do it?
- If I set a limit about that behavior, what will he think is my motive?
- What is my motive for being concerned about it?
- Do I think that his behavior says something about me as parent, and if so, does that influence how I see it and deal with it?
- Is my response to his behavior influenced—for better or worse— by my own attachment history?
- How do I see that behavior as related to our relationship?
- If I really try to take his perspective, does that help me to understand what he did better?
- If I really take his perspective, does that help me to know how to best handle it?
- Am I open to understanding his perspective? If not, why not?

Reflective functioning does not consist of simply asking these questions in an analytical or judgmental way. It requires that as you explore the possible factors that are the context of the behavior—its meaning—that you accept these factors and not evaluate them. Your intention here is to understand, not judge. In this open, reflective mode, you turn the light of your curiosity on all possible factors, within your child and yourself, that might help you to understand the behavior better. There is no need to avoid thinking about certain possibilities. Your approach system is fully "on," enabling you to move toward and explore whatever is going on with your child. Both you and your child are safe with any of the emerging thoughts you both may have about the meaning of the behavior. There is no reason to experience shame for a thought, emotion, or wish. Reflective functioning also requires that you be open to your emotional responsiveness to your child as you are being curious and trying to understand the meaning of his or her behavior. The understanding that you are able to attain when you include your experience of empathy for your child and are engaged in open attunement with his or her experience is much richer and extends much further into the child's inner world than would occur if you took an evaluative, analytical, stance.

An Example of Reflective Functioning with Affective–Reflective Dialogue

Emily (mom) received a phone call from the school that her 16-year-old son Frank attends. She was told that Frank had yelled at his teacher in a manner that was seen as being very inappropriate. Emily believes that teachers ought to be treated with respect, and she also was confused as to why her son would mistreat his teacher. She sees him coming up the driveway and she meets him at the door.

Emily: Hi, Frank.
Frank: Hi, Mom.
Emily: Before you get ready to head out for your soccer game, after you get a snack, would you stop back here? I'd like to talk to you a bit.
Frank: What about?
Emily: I got a call from school.
Frank: They called you! Why don't they just let it drop!
Emily: Sounds like it's still bothering you!
Frank: Yeah, it is! I got in trouble for telling Mrs. Stephenson to back off. Why doesn't she get in trouble for nagging me so much?

Emily: Why don't you tell me about it.

Frank: She just doesn't stop! She says that I've got to study more! And more! And more!

Emily: I don't understand, Son. I thought that you were doing well in her class.

Frank: I am! So it doesn't seem that it's any of her business if I don't do great on the college exams.

Emily: What do you mean?

Frank: She got me this book to study for the college exams and wants me to go over it with her after school. When I thanked her but said that I've got a lot going on after school and don't have the time to stay, she said that she wanted me to do a chapter at home twice a week and she'd ask me questions about it during my recess. I again said, that I'd pass—I've got a lot going on.

Emily: She wanted to help you get ready for the college exams—and you thanked her but said that you'll manage on your own? Is that right?

Frank: Yeah. Eveything was cool, if she'd have just let it rest at that.

Emily: So then what happened?

Frank: She got annoyed and said that I wasn't taking it seriously enough. It would have big implications for my future.

Emily: And then?

Frank: When I still said that I wasn't interested, she said that she was disappointed in me and that if I wanted her to be proud of me, I'd better do what she wanted.

Emily: And you said . . .

Frank: Well, that's where I lost it a bit. I kinda told her I really didn't care.

Emily: In those words?

Frank: That I didn't give a shit if she was proud of me or not.

Emily: Ah, now I understand better, Frank. Thanks for letting me know. So why do you think that you lost it and said that? What was going on for you right then?

Frank: She didn't seem to have a right to say that! I'm doing fine in her class. I get good grades and don't cause her any grief.

Emily: So it seems to you that she should be fine with you . . . or proud of you already.

Frank: Yeah! Why should she pull that on me? I should be able to say how much studying I want to do for the exams without her judging me like that if I'm not doing everything that she wants me to do. It has nothing to do with her class!

Emily: I hear you saying that you would have been OK if she'd pushed you about her class, but this seemed like it was too much pushing about something that was your call.

Frank: Yeah, mom, it doesn't seem right! Saying that she's disappointed in me, that she won't be proud of me. You never talk to me like that! Maybe you'd have a right to say those things, I don't know, but I do know that she doesn't.

Emily: I see why this was so hard for you. I see you as someone who tries to handle his responsibilities and really does quite well. I think that you're proud of the job you do at school and of the relationships you have with your teachers . . .

Frank: Yeah, I am. And it's like none of that matters to her.

Emily: And you're right. I might say that I'm disappointed or not proud of something that you do, but never that I'm disappointed in *you*, or not proud of *you* . . .

Frank: So why did she say that?

Emily: What do you think?

Frank: Seemed like a power trip.

Emily: Maybe. Does she seem that way to you—that she likes to use power over the students?

Frank: No, she doesn't. And that's why it seemed so unfair. I thought that we had a good relationship and that she liked me and what I do in her class.

Emily: Then why do you think she said that?

Frank: Wants me to do well? Thought that would motivate me to try harder?

Emily: Do you think?

Frank: Maybe. But she really has a poor way of showing it!

Emily: So you're saying that if she wanted to help you, she might have done it differently or said it differently. She gave you that book to help, I'd guess, not to have power over you.

Frank: Yeah, and that was really nice. But why pull out that "disappointed" and "not proud" stuff?

Emily: I don't know, Frank. Maybe she felt that she was giving you a gift and you were not appreciating it. And she is trying hard to help and, to her, you don't seem to care.

Frank: But I did feel good about it! If she had just left it alone.

Emily: Then you would not have said "I don't give a shit!"

Frank: So they told you what I said?

Emily: Yeah, they did.

Frank: Are you disappointed in me now?

Emily: No, Frank, not in you. Never in you.

Frank: Maybe in what I said?

Emily: That's right. Are you OK that I wish you hadn't said that?

Frank: I guess. I guess I wish that I hadn't either.

Emily: Any thoughts about what you might do about it?

Frank: Tell Mrs. Stephenson that I'm sorry.

Emily: That would be hard, I'd bet.

Frank: Yeah, it would. But I shouldn't have said that to her. And maybe I could ask her if I could borrow her book and maybe study it some on the weekends when I have extra time.

Emily: My guess is that she'd like that. And like that you worked it out with her.

Frank: Yeah, she probably would.

Emily: Frank . . . I'm always proud of you. And now I'm proud of how you're handling this. You made a mistake, you admit it, and you're fixing it. I like how you're handling this.

Frank: Thanks, Mom. Now I got to handle my friends. The word got around what I said to Mrs. Stephenson, and I think they're going to really try to jerk me around about it.

Emily: I bet they do. And if they do . . . you're going to say to them . . .
Frank: Don't worry, mom. You won't get any phone calls about it!

Such a dialogue is realistic when parents engage their children with an open, accepting, curious, and empathic attitude. This kind of attitude reduces defensiveness in children and fosters their readiness—and ability—to explore their inner lives. When your children know that you just want to understand what is going on, and that they will not be judged for what they say to you, they are more likely to be open and honest about what they are thinking, feeling, and wanting. Then, through such a dialogue, their decisions about their past or future behaviors are likely to be more productive and appropriate. Such dialogues help both you and your children make more sense of what happened and develop your reflective functioning skills. And you are both making your brains better and healthier in the process.

In contrast to that dialogue is one in which stressed-out parents have already evaluated their children's behavior and found it to be wrong. These parents are likely to have made negative assumptions about their children's thoughts, emotions, and motives that led to the behavior (e.g., "You always want your own way," "You are being selfish," "You shouldn't be jealous of your brother's success"). Such assumptions about children's inner lives lead to parents demanding to know "why" their children behaved as they did, with the expectation that their children will acknowledge their inappropriate motives. If their children do not agree that the parents' negative assumptions are valid, the parents then accuse the children of being defensive and unwilling to "own up" to their faults.

This second dialogue seldom leads to productive understanding about the event being explored. There is little openness to discovering together what it means. An even greater worry is that these judgmental, fault-finding examinations lead to greater secrecy by children, leaving parents even less aware of their children's inner lives. Stress-based interactions also lead to reduced relationship repair after a conflict. Rather than parents and children ending the discussion with a quick smile and maybe even a hug over their joint efforts to understand and resolve an issue, they are likely to go their separate ways, each resenting the behaviors of the other, each feeling defensive over their stance, neither feeling understood. This creates emotional distance in the relationship. Eventually, parents and children agree to "forget" what happened and get back to normal. This new "normal," sadly, contains less openness, laughter, sharing, and desire to be together than existed prior to the conflict. When this sequence becomes a repetitive pattern, the relationship is likely to offer partners few reasons for seeking each other out for "comfort and joy."

Mindfulness

The rapidly growing interest within the mental health field in the centuries-old practice of mindfulness offers a deeper understanding of reflective functioning and ways to facilitate it. Recent brain-imaging studies of the effects of mindfulness practices on our brains have added a whole new dimension to this interest, showing that this "mindfulness stuff" has real substance, that there is a scientific basis to its beneficial effects on our functioning (Tang, Lu, Geng, et al., 2010; Posner, Sheese, Odludas, & Tang, 2006). Even more exciting for those of us interested in parenting is new neuroscientific evidence of strong links between mindulness and sensitive, attuned parenting (Fleming, Gonzalez, Afonso, & Lovic, 2008). This line of research strongly suggests that mindfulness practices, including reflective thinking, can strengthen brain processes that are important to parenting.

Definitions of mindfulness are varied, but they consistently focus on the person's open acceptance of the here-and-now experience, focusing on it without judgment, evaluation, or efforts to change it. Within such acceptance the individual goes deeper into the present moment, trying to experience it, understand it more fully, and to especially experience what is unique about it, what lies under the concept of a tree, person, or the sound of a bird singing. A person is open to whatever is present in the here-and-now moment, being influenced by it, flexibly responding to it in a manner congruent with the person's narrative. A person in a mindful state is not standing against, in opposition to, the event or object in the present. Rather the distinction between self and other, inside the person and outside the person, is blurred, and in fact, is itself a concept that is gently set aside in the mindful experience. There is a reciprocal influence, a back-and-forth flow of energy and openness between the "self" and "other."

- Dan Siegel summarizes our understanding of mindfulness by describing it as "being aware, on purpose and nonjudgmentally, of what is happening as it is happening in the present moment" (2010, p. xxv).
- Tara Brach defines mindfulness as "the quality of awareness that recognizes exactly what is happening in our moment-to-moment experience" (2003, p. 27).
- James Austin tries to capture the one-of-a-kind nature of mindful awareness when he speaks of "being mindfully attuned to the fresh individuality of each present moment as it evolves into the next one, and then the next one" (2006, p. 237).
- One aspect of this mindful awareness that is focused on someone you love, is known as loving-kindness, blending mindfulness into the experience of the relationship itself (see Jon Kabat-Zinn [2005] on lovingkindness meditation).

It is not surprising that mindfulness involves the very areas of the brain that are involved in the brain-based parenting that we have been advocating. This finding supports Daniel Siegel's (2010) contention that we can improve our capacity for compassion and intersubjectivity in two ways: (1) *inter*personally, by practicing being openly engaged and empathic with another person, and (2) *intra*personally, through practicing mindfulness in ways that enhance our ability to let go of judgmental processes and stay more "present."

Brain-imaging studies are showing that meditation can change the brain and that the changes occur in regions of the brain that are associated with empathy and attunement—that is, with being very attentive to your own or another person's unfolding experience. Expert meditators show high levels of prefrontal activity, especially in the very highest regions, combined with very low levels of limbic activity. In other words, the brains of these long-time meditators look quiet and alert (Cahn & Polich, 2006; Davidson, Kabat-Zinn, Schumacher, et al., 2003; Fehmi & Robbins, 2007; Lazar, Kerr, Wasserman, et al., 2005). Even newcomers to meditation, though, appear to be able to change their brains, fostering growth in the regions that are considered to be part of the "executive attention network," including the upper part of the anterior cingulate and part of the medial prefrontal cortex that is known to be associated with mentalizing and empathic awareness (Tang et al., 2010).

Mindfulness, Parenting, and PACE

Mindfulness, then, is essentially a process of turning our attention to the present moment more fully than we ordinarily do. It involves strengthening our ability to bring our attention into the present, to suspend the usual processes we use to make quick appraisals and rapid judgments, and to enable our brains to slow down and take a longer, deeper look at what is right in front of us now, what we are actually experiencing right now.

Children are exquisitely aware of their parents' attention and where it is being directed. Even babies track their parents' gazes and react if a parent looks away and breaks eye contact. Maybe you've had the experience of your child demanding your attention when you are talking on the phone, when the moment before he or she was playing contentendly, apparently oblivious to whether you were paying attention or not. Children know instinctively whether or not we are paying attention to them.

When we are stressed out, children may draw our attention mostly by doing something annoying or by not doing something we need them to do. This kind of parental attention is very different from the kind of attention we pay when we are tuning in to what our child is saying or doing, with the intention to understand and to be with him or her in the moment, not distracted, not multitasking, not paying attention reluctantly or in anger. This "mindful" form of parental attention feels very different to children than those other kinds of attention, the annoyed kind or the distracted kind. Being the object of mindful attention makes children feel "seen" and cared about much more than the other kinds of attention.

This is why there is a strong connection between a parent's mindfulness and the quality of the parent–child interactions. Mindful attention promotes intersubjectivity and interpersonal "resonance"— mutual feelings of being in connection. Improving your ability to pay attention in this deeper way, then, can be extremely helpful to your relationship with your child (Atkinson et al., 2005).

Mindfulness facilitates reflective functioning in that it moves the mind of the individual into the core experience of the present event, without assumptions or judgments. It suspends our values, beliefs, or biases as to what is right or wrong, appropriate or inappropriate, good or bad. The value of mindfulness for reflective parenting is that it facilitates clear awareness and understanding. It creates an openness that enables parents to be receptive to whatever is present, rather than channeling their attention to areas of awareness that involve evaluations. A mindful awareness enables parents to be deeply aware of the thoughts, emotions, and wishes of their children. Such an awareness is invaluable in deepening parents' knowledge of their children and their relationship with those children.

Mindfulness also is crucial if parents want to know how best to evaluate a given behavior, and what, if any, consequences might be of value in influencing that behavior in the future. Being aware of how a behavior emerged from your child's world is likely to be the best way to know how to respond to that behavior. For many valuable insights into various ways of joining mindfulness with parenting, consider reading *Everyday Blessings: The Inner Work of Mindful Parenting*, by Myla and Jon Kabat-Zinn (1997).

PACE is a beneficial attitude to assume in developing a mindful approach to parenting. When PACE permeates parents' interactions with their children, it fosters and nourishes the same mindful attitude within the children. PACE creates this mindful awareness by virtue of its components:

• *Playfulness.* A lightness of experience and an openness to possibility and meaning are inherent in playfulness. Without this lightness, parents are more likely to adopt a very serious stance in which they cling to one way of looking at an event and responding to it. When children experience their parents' light manner of addressing an event, they are likely to feel safer, knowing that their parents are able to explore the event within the larger context—including their relationship—which is more important than the event.

• *Acceptance.* By removing judgment from experience, parents are more open to fully and deeply understanding a given experience. Within the context of acceptance, this deeper awareness enables parents to discover the best response to a given child behavior. Children, when experiencing their parents' acceptance, are also more likely to accept the event that occurred and its meaning to them, and to participate more safely in the act of understanding it and in changing their behavior if needed.

• *Curiosity.* Within the clear awareness of the present experience, parents are then able to adopt a not-knowing approach to its meaning. Their intent is to understand, not judge, their children's experiences. They are engaged in an act of exploration to discover which aspects of their children's inner lives led to their behavior. In a mindset of curiosity, parents intend to experience their children's perspectives of the immediate situation, and in so doing, they are able to understand the situation in a way that respects their children's perspectives. The children, when experiencing their parents' open interest in, and desire to understand, their experiences and perspectives, are more likely to explore their own inner lives alongside their parents with the same open, nondefensive attitude. With curiosity, parents are fascinated with their children and their world.

• *Empathy.* This clear awareness of their children's experience of a situation or event, when associated with an attitude of loving-kindness and compassion, enables the best possible, flexible response to their children's behavior. The children, experiencing their parents' loving-kindness and compassion, are likely to feel safe and to be much more open when their parents focus on some sensitive issue that concerns them. The children are less likely to become defensive and more likely to explore the meaning of their behavior with their parents. When parents initiate a dialogue about an area of concern, bringing an empathic stance into the interaction, children are likely to feel that their parents want to understand and help them rather than devalue, criticize, or change them.

Reflective Functioning in the Therapy Room

In the preceding chapter we explored how therapists need to be aware that parents seeking treatment for concerns with their children are likely to be experiencing intense negative emotions about themselves, their children, their relationship, and the entire parental experience. From that awareness, the therapist needs to co-regulate these negative emotional experiences before addressing the particular content associated with such states. Once their negative emotions are regulated, parents are likely to be more open to the task of making sense of the past and present family difficulties through developing and enhancing their reflective functioning. Such reflective functioning is crucial to the sensitive, high-quality parenting that we are proposing as a realistic therapeutic goal. Such functioning is crucial in efforts to reduce blocked care and to activate the brain systems that are necessary for this level of parenting.

When parents are experiencing blocked care, they are most likely in a defensive mental state wherein their focus is on the "badness" of their children's behavior, not on making sense of the behavior. They want the behavior to stop, plain and simple. They consider behavioral change as the solution to their stress and the condition for any return to a sense of psychological safety within their home. Such a behavioral focus tends to lead parents toward a heightened focus on consequences, whether changing the consequences given for specific behaviors or making the current consequences bigger. When the solution to the problem involves such a narrow focus, it is no wonder that parents find themselves trapped. They exclaim, often in desperation: *"If I let him get away with it, he'll never stop what he's doing!"*

This is followed by: *"I know that taking away his [privileges, playing sports, going out in the evening, favorite game, bike, etc.] seems harsh, but what else can I do? He can't get away with it!"*

Along with that comment is often: *"He's so mad about what I've done. But can't he see that he's brought it on himself?"*

Finally, the parent is likely to say: *"I just don't enjoy parenting anymore. We never talk, or laugh, or share things like we used to. But I don't know what else to do."*

Such comments, in the context of increasing spirals of behaviors and consequences, often only find temporary relief when the therapist focuses primarily on refining the consequences through behavioral analysis, making them more positive rather than negative, and negotiating (with the parents in control of the deck of cards) new contracts with the children. Continuing to focus on children's unwanted behaviors and parents' responses in terms of behavioral consequences often proves to be insufficient for the following reasons:

1. Blocked care is not addressed, making it difficult for parents to change their own behaviors sufficiently to maintain changes in their children's behaviors.
2. Insufficient attention is given to increasing the parents' approach, reward, child-reading, and meaning-making systems. Parenting remains a job, even a tedious or dreaded job, not the development of a deeply reciprocal parent–child relationship.
3. Parents remain in a defensive, evaluative state rather than in the open, engaged, accepting state that tends to have the greatest positive influence on the parent–child relationship. In brain terms, parents are not maintaining good vagal tone. The lower

vagal circuit remains active rather than the upper "smart" vagal circuit.

4. The lack of activation of the child-reading system impedes parents' ability to make sense of their children's behavior.

5. All of the above suggest that the parents' reflective functioning is not sufficiently engaged to ensure that they are able to see and succeed with the big picture—the parent–child relationship—within which the little picture—children's behaviors—has both its meaning and its solution. In short, reflective functioning creates the understanding of the need for "correction within connection" and also that "connection precedes correction."

Once parents have shifted out of the defensive state of mind, which is highly influenced by the amygdala and limbic system, and into the open, engaged, smart vagal state, it becomes possible to access the higher regions of the prefrontal cortex that are needed for reappraisal and for "making new sense" of their relationships with their children, and for accessing the deeper meaning of their role as parents. PACE is a way of engaging parents' right-brain defense system first and then linking it to the therapist's open, engaged, right brain, thereby helping parents to disengage from their protective stance and shift into engagement. Then, by maintaining the PACE process, the ongoing affective–reflective dialogue opens connections in parents' brains between both the right and left hemispheres and also between the lower affect regulation system that connects the orbital prefrontal cortex and lower anterior cingulate regions to the limbic system and the higher flexible, reflective processes that depend upon the middle prefrontal cortex and the dorsolateral prefrontal cortex.

Example: Earlier we gave an example of a parent, Emily, who managed to have an affective–reflective dialogue with her 16-year-old son Frank. Frank had yelled at his teacher, and Emily was able to help both her son and herself make sense of the event and discover what he might do about it. Let's now imagine that Emily had not been able to reflect on her son's behavior. Instead she became judgmental and defensive and expressed her anger about it to a therapist for whom she sought help in deciding what to do about the behavior.

Mom: When I heard what he said to the teacher, I was waiting for him to get home from school, and when he walked through the door I let him have it!

Therapist: What did you say?

Mom: I let him know that what he did was unacceptable, that he would apologize to his teacher tomorrow, and that he was going to have some consequences for what he did that will make him think twice about being so disrespectful again.

Therapist: And how did he respond?

Mom: He got angry with me for not letting him tell his side! I let him know there was no side when he talked that way to his teacher! I didn't want any excuses!

Therapist: And he . . .

Mom: He screamed "Whatever!" and headed for his room. And I let him know that talking to me that way would just make it worse for him.

Therapist: So, that was difficult for you . . . and for him. What do you think bothered you the most about it?

Mom: That he would talk that way to a teacher. He actually said to her that he did not "give a shit" about what she thought! I taught him better than to talk like that to an adult—any adult—and he says it to his teacher! Someone whom he should really respect.

Therapist: I think that you're saying that it's very important to you that your son respect his teacher, and it bothered you a lot that he said that to her.

Mom: Are you saying that I shouldn't have gotten upset about that?

Therapist: I'm sorry, Emily, if that's the impression that I gave you. I didn't mean that at all. I'm trying to understand what you were thinking and feeling when he walked in the door.

[When parents move into a defensive stance during the conversation, it is often helpful for the therapist to apologize for communicating in a manner that would elicit such a response. This is not about parents being "overly sensitive." If they experienced themselves as being judged by the therapist, then they are likely to re-engage without defensiveness *only if* the therapist is sorry for their sense of being blamed or judged poorly.]

Mom: You're right! It is important to me that he treats adults with respect.

Therapist: I think I understand. You raised Frank to know that respect is very important. What do you think was behind his comment to his teacher?

Mom: He's been acting more that way lately. Arguing a lot. Like he doesn't think he has to do what he's told to do. I think that he's just too full of himself lately.

Therapist: Any sense as to what that might be about? Arguing more, not accepting your authority so much, and maybe not accepting his teacher's authority too?

Mom: I don't know. Probably just that adolescent thing where he thinks he knows everything. His parents and teachers don't know anything. He never tells me what he's thinking, so I don't know.

Therapist: I see. So you think it may be adolescence. Do you think that is why he doesn't tell you anything too?

Mom: Probably. Aren't all adolescents that way?

Therapist: No. Though some certainly are. Do you wish that he'd talk to you more?

Mom: Of course I do. He used to talk all the time when he was a little kid. Even when he was around 13 or so. And then he just stopped. We used to be very close.

Therapist: Sounds like you wish that you two were close like that again.

Mom: I do. But I'm not going to let him get away with being disrespectful just so he'll talk with me.

Therapist: Oh, Emily, I'm sorry if I am giving you the impression that I think you should overlook what he said to the teacher. I don't mean that at all.

Mom: Then why do you keep talking about why he did it, what's he thinking, do I want him to talk more? He did what he did, and there is no excuse.

Therapist: I certainly am not looking to excuse him. I'm simply looking to understand it better and maybe to help you to figure out the best way to approach it. You're guessing that it is simply his adolescence, partly because he doesn't talk with you, so it is hard to know what he is thinking about why he did it.

Mom: Why isn't that searching for an excuse? Finding out why?

Therapist: It would only be an excuse if it meant he is not accountable for what he did. With knowing why, he is still accountable. But if we have the reason, it would help us in knowing what is the best response to it—how best to respond so that it doesn't happen again.

Mom: So how am I supposed to know if he won't talk to me?

Therapist: Great question. We could guess. Especially if we knew of something that is happening in his life lately—with family, friends, activities. Easier, though, if he'd tell us what is going on . . . why he said that to his teacher and other things too.

Mom: He just won't say anything to me anymore.

Therapist: And you sound like you're sad about that.

Mom: I am! He's my son and we used to be so close!

Therapist: And if we could help to get that closeness back, maybe he wouldn't be so likely to talk like that with his teacher.

Mom: So it's my fault that he disrespected his teacher!

Therapist: Emily, I don't think that at all. I'm sorry if I gave that impression. I meant more that if he talked with you like he used to, maybe whatever was going on in him that led him to say that to his teacher—whatever that was, maybe he would have told you and you could have helped him to manage it better.

Mom: So how do I get him to talk to me?

Therapist: We can't make him talk, but maybe if we helped him to feel confident that whatever he says to us about his inner life won't be judged. He is safe in knowing that what he thinks or feels or wants will be accepted, not evaluated.

Mom: I'm going to need some help.

(*The therapist and Emily now discuss the value of Emily accepting her son's inner life and limiting her evaluations to his behaviors alone. Gradually she agrees that such dialogues were likely to help her son to speak with her more openly and to help them both make better sense of what was happening in his life.*)

Mom: So I think that you're saying I have to get back to the basics with Frank.

Therapist: Yes, getting to know his inner life again, from his perspective and with your mind holding on to your love for him and your confidence in who he really is, under the rude words that he used with his teacher.

Mom: I can do that, especially if you're willing to coach me a bit.

The brain-based research that we have referenced suggests that therapy would do well to combine the interpersonal and intrapersonal processes of empathy and mindfulness as robustly and intensively as possible. The therapist could incorporate these attributes through first facilitating the intersubjective experience of PACE within an affective–reflective dialogue and the resulting open engagement of parents' smart vagal system. This experience leads to the strengthening of the anterior cingulate/ insula regions, integrating areas of the prefrontal cortex and the amygdala, hippocampus, nucleus accumbens, and limbic system. Strengthening these pathways enhances the parents' abilities to focus attention, be mindfully aware of self and other, and experience empathy. From there the therapist might encourage specific mindfulness practices for parents as well as related attention and empathy training tasks.

Summary

Reflective functioning results from the full integration of the five brain systems that are central in providing the quality parenting that we are advocating in this book. With reflective functioning, parents are able to both engage their emotional responses to their child, and guide these responses so that they are influenced by the meanings of their joint behaviors and the immediate situation. Within reflective functioning both the minds and hearts (the inner lives) of parents are able to openly engage the minds and hearts of their children.

CHAPTER 7

Quick Review
Nine Strategies to Develop the Parenting Brain

We would now like to offer a brief summary of activities for parents to consider if they want to enhance their parenting based on the concepts that we have presented.

1. Feed Your Brain with PACE

Being highly social mammals, we were given the smart vagal system to use, so be smart and use it. That means, stay in the open and engaged stance when with your children, rather than sliding into the defensive, self-protective stance. That stance was given to us for tigers and bears, not for our children. OK, maybe not all the time, but try for more often than not every day and in every situation—easy when having fun, harder during conflict and discipline. What will help? PACE. Nothing works better for staying engaged in most situations, experiencing your child's world with thought and feeling, while remaining in an open and available state yourself, and all without losing your position as parent. What is especially nice is that when you approach your child with PACE, you immediately increase the likelihood that he or she will engage with you.

2. Befriend Your Amygdala

Since your amygdala is always trying to keep you safe by detecting even the slightest threat to your well-being, it is your friend even though it's a friend that can easily give you misleading, if well-intended, information. We call this misleading information "false alarms"—amygdaloid moments that make you start to play defense when there is really no threat that requires you to fight, flee, or hide. So, learn to hear your amygdala, to know when it has fired off a "warning" (you will feel it in your gut as your stomach drops or in your chest as your heart starts pumping faster), while also learning to take a "second look" at what is going on, using your big prefrontal cortex and that good old anterior cingulate bridge, before you really go into a defensive state of mind that will make you put up a wall between you and your child. It's always good to thank your amygdala for being so vigilant even when it is overdoing its job. It's also good to figure out whether you have a sleepy amygdala or a quick-reacting, kind of squirrel-like one that can keep you on high alert for danger. If you have a sleepy alarm system, you may need to learn to pay more attention to possible harmful things, and if you have the hyperactive alarm system, you would do well to learn to recognize a false alarm when you get one. Part of this process is a matter of good old genetics, since certain genes that you carry have a lot to do with how your amygdala works. The main thing is that you can learn to deal with your particular amygdala if you get to know it, appreciate it for what it does, and not take it to be the "voice of the truth."

3. Welcome the Elephants in Your Attachment History

While living with your parents as their child, you were learning how to be the parent of your child. You can see the wisdom of that sequence; it saves a lot of time and neural connections for learning new things that your parents did not know about, like smart phones and even microwaves. Our parents most likely were in the defensive, self-protective stance more than we would like to be, partly because basic survival was harder back then. As a result, our attachment history is likely to contain many elephants that we try to avoid, and when we can't avoid them, we defend against them.

These elephants are memories that exist in various regions of the cortex that, when activated and flashed to the prefrontal cortex and anterior cingulate to aid us in caregiving, they instead deactivate the smart vagal and make us defensive. Why? Because these memories are coated with fear, anger, discouragement, and shame, and these emotions—when associated with those memories—are hard to regulate. But we must remember them and regulate them. When there are no longer memories from our own attachment history that move us into shame and fear—and the resulting focus on our own self-protection—then we are less likely to move into self-protection when we enter similar experiences with our children. When we welcome the elephants—a welcoming that releases them to return to their homes (allows you to integrate your shameful and frightening memories)— we are developing what researchers call a *coherent autobiographical narrative* with respect to attachment relationships (Main, 2000). When this occurs for us as parents, we are more able to generate a similar narrative within our children's autobiographies. Even if we had a hard attachment history, we can still develop a coherent narrative—researchers call that *earned security* (Hesse, 2008) because we had to work at it. From this position of our own security, we are able to generate security for our child. Another way of saying this is that our smart vagal activates our children's smart vagal. Or when our elephants are welcomed and eventually leave, our children are less likely to be surprised by any elephants that would trample on their prefrontal cortex, anterior cingulate, hippocampus, and related regions.

4. Think with Your Heart and Feel with Your Mind

As we have said in a number of ways throughout this book, our brains work best when the activity of our more cognitive–reflective areas are integrated with our more emotional areas. Your emotions are less likely to take over and lead you to behaviors and words that you regret if you are able to tap into the reflective elements of your empathy for your children, your intuition about them, your history together combined with your attachment history, along with the larger meaning of what it is to you to be a parent.

When your reason fails to help you to decide how best to manage a situation, this time it is the emotional components of intuition, empathy, history, and meanings that will probably guide you to the best decision. What we have referred to as the bridge between the emotional and reflective—the anterior cingulate and insula—is actually where a lot of the action is. The more you know your children, the deeper you will love them. The more you love your children, the more comprehensive will be your knowledge of them.

5. Have a Friend or Two

It would be great if your partner were also your best friend and that you have one or two more. You want your friend to be someone you can, and do, turn to when you are struggling, and of course that works best if you are willing to aid your friend when he or she is struggling, too. When you experience the care of your friend, you will be more ready and able to care for your children again.

Just as important, though, is having a friend to laugh with and with whom you can share ideas and experiences. You also want your friend to discover who you truly are, which is deeper than any role you play. You need a friend who will discover the best in you and then remind you of your strengths, your helpfulness and openness, when you forget. Under the stress of raising your children, you will have doubts and move into shame at times. Your friend sees those times too and comforts you while also seeing your gifts and celebrating them.

6. Be Mindful

In suggesting that you be mindful, we are also suggesting that you be your own friend. Accept yourself and your child. Reflect on your experience and your children's experiences. Be fully present when with your children so that there is no doubt that they are in your mind and heart—and they will remain there when you are separate.

Be mindful, step back, and become aware of the big picture of your development as a parent, your hopes and dreams, and your children's development as their own unique persons. Be in awe of your children's individuality; discover that individuality and do not see only an ideal created in your mind.

7. Discover Your Children with Comfort and Joy

Yes, these are the "good tidings"! Comfort and joy—when experienced for and with your children—will facilitate their development and your relationships with them across all of the challenges, opportunities, ordeals, and celebrations that you are likely to encounter. Please remember what we have been saying about the primary way in which children learn about the social and emotional realities of their world: through reciprocal intersubjective experiences with their parents—you. These experiences of shared affect, joint awareness, and complementary intentions join your brain with their brains in such a way that your brain is influencing the development of the structure and functioning of their brains! Yes, your influence over the development of your child is profound, if you use your brain as it was designed. Be with them in their worlds and invite them to be with you in your world—openly and fully. They will want to learn from you.

8. Connect and Correct

Remember that your relationships with your children are the primary way that you will influence their development within the family today and throughout their lives. When your relationships are regularly characterized by intersubjective experiences of learning and shared meanings, your children will want to be like you (i.e., identify with you) and they will naturally lean toward your values, interests, and habits. When you specifically teach them something (i.e., provide discipline), they will be more receptive to your teaching, trusting its value and your good intent, even when they moan about a restriction that you are imposing.

Please remember that when you connect with your child after he or she did something that you had to correct, you are not "rewarding bad behavior"! Rather you are communicating that your relationship is more important than any behavioral conflict and that he or she is not the behavior. He is your son—she is your daughter—and your love is unconditional.

9. Tinker and Repair

Please remember that life goes on and that what worked yesterday may not work today. Being open means being receptive to what makes a given situation unique and responding in the best way possible to it. This level of nuanced responding requires flexibility, not a cookbook with a list of behaviors and consequences. This sort of tinkering with family situations and relationships requires that you fully use your dorsolateral prefrontal cortex and the valuable input that it is receiving from your anterior cingulate and insula and the other regions and systems that we mentioned. Trust all parts of your brain to know what is the best thing to do—now and here.

And you will make mistakes. You will. Please do. Not that we encourage that you deliberately make mistakes but rather that—since you will make them regardless—admit that to yourself and your children when you do. You do not lose authority when you apologize to your children for not using your brain well. You will gain authority because they will be impressed with your honesty and your willingness to acknowledge that you are not all-knowing and not always right.

And you will have conflicts with your children that cause disruptions in the relationships. These disruptions actually can deepen your relationships with your children and increase their sense of safety with you if you ensure that the disruptions are repaired. You're the parent, and it is your responsibility to see that the repair happens as soon as you are both ready and able—sooner rather than later is preferable. Be in your smart vagal stance and acknowledge the break, communicate PACE about it, invite your children to communicate their experience, bring in an apology if it fits, and reconnect as you move into your lives together again.

Summary

We truly hope that you will find this book to be helpful in your efforts to have the kinds of relationships that you want with your children, to participate in your children's development in ways that you want, and to experience the joy and meaning that parenting can provide. Your brain is designed to help you to achieve those goals—the full brain, working in integrated ways and working in concert with your child's brain. Yes, the news is that there is a Wi-Fi connection between your brain and your children's brains. For better or worse. We hope that we have increased your awareness of how this wireless connection—with its open, engaged, intuitive, empathic, reciprocal features—is capable of working. You have a brain designed for parenting. Take advantage of it.

Appendix
Seeking Help

You may decide to seek psychological treatment for your concerns regarding aspects of your children's functioning or your relationships with your children. You may have read books such as this one, spoken with family and friends, reflected on the difficulties on your own, and tried new ways of addressing these issues on your own. If your concerns remain, seeking professional services to assist you certainly makes sense.

It is our belief that family treatment be considered first regardless of the nature of the psychological difficulties demonstrated by your child (or children). These difficulties might be expressions of family relationship patterns that were present long before the problems began to manifest themselves. Even if the difficulties emerged outside the immediate family, the interventions of choice might well involve assisting your child to turn to you in making sense of his or her struggles and in assisting you in helping your child with whatever he or she presents. The family format also communicates to the child that whatever the difficulties are, his or her parents will be present and active in assisting him or her with them. The child is not alone with the difficulties, nor are those difficulties a sign that he or she is sick or deficient in some way. All are involved, all are in it together, and all will enjoy their resolution together.

It is possible that you and the therapist may decide that there is some value in giving the child the opportunity to speak with the therapist alone, at least once or more. Or the child may request this, and all involved may certainly think that his or her request might best be honored. However, the family format might still be available, and your presence or background support and availability might well communicate to your child your acceptance and involvement in whatever way is best.

As we've suggested in this work, our recommendation is that you and the therapist meet alone without the child at the onset of the professional interventions. This meeting will:

1. Enable you and the therapist to get to know each other and for you to feel safe with him or her while you share the intimate aspects of your family life.
2. Enable you to establish an open, engaged state rather than a defensive and self-protective one that you might have felt when you met the therapist for the first time.
3. Give you the opportunity to reflect on your strengths and vulnerabilities as a parent, and become willing and able to explore your own attachment history for connections with the current difficulties.
4. Enable you to discuss with the therapist the nature of the family therapy sessions, what the therapist's goals and interventions will be, and his or her expectations for you and your child.
5. Enable you to feel safe when your child is present so that you and the therapist together will be able to help your child to feel safe rather than defensive.

We believe that family therapy functions best when it is structured around the goal of having the family members engage in open, nonjudgmental, affective, and reflective communication wherein the experiences of all are shared with an attitude of PACE. If you are able to remain in an open, intersubjective stance, possibly with the assistance of the therapist, soon your child is likely to join you both in the same stance. It is best for you, as the parent, to assume the responsibility of maintaining this state. If your child's defensiveness is not met by a defensive reaction by you, nor a judgmental reaction by the therapist, it is likely that he or she will gradually become more open and self-disclosing. If your child's experience is met with acceptance, curiosity, and empathy, he or she will likely begin to view your experience in the same way, breaking cycles of defensiveness that may have been present for years.

This model of family treatment is based on attachment principles that emphasize the importance of parents providing both physical and psychological safety for their children. These principles are supported in many ways by the brain-based approach that we have spoken about throughout this work. Stephen Porges's (2011) emphasis on the need for safety to maintain the functioning of the social engagement process and the smart vagal system is one central example. However, we also have stressed that your safety, as a parent, is equally important since your parenting brain also works best when you feel safe. You need to know that the family therapist is not judging you. If you and your therapist differ, the therapist needs to be willing and able to ensure your sense of safety while maintaining his or her own sense of safety so that he or she does not become defensive and self-protective. You both will have to commit to addressing differences in an open, intersubjective manner rather than pretending that they are not there.

We also have certainly stressed our belief that your relationship with your children is central to their development and your own development as a parent. We have emphasized that being able to reflect on the meaning of your behaviors and your children's behaviors is likely to be central in the long-term development of your relationships and the functioning of your family. We would encourage you to avoid simply looking for a way to manage, change, or eliminate your children's problematic behaviors. This, we believe, is less likely to be a long-term solution than if you and your children work on understanding the meaning of the behaviors, while you develop and maintain your relationship with one another in good times and bad times.

References

Admon, R., Lubin, G., Stern, O., Rosenberg, K., Sela, L., Ben-Ami, H., et al. (2009). Human vulnerability to stress depends on amygdala's predisposition and hippocampal plasticity. *Proceedings of the National Academy of Sciences, 106*(33), 14120–14125.

Allman, J.M., Hakeem, A., Erwin, J., Nimchinsky, E., & Hof, P. (2001). The anterior cingulate cortex: The evolution of an interface between emotion and cognition. *Annals of the New York Academy of Sciences, 935,* 107–117.

Allman, J.M., Tetreault, N.A., Hakeem, A.Y., & Park, S. (2011). The von Economo neurons in apes and humans. *American Journal of Human Biology, 23,* 5–21.

Andari, E., Duhamel, J., Zalla, T., Herbrecht, E., Lebayer, M.,& Sirigu, A. (2010). Promoting social behavior with oxytocin in high-functioning autism spectrum disorders. *Proceedings of the National Academy of Sciences.* Published online before print February 16, 2010, doi: 10.1073/pnas. 0910249107 PNAS February 16, 2010.

Andersen, P., Morris, R., Amaral, D., Bliss, T., & O'Keefe, J. (Eds.). (2007). *The hippocampus book.* Oxford, UK: Oxford University Press.

Atkinson, L., Goldberg, S., Raval, V., Pederson, D., Benoit, D., Gleason, K., et al. (2005). On the relation between maternal state of mind and sensitivity in the prediction of infant attachment security. *Developmental Psychology, 41*, 42–53.

Atzil, S., Hendler, T., & Feldman, R. (2011). Specifying the neuro-biological basis of human attachment: Brain, hormones, and behavior in synchronous and intrusive mothers. *Neuropsychopharmacology.* Retrieved Sept. 9, 2011, from www.nature.com/npp/journal/vaop/ncurrent/full/npp2011172a.html.

Austin, J. H. (2006). *Zen-brain reflections.* Cambridge, MA: MIT Press.

Bales, K.L., & Carter, C.S. (2003). Sex differences and developmental effects of oxytocin on aggression and social behavior in prairie voles. *Hormones and Behavior, 44,* 178–184.

Banfield, J., Wyland, C., Macrae, C., Munte, T., & Heatherton, T. (2004). The cognitive neuroscience of self-regulation. In R. Baumeister & K. Vohs (Eds.), *Handbook of self-regulation* (pp. 62–83). New York, NY: Guilford Press.

Baron-Cohen, S. (2003). *The essential difference: The truth about the male and female brain.* New York: Basic Books.

Baynes, K. & Gazzaniga, M. (2000). Consciousness, introspection, and the split-brain: The two minds/one body problem. In M. Gazzaniga (Ed.), *The new cognitive neuroscience*, 2nd edition (pp.1355–1364), Cambridge, MA: MIT Press.

Beuregard, M., Levesque, J., & Bourgouin, P. (2001). Neural correlates of conscious self-regulation of emotion. *Journal of Neuroscience, 21*(RC165), 1–6.

Brach, T. (2003). *Radical acceptance: Embracing your life with the heart of a Buddha.* New York, NY: Bantam Books.

Bridges, R. (Ed.). (2008). *Neurobiology of the parental brain.* San Diego, CA: Academic Press.

Cahn, B. & Polich, J. (2006). Meditation states and traits: EEG, ERP, and neuroimaging studies. *Psychological Bulletin, 132*(2), 180–2111.

Canli, T., Qui, M., Omura, K., Congdon, E., Haas, B.W., Amin, Z., et al. (2006). Neural correlates of epigenesis. *Proceedings of the National Academy of Sciences, 103,* 16033–16038.

Carr, L., Iacoboni, M., Dubeau, M.C., Maziotta, J.C., & Lenzi, L.G. (2003). Neural mechanisms of empathy in humans: A relay from neural systems for imitation to limbic areas. *Proceedings of the National Academy of Sciences, 100,* 5497–5502.

Carter, C.S. (2007). Neuropeptides and the protective effects of social bonds. In E. Harmon-Jones & P. Winkielman (Eds.), *Social neuroscience* (pp. 425–438). New York, NY: Guilford Press.

Carter, C.S. & Keverne, E.B. (2002). The neurobiology of social affiliation and pair bonding. In D. Pfaff (Ed.), *Hormones, brain, and behavior, Volume 1* (pp. 299–337). San Diego, CA: Academic Press.

Cassidy, J., & Shaver, P.R. (Eds.). (2011). *Handbook of attachment: Theory, research, and clinical applications,* 2nd Ed. New York, NY: Guilford Press.

Champagne, F. (2008). Maternal influence on offspring reproductive behavior: Implications for transgenerational effects. In R. Bridges (Ed.), *Neurobiology of the parental brain* (pp. 307–318). San Diego, CA: Academic Press.

Cohen, R., Grieve, S., Hoth, K., Paul, R., Sweet, L., Tate, D., et al. (2006). Early life stress and morphometry of the adult anterior cingulate cortex and caudate nuclei. *Biological Psychiatry, 59,* 975–982.

Corter, C., & Fleming, A. (2002). Psychobiology of maternal behavior in human beings. In M. Bornstein (Ed.), *Handbook of parenting: Biology and ecology of parenting* (pp. 141–182). Mahwah, NJ: Erlbaum.

Cozolino, L. (2006). *The neuroscience of human relationships.* New York: Norton.

Craig, A.D. (2009). How do you feel now?: The anterior insula and human awareness. *Nature Reviews Neuroscience, 10,* 59–70.

Cushing, B.S., & Kramer, K.M. (2005). Mechanisms underlying epigenetic effects of early social experience: The role of neuropeptides and steroids. *Neuroscience and Biobehavioral Reviews, 29,* 1089–1105.

Damasio, A. (1996). *Descartes'error: Emotion, reason, and the human brain*. New York, NY: Putnam.

Davidson, R.J., Kabat-Zinn, J., Schumacher, J., Rosenkranz, M., Muller,D., Santorelli, S.F., et al (2003). Alterations in brain and immune function produced by mindfulness meditation. *Psychosomatic Medicine, 65*, 564–570.

Davis, M., & Whalen, P.J. (2001). The amygdala: vigilance and emotion. *Molecular Psychiatry, 6*, 13–34.

DeBellis, M. (2001). Developmental traumatology: The psychophysiological development of maltreated children and its implications for research, treatment, and policy. *Development and Psychopathology, 13*, 539–564.

deHaan, M., & Gunnar, M. (Eds.). (2009). *Handbook of developmental social neuroscience*. New York, NY: Guilford Press.

Domes, G., Heinrichs, M., Glascher, J., Buchel, C., Braus, D.F., & Herpetz, S.C. (2007). Oxytocin attenuates amygdala responses to emotional faces regardless of valence. *Biological Psychiatry, 10*, 1187–1190.

Dozier, M., Stovall, K.C., Albus, K.E., & Bates, B. (2001). Attachment of infants in foster care: The role of caregiver state of mind. *Child Development, 72*, 1467–1477.

Drevets, W.C. (2000). Functional anatomical abnormalities in limbic and prefrontal cortical structures in major depression. *Progress in Brain Research, 126*, 413–431.

Eluvathingal, T., Chugani, H., Behen, M., Juhasz, C., Muzik, O., Maqbool, M., et al. (2006). Abnormal brain connectivity in children after severe socioemotional deprivation: A diffusion tensor imaging study. *Pediatrics, 117*(6), 2093–2100.

Fehmi,L. & Robbins, J. (2007). *The open-focus brain: Harnessing the power of attention to heal mind and body*. Boston, MA: Trumpeter Books.

Feldman,R., Gordon,I., Schneiderman,I.,Weisman, O., & Zagoory-Sharon, O. (2010). Natural variations in maternal and paternal care are associated with systematic changes in oxytocin following parent–infant contact. *Psychoneuroendocrinology, 35*, 1133–1141.

Feldman, R., Gordon, I., & Zagoory-Sharon, O. (2010). The cross-generation transmission of oxytocin in humans. *Hormones and Behavior, 58,* 669–676.

Field, T. (2002). Massage therapy. *Medicine Clinics of North America, 86,* 163–171.

Fields, R.D. (2009). *The other brain: From dementia to schizophrenia, how new discoveries about the brain are revolutionzing medicine and science.* New York, NY: Simon and Schuster.

Fleming, A.S., & Li, M. (2002). Psychobiology of maternal behavior and its early determinants in nonhuman mammals. In M. Bornstein (Ed.), *Handbook of parenting, Volume 2* (pp. 61–97). Mahwah, NJ: Erlbaum.

Fleming, A.S., Gonazalez, A., Afonso, V., & Lovic, V. (2008). Plasticity in the maternal neural circuit: Experience, dopamine and mothering. In R. Bridges (Ed.), *Neurobiology of the parental brain* (pp. 519–536). San Diego, CA: Academic Press.

Fonagy, P., Gergely, G., Jurist, E., & Target, M. (2002). *Affect regulation, mentalization, and the development of the self.* New York, NY: Other Press.

Fosha, D. (2000). *The transforming power of affect.* New York, NY: Basic Books.

Francis, D.D., Champagne, F., & Meaney, M.J. (2000). Variations in maternal behavior are associated with differences in oxytocin receptor levels in the rat. *Journal of Neuroendocrinology, 12,* 1145–1148.

Frith, U., & Frith, C.D. (2003). Development and neurophysiology of mentalizing. Philosophical Transactions of the Royal Society of London. *Series B: Biological Sciences, 358,* 459–473.

Fuchs, E., & Flugge, G. (2003). Chronic social stress: Effects on limbic brain structures. *Physiology and Behavior, 79,* 417–427.

Gerhardt, S. (2004). *Why love matters: How affection shapes a baby's brain.* New York, NY: Brunner-Routledge.

Giedd, J., Stockman, M., Weddle, C., Liverpool, M., Alexander-Block, A., Wallace, G., et al. (2010). Anatomic magnetic resonance imaging of the developing child and adolescent brain and effects of genetic variation. *Neuropsychology Review, 20,* 349–361. doi: 10.1007/11065-010-9151-9.

Gil, E. (2006). *Helping abused and traumatized children: Integrating directive and nondirective approaches.* New York, NY: Guilford Press.

Gordon, H., Zagoory-Sharon, O., Leckman, J.F., & Feldman, R. (2010). Oxytocin and the development of parenting in humans. *Biological Psychiatry, 68,* 377–382.

Gouin, J-P., Carter, C., Pournajafi-Narzarloo, H., Glaser, R., Malarkey, W., Loving, T., Stowell, J., & Kiecolt-Glaser, J. (2010). Marital behavior, oxytocin, vasopressin, and wound healing. *Psychoneuroendocrinology, 35*(7), 1082–1090. doi:10.1016/j.psyneuen.2010.01.009.

Gundel, H., Lopez-Sala, A., Ceballos-Bauman, A.O., Deus, J., Cardoner, N., Marten-Mittag, B., et al. (2004). Alexithymia correlates with the size of the right anterior cingulate. *Psychosomatic Medicine, 66,* 132–140.

Guastella, A.J., Mitchell, P.B., & Dadds, M.R. (2008). Oxytocin increases gaze to the eye region of human faces. *Biological Psychiatry, 63,* 3–5.

Guastella, A.J., Mitchell, P.B., & Matthews, F. (2008). Oxytocin enhances the encoding of positive social memories in humans. *Biological Psychiatry, 64,* 256–258.

Heim, C., & Nemeroff, C.B. (2002). Neurobiology of early life stress: Clinical studies. *Seminars in Clinical Neuropsychiatry, 7,* 147–159.

Heinrichs, M., von Dawans, B., & Domes, G. (2009). Oxytocin, vasopressin, and human social behavior. *Frontiers in Neuroendocrinology, 30,* 548–557.

Heinz, A., Braus, D., Smolka, M., Wrase, J., Puls, F., Hermann, D., et al. (2005). Amygdala–prefrontal coupling depends on a genetic variation of the serotonin transporter. *Nature Neuroscience, 8,* 20–21.

Hesse, E.(2008). The adult attachment interview: Protocol, method of analysis, and empirical studies. In J. Cassidy and P.R. Shaver (Eds.), *Handbook of attachment,* 2nd edition (pp. 552–598). New York, NY: Guilford.

Hughes, D. (2006). *Building the bonds of attachment* (2nd ed.). Lanham, MD: Jason Aronson.

Hughes, D. (2009). *Attachment-focused parenting.* New York, NY: Norton.

Hughes, D. (2011). *Attachment-focused family therapy workbook.* New York, NY: Norton.

Insel, T.R., & Shapiro, L.E. (1992). Oxytocin receptor distribution reflects social organization in monogamous and polygamous voles. *Proceedings of the National Academy of Sciences, 89,* 5981–5985.

Iversen, L.L., Iversen, S.D., Dunnett, S.B., & Bjorklund, A. (Eds.). (2010). *Dopamine handbook.* New York, NY: Oxford University Press.

Kabat-Zinn, J. (2005). *Coming to our senses: Healing ourselves and the world through mindfulness.* New York, NY: Hyperion.

Kabat-Zinn, M. & J. (1997). *Everyday blessings: The inner work of mindful parenting.* New York, NY: Hyperion Press.

Kagan, J. (1994). *Galen's prophecy: Temperament in human nature.* New York, NY: Basic Books.

Kosfeld, M., Heinrichs, M., Fischbacher, U., & Fehr, E. (2005). Oxytocin increases trust in humans. *Nature, 435,* 673–676.

Lazar, S.W., Kerr, C.E., Wasserman, R.H., Gray, J.R., Greve, D.N., Treadway, M.T., et al. (2005). Meditation experience is associated with increased cortical thickness. *NeuroReport, 16*(17), 1893–1897.

LeDoux, J. (2002). *The synaptic self.* New York, NY: Viking.

Leuner, B., Glasper, E., & Gould, E. (2010). Parenting and plasticity. *Trends in Neuroscience, 33,* 465–473. doi:10.1016/jtins.2010.07.003.

Linehan, M. (1993). *Cognitive-behavioral treatment of borderline personality disorder.* New York, NY: Guilford.

Lorberbaum, J. P., Newman, J.D., Horwitz, A.R., Dubno, J.R., Lydiard, R.B., Hamnerer, M.B., et al., (2002). A potential role for thalamocingulate circuitry in human maternal behavior. *Biological Psychiatry, 51,* 431–445.

Main, M. (2000). The adult attachment interview: Fear, attention, safety, and discourse process. *Journal of the American Psychoanalytic Association, 48,*1055–1096.

Marrazziti, D. (2009). Neurobiology and hormonal aspects of romantic relationships. In M. deHaan & M.R. Gunnar (Eds.), *Handbook of social developmental neuroscience* (pp. 265–280). New York, NY: Guilford Press.

Mayes, L., Magidson, J., Lejuez, C., & Nicholls, S. (2009). Social relationships as primary rewards: The neurobiology of attachment. In M. deHaan & M. Gunnar (Eds.), *Handbook of developmental social neuroscience* (pp. 342–76). New York, NY: Guilford Press.

McEwen, B. (2004). Protection and damage from acute and chronic stress: Allostasis, allostatic overload, and relevance to the pathophysiology of psychiatric disorders. In R.Yehuda & B. McEwen (Eds.), Biobehavioral stress: Protective and damaging effects (pp. 1–7). *Annals of the New York Academy of Sciences, 1032.*

National Scientific Council on the Developing Child. (2008). The timing and quality of early experiences combine to shape brain architecture. Center on the Developing Child, Harvard University, Working Paper 5.

National Scientific Council on the Developing Child. (2010). Early experiences can alter gene expression and affect long-term development. Center on the Developing Child, Harvard University, Working Paper 10.

Noriuchi, M., KiKuchi, Y., & Senoo, A. (2008). The functional neuroanatomy of maternal love: Mother's response to attachment behaviors. *Biological Psychiatry, 63,* 415–423.

Norris, C.D., & Cacioppo, J.T. (2007). I know how you feel: Social and emotional information processing in the brain. In E. Harmon-Jones & P. Winkielman (Eds.), *Social neuroscience* (pp. 84–105). New York, NY: Guilford Press.

Numan, M.T., & Stolzenberg, D.S. (2008). Hypothalamic interaction with the mesolimbic dopamine system and the regulation of maternal responsiveness. In R. Bridges (Ed.), *Neurobiology of the parental brain* (pp. 3–22). London: Academic Press.

Numan, M. & Insel,T.R. (2003) *The neurobiology of parental behavior.* New York, NY: Springer-Verlag.

Ochsner, K.N., Knierim, K., Ludlow, D.l., Hanelin, J., Ramachanran, T., Glover, G., et al. (2004). Reflecting upon feelings: An fMRI study of neural systems supporting the attribution of emotion to self and other. *Journal of Cognitive Neuroscience, 16,* 1746–1772.

Ochsner, K.N., Ray, R., Cooper, J., Robertson, E., Chopra, S., Gabrielli, J., et al. (2004). For better or for worse: Neural systems supporting the cognitive down-and-up regulation of negative emotion. *NeuroImage, 23,* 483–499.

Ochsner, K.N., Zaki, J., Hanelin, J., Ludlow, D.H., Knierim, K., Ramachandran, T., et al. (2008). Your pain or mine?: Common and distinct neural systems supporting the perception of pain in self and other. *Social Cognitive and Affective Neuroscience, 3*(2), 144–160.

Ogden, P., Minton, K., & Pain, C. (2006). *Trauma and the body: A sensorimotor approach to psychotherapy.* New York, NY: Norton.

Panksepp, J. (1998). *Affective neuroscience.* New York, NY: Oxford University Press.

Panksepp, J., & Burgdorf, J. (2000). 50 kHz chirping laughter in response to conditioned and unconditioned tickle-induced reward in rats: Effects of social housing and genetic variables. *Behavioral Brain Research, 115,* 25–38.

Panksepp, J. (2004). Emerging neuroscience of fear and anxiety: Therapeutic practice and clinical implications. In J.Panksepp (Ed.), *Textbook of biological psychiatry* (pp. 489–512). Hoboken, NJ: Wiley-Liss.

Pellis, S.M., & Pellis, V.C. (2006). Play and the development of social engagement: A comparative perspective. In P. Marshall & N. Fox (Eds.), *The development of social engagement* (pp. 247–274). New York, NY: Oxford University Press.

Perry, B. (1997). Incubated in terror: Neurodevelopmental factors in the "cycle of violence." In J. Osofsky (Ed.), *Children in a violent society* (pp. 124–148). New York, NY: Guilford Press.

Pollak, S.D. (2003). Experience-dependent affective learning and risk for psychopathology in children. In R. King, C.F. Ferris, & I.L. Lederhendlerk (Eds.), *Roots of mental illness in children* (pp. 102–111). New York, NY: Annals of the New York Academy of Sciences.

Porges, S. (2011). *The polyvagal theory: Neurophysiological foundations of emotions, attachment, communication, and self-regulation.* New York, NY: Norton.

Posner, M., & Rothbart, M. (2007). *Educating the human brain.* Washington, DC: American Psychological Association.

Posner, M.I., Rothbart, M.K., Sheese, B.E., & Tang,Y. (2007). The anterior cingulate gyrus and the mechanism of self-regulation. *Cognitive, Affective, and Behavioral Neuroscience, 7*(4), 391–395.

Posner, M., Sheese, B.E., Odludas, Y., & Tang, Y. (2006). Analyzing and shaping human attentional networks. *Neural Networks, 19,* 1422–1429.

Ross, H.E., & Young, L. (2009). Oxytocin and the neural mechanisms regulating social cognition and affiliative behavior. *Frontiers in Neuroendocrinology, 4,* 534–547.

Roth, T.L., Lubin, F.D., Funk, A.J., & Sweatt, J.D. (2009). Lasting epigenetic influence of early-life adversity on the BDNF gene. *Biological Psychiatry, 65,* 760–769.

Rothschild, B. (2010). *8 keys to safe trauma recovery.* New York, NY: Norton.

Sapolsky, R.M., Meaney, M.J., & McEwen, B.S. (1985). The development of the glucorticoid receptor system in the rat limbic brain III: Negative-feedback regulation. *Brain Research, 350,* 169–173.

Schore, A. (1994). *Affect regulation and the origin of the self: The neurobiology of emotional development.* Hillsdale, NJ: Erlbaum.

Schore, A. (2003). *Affect regulation and the repair of the self.* New York, NY: Norton.

Seltzer, L.J., Ziegler, T.E., & Pollak, S. (2010). Social vocalizations can release oxytocin in humans. *Proceedings of the Royal Society B: Biological Sciences, 7,* 2661–2666.

Shonkoff, J.P., & Levitt, P. (2010). Neuroscience and the future of early childhood policy: Moving from why to what and how. *Neuron, 67*(5), 689–691.

Siegel, D. (1999). *The developing mind.* New York, NY: Guilford Press.

Siegel, D. (2010). *The mindful therapist.* New York, NY: Norton.

Siegel, D.J., & Hartzell, M. (2003). *Parenting from the inside out.* New York, NY: Penguin.

Stern, D. (2000). *The interpersonal world of the infant: A view from psychoanalysis and developmental psychology*. New York, NY: Basic Books.

Strathearn, L., & Fonagy, P. (2009). Adult attachment predicts maternal brain and oxytocin response to infant cues. *Neuropsychopharmacology, 34*, 2655–2666.

Suomi,S. (2003). Gene-environment interactions and the neurobiology of social conflict. In J.King, C.Ferris, & I.Lederhendler (Eds.), Roots of mental illness in children (pp. 132-139). *Annals of the New York Academy of Sciences*, volume 1008.

Swain, J.E., & Lorberbaum, J. (2008). Imaging the human brain. In R. Bridges (Ed.), *Neurobiology of the parental brain* (pp. 83–100). San Diego, CA: Academic Press.

Swain, J.E., Lorberbaum, J.P., Kose, S., & Strathearn, L. (2007). Brain basis of early neuroimaging studies. *Journal of Child Psychology and Psychiatry, 48*, 262–287.

Tang, Y.Y., Lu, Q., Geng, X., Stein, F.A., Yang, Y., & Posner, M.I. (2010). Short-term meditation induces white matter changes in the anterior cingulate. Proceedings of the National Academy of Sciences, 107, 15649–15652.

Teicher, M.H., Andersen, S.L., Polcari, A., Anderson, C.M., Navalta, C.P., & Kim, D.M. (2003). The neurobiological consequences of early stress and childhood maltreatment. *Neuroscience Biobehavioral Review, 27*, 33–44.

Trevarthen, C. (2001). Intrinsic motives for companionship in understanding: Their origin, development, and significance for infant mental health. *Infant Mental Health, 22*, 95–131.

Trevarthen, C., & Aitken, K.J. (2001). Infant intersubjectivity: Research, theory, and clinical applications. *Journal of Child Psychology and Psychiatry, 42*, 3–48.

Tronick, E. (2007). *The neurobehavioral and social–emotional development of infants and children*. New York, NY: Norton.

Van IJzendorn, M. (1995). Adult attachment representations, parental responsiveness, and infant attachment. *Psychological Bulletin, 117*(3), 387–403.

van Reekum, C.M., Urry, H. L., Johnstone, T., Thurow, M.E., Frye, C.J., Jackson, C.A., et al. (2007). Individual differences in amygdala and ventromedial prefrontal cortex activity are associated with evaluation speed and psychological well-being. *Journal of Cognitive Neuroscience, 19*(2), 237–248.

Veenama, A.A., & Neuman, I.D. (2008). Central vasopressin and oxytocin release: Regulation of complex social behaviors. *Progress in Brain Research, 170,* 261–276.

Vuilleumier, P. (2009). The role of the human amygdala in perception and attention. In P. Whalen and E. Phelps (Eds.), *The human amygdala* (pp. 220–249). New York, NY: Guilford.

Wall, P., & Messier, C. (2001). The hippocampal formation–orbito medial prefrontal cortex circuit in the attentional control of meaning. *Behavior and Brain Research, 127,* 99–111.

Wesselman, D. (1998) *The whole parent: How to become a terrific parent even if you didn't have one.* Cambridge, MA: Perseus Publishing

Whalen, P. & Phelps, E. (2009). *The human amygdala.* New York, NY: Guilford.

Winstanley, C. (2007). The orbitofrontal cortex, impulsivity, and addiction: Probing orbitofrontal dysfunction at the neural, neurochemical, and molecular level. In G. Schoenbaum, J. Gottfried, E. Murray, & S. Ramus (Eds.), *Linking affect to action: Critical contributions of the orbitofrontal cortex* (pp. 639–655). New York, NY: Annals of the New York Academy of Sciences.

Zubietta, J.K., Ketter, T.M., Bueller, J.A., Xu, Y., Kilbourn, M.R., & Young, E.A. (2003). Regulation of human affective responses by anterior cingulate and limbic mu-opioid neurotransmission. *Archives of General Psychiatry, 60,* 1145–1153.

Index

The Norton Series on Interpersonal Neurobiology
Allan N. Schore, PhD, Series Editor
Daniel J. Siegel, MD, Founding Editor

The field of mental health is in a tremendously exciting period of growth and conceptual reorganization. Independent findings from a variety of scientific endeavors are converging in an interdisciplinary view of the mind and mental well-being. An interpersonal neurobiology of human development enables us to understand that the structure and function of the mind and brain are shaped by experiences, especially those involving emotional relationships.

The Norton Series on Interpersonal Neurobiology will provide cutting-edge, multidisciplinary views that further our understanding of the complex neurobiology of the human mind. By drawing on a wide range of traditionally independent fields of research—such as neurobiology, genetics, memory, attachment, complex systems, anthropology, and evolutionary psychology—these texts will offer mental health professionals a review and synthesis of scientific findings often inaccessible to clinicians. These books aim to advance our understanding of human experience by finding the unity of knowledge, or consilience, that emerges with the translation of findings from numerous domains of study into a common language and conceptual framework. The series will integrate the best of modern science with the healing art of psychotherapy.